Bridges to Consciousness

This book investigates consciousness as an emergent state arising from the global functioning of the brain and the body. In this research Krieger applies these concepts to analytical psychology, particularly to the constellation of the complex and of the archetype. Global brain functioning is considered as a complex system whose macroscopic, emergent patterns such as thoughts and behaviours are determined by physical parameters including emotion, memory and perception.

The concept of the feeling-toned complex was among the first of the theories to be developed by Jung, and the theories of complexity and dynamical systems which subsequently developed in the physical sciences did not exist at the time. This book takes a new look at the feeling-toned complex as a basin of attraction which competes for consciousness against other complexes to determine behaviour. By drawing parallels between current ideas in neuroscience and Jung's more traditional theories, Krieger discusses the relevance for both psychotherapy and everyday life.

Bridges to Consciousness considers the importance of the link between emotion and the complex in both the establishment of consciousness and the determination of self-esteem, making the work relevant to therapists and analysts. This book will also awaken interest in complexes in both Jungian and wider neuroscientific research communities and will therefore interest researchers and academics in the field of psychology who want an insight into how the ideas of Jung can be applied beyond the traditional analytic field.

Nancy M. Krieger has a PhD from the Centre for Psychoanalytic Studies, Essex University, UK. She graduated from the International School of Analytical Psychology in Zurich, Switzerland, where she is now a training analyst and teaches regularly. She has a private practice in France near Basel.

Research in Analytical Psychology and Jungian Studies Series

Series Advisor: Andrew Samuels, Professor of Analytical Psychology, Essex University, UK

The *Research in Analytical Psychology and Jungian Studies* series features scholarly works that are, broadly speaking, of an empirical nature. The series comprises research-focused volumes involving qualitative and quantitative research, historical/archival research, theoretical developments, heuristic research, grounded theory, narrative approaches, collaborative research, practitioner-led research, and self-study. The series also includes focused works by clinical practitioners, and provides new research informed explorations of the work of C.G. Jung that will appeal to researchers, academics, and scholars alike.

Books in this series:

Time and Timelessness
Temporality in the theory of Carl Jung
Angeliki Yiassemides

Apophatic Elements in the Theory and Practice of Psychoanalysis
Pseudo-Dionysius and C.G. Jung
David Henderson

C.G. Jung and Hans Urs von Balthasar
God and evil – A critical comparison
Les Oglesby

Bridges to Consciousness
Complexes and complexity
Nancy M. Krieger

Bridges to Consciousness

Complexes and complexity

Nancy M. Krieger

Routledge
Taylor & Francis Group
LONDON AND NEW YORK

First published 2014
by Routledge
2 Park Square, Milton Park, Abingdon, Oxfordshire OX14 4RN

and by Routledge
711 Third Avenue, New York, NY 10017

First issued in paperback 2016

Routledge is an imprint of the Taylor & Francis Group, an informa business

British Library Cataloguing in Publication Data
A catalogue record for this book is available from the British Library

Library of Congress Cataloging in Publication Data
Krieger, Nancy M.
Bridges to consciousness : complexes and complexity / Nancy M. Krieger.
pages cm
Includes bibliographical references.
ISBN 978-0-415-82875-8 (hardback) -- ISBN 978-0-203-58147-6 (ebook) 1. Consciousness. 2. Jungian psychology. I. Title.
BF311.K6975 2013
153--dc23
2013024066

ISBN 13: 978-0-415-79172-4 (pbk)
ISBN 13: 978-0-415-82875-8 (hbk)

Typeset in Bembo
by GreenGate Publishing Services, Tonbridge, Kent

Contents

Figures

Tables

Preface

My first encounter with dynamical systems was as an undergraduate physics student in the late 1960s. The physics building at the University of Michigan at that time was a modern, rectangular eyesore amidst the otherwise beautiful gothic architecture of the campus, but its long, straight hallways were an excellent place to calibrate the then new lasers. It is the work of Herman Haken, who was then developing much of the mathematical explanation behind the working of lasers, which forms the theoretical basis for my investigation of the psyche as a dynamical system. For over 40 years since then I worked in IT. I spent many of the later years designing message flows in distributed systems, determining which system had what information at what time and how it could get to where it was needed using, for the most part, standardised messages.

In 1999 I started my training at the C.G. Jung Institute in Küsnacht. The research for this paper started with my diploma thesis (completed in 2006) for the newly founded International School of Analytic Psychology (ISAP) in Zurich. The principle orientation of that paper, 'The Experience of the Self in the Analytic Relationship', was clinical, although it did address the topic of the neurological underpinnings of consciousness. I made no specific reference to complexity theory at that time.

My interest in complexity theory developed quickly with my reading during the first months of research for my PhD, principally from my readings in consciousness studies around the theories of Bernard Baars and the Global Workspace (2005). By 2008, one and a half years into the thesis, the idea of including the complex as an attractor in a dynamical system had become a central element in my research. That Autumn I visited Dr Harald Atmanspacher at the Institut für Grenzgebiete der Psychologie und Psychohygiene (IGPP) in Freiburg. Dr Atmanspacher works in theoretical neuroscience. His background in the physical sciences gives him a different perspective from others coming from a medical, psychological, or philosophical discipline. He encouraged me to orient my research to track the correlation between the micro- and macro-levels of the emerging brain-psyche system.

After working on this for a while I realised that I needed to investigate in depth the ego-complex, its formation and the role it plays within the normal functioning of the psyche.

At this point the structure and content of the thesis was fixed. Although the range of topics covered is unusually broad, this thesis begins with a single premise: that a feeling-toned complex, as defined by Jung, is an attractor in a dynamical system. It attempts to substantiate this (although physical proof is beyond the practical limits of this research) and then investigates the resulting implications for the major concepts of Analytical Psychology.

Since my natural way of thinking is principally mathematical, I think more in images than in words. In struggling to understand a concept it helps me more to form an image than to formulate the concept in words. Throughout this thesis, I have inserted images of several Jungian concepts, which I have created and which I hope add to the reader's understanding.

Foreword

Approximately 100 years ago, C.G. Jung underwent a series of experiences that transformed his view of himself, the world and the psyche. Just prior to this in 1912 he delivered nine lectures at Fordham Medical College (present day Fordham University) in New York City on 'The Theory of Psychoanalysis'. These lectures mark the acme of Jung's early objective writing style; the lectures were presented in the positivistic scientific idiom of the day and very well received by the physicians in the audience. However, an alternative mode of observation and writing was already beginning to emerge for him this year as can be seen in the second part of *Wandlungen und Symbole der Libido* (1912, later translated as *The Psychology of the Unconscious*) in which he gave voice to his inner experiences. The following year (1913), Jung embarked on a life-altering voyage into the interior, as he plunged into his own unconscious material, wrestling with it until he gradually produced his *Red Book* (2009), only recently available to the general public. This was the definitive self-exploration that made Jung into the *Jung* we now identify with his name; and he claims to have stopped his work on it as he needed to return to the world and to science. In the process he drew upon old, seemingly outdated modes of discovery while also pioneering new ways to conceive, examine and engage the fullness of the psyche. He was crafting a new vision of the world, a cosmology, with a science that included subjective meaning. The intuitive leaps in Jung's formulations left him anticipating the paradigm shifts that are only now beginning to emerge in cosmology and the neurosciences.

It is against this backdrop that we may be best able to appreciate Dr Nancy Krieger's accomplishments in her exciting, rich book. First educated in contemporary science but then feeling the pull of the psyche, she trained as a Jungian analyst. The combination she sought to craft out of her diverse interests led her to seek a PhD in a new, burgeoning area of study – complex systems applied to analytical psychology – and ultimately has produced this book. I had the privilege and pleasure of being a reader of Dr Krieger's dissertation as the dual background of science and analytical psychology is something we share, though with different formal fields of initial scientific study. I too have found a synthesis of interests in the study of complex systems. Dr Krieger's unique approach has brought her to apply complexity to Jung's theory of complexes, a contribution which will benefit various disciplines as it helps modernise and provide a neuroscientific base for many of Jung's hypotheses, while correcting and amending others.

The line of inquiry followed in this book is one I feel certain would have been close to Jung's own interests. From explorations in the history of ideas associated with analytical psychology, we have learned that Jung was strongly influenced by the strands of emergentism available during his lifetime; this field did not find fuller scientific footing until some 20 years after Jung's death with the advent of Complexity Theory, especially as articulated by the scientists of the Santa Fe Institute. Modern complexity theory includes the study of self-organizing systems with emergent properties, ideas Jung intuited but could only ground phenomenologically. In the process he did draw upon the work of others interested in similar perspectives. For example, Jung turned to the British philosopher, psychologist and ethologist Conway Lloyd Morgan for the biological aspects of his theories of archetypes, as from Morgan's book *Habit and Instinct* (1896)—in particular Morgan's portrayals of the yucca moth and leaf-cutting ant's behavioral patterns. This in turn links with both Morgan's later publication from his Gifford lectures, *Emergent Evolution* (1927), and with the work of his friend and colleague James Mark Baldwin, whose ideas have been experiencing a renaissance in complexity studies, especially 'the Baldwin Effect' linking culture and evolution; the mind is thus always embedded in its environment. These ideas have ably been shown to stand behind Jung's own thinking on archetypes by George Hogenson (2001).

Similarly, study of Jung's methodology for observing and engaging unconscious material can now be straightforwardly revisioned as offering the means for exploring emergent processes (Cambray and Carter 2004, Chapter 5). In this book Dr Krieger further extends the use of complexity theory to Jung's early discoveries and refinements of 'the feeling-toned complex', a concept that he retained throughout his entire career and which remains a keystone of modern analytical psychology. At one point Jung even thought of calling his approach 'Complex Psychology'. By making manifest the link between the formulation of complexes and complexity, Dr Krieger helps to ground, clarify and reshape where needed, Jung's intuitive insights, moving various ideas of his from hypotheses to proto-theories capable of being more fully and rigorously tested; she has made a major contribution to advancing Jung's original ideas.

In the past decade there has been a growing body of university based researchers and academics in addition to analysts studying the postulates of analytical psychology. While the clinical dimension of this discipline is vital, it is equally important to the health of the field for there to be in-depth exploration, evaluation and reformulation of its main tenets as well as articulating the limits of present knowledge as applied to the underlying concepts. With experience and training in multiple areas, Dr Krieger serves as a valued guide into the frontiers of complex psychology.

Joseph Cambray

References

Jung, Carl, G. (1912). *Wandlungen und Symbole der Libido* (*The Psychology of the Unconscious*). Leipzig & Vienna: Franz Deuticke.

Jung, Carl, G. (2009). *The Red Book: Liber Novus*. New York and London: W.W. Norton and Co.

Cambray, Joseph and Linda Carter (2004). *Analytical Psychology: Contemporary perspectives in Jungian analysis*. Hove and New York: Brunner-Routledge.

Hogenson, George B. (2001). 'The Baldwin effect: A neglected influence on C.G. Jung's evolutionary thinking'. *Journal of Analytical Psychology*, 46(4), 591–611.

Morgan, C. Lloyd (1896). *Habit and instinct*. London: Arnold.

—— (1927). *Emergent evolution*. New York: Henry Holt.

Acknowledgements

I'd like to thank Anne Blonstein for the long hours of conversation before she took ill, Andrew Fellows for his careful reading and helpful suggestions, Roderick Main and Renos Papadopoulos for their guidance over the many years it took for this project to mature, and most of all my doctoral supervisor Andrew Samuels, without whom it never would have existed, and who gave me the benefit of his vast experience as a Jungian, an academic and an author.

I am especially indebted to Dr Christian Hess, Professor Emeritus of Neurology at the University of Bern for his reading of and advice on the medical arguments in my manuscript. Also to Dr Johannes Bircher for his assistance.

Chapter 1

A Jungian neuroscience of consciousness

This book is based on an investigation of consciousness as an emergent phenomenon of the brain and body. My starting point is what Jung described as the constellation of an autonomous complex because in this process consciousness is noticeably affected. I am not trying to validate Jungian theory with regard to neuroscience. Since both are describing the same physical responses, albeit from different perspectives, they must overlap. Instead, I start with a phenomenological investigation of the autonomous complex. Based on an analysis of the times of the various physical reactions, I consider them as a hierarchy of dynamical systems culminating in the emergence of consciousness. I believe this analysis is reasonable. Interaction of the subject with his or her environment and society is also a factor. I approach this only indirectly, first as perception during the constellation of the complex and second as intersubjectivity in the formation of the ego-complex.

Although some of my work may be applied to therapy, my background is in the physical sciences and information technology. Consequently, my approach is different from that of Jungian authors whose principal interest is clinical.

In my opinion, the theory of complexes has been left too much in the background of Jungian thinking. I would hope that this work reawakens interest in complexes in both the Jungian and wider neuroscientific research communities.

By applying Dynamical Systems Theory and modelling of the neural correlates of psychological states, the feeling-toned complex can be seen as an attractor state in the psychic landscape. I conclude that three concepts or processes are of primary importance to the emergence of consciousness:

- symbolisation and the emergence of meaning,
- the concept of self,[1]
- coordination/synchronisation over many psychological and physical levels forming a global workspace.

Our need to understand, to find meaning within the context of one's self and the current situation is, I believe, our most distinguishing characteristic as human beings. This process goes on continually in our everyday lives, during the functioning of the ego-complex, but is more visible in the sudden eruption into consciousness of an autonomous complex. It can also be experienced in the insight brought by the constellation of an archetype.

One of the principal findings of this research reinforces Jung's intuitive understanding of the central role played in the manifestation of consciousness by the coalescing of lower-level processes into a symbolic image and the sudden realisation of the meaning of that image for the subject.

A complex system is made up of a large number of individual elements that interact amongst themselves and with the environment, so there is an exchange of energy and information. The fact that it changes over time gives it a dynamical nature. Nonlinear means that the changes are not regular and may be quite radical. Complexity theory is the study of such systems. Dynamical systems theory is the area of study within applied mathematics which is used to describe the behaviour of such systems. I use the terms 'complexity' and 'dynamical systems' interchangeably. In popular literature such systems are often referred to as 'chaotic' and the area of study as 'chaos theory'. This is technically incorrect and I avoid the term. Chaos is a more restrictive term than complexity as chaotic systems have specific mathematical properties. It is not my intention to investigate chaos *per se*, only the broader properties of complexity. Complexity is closely related to emergence. As a system changes it may enter a state where a property or behaviour develops which appears foreign to its original configuration. I investigate the psyche as an emergent state arising from the global functioning of the brain and the body. In this research I apply these concepts to Analytical Psychology, particularly to the constellation of the complex and of the archetype. Global brain functioning is considered as a complex system whose macroscopic, emergent patterns (i.e. thoughts and behaviour) are determined by physical parameters (i.e. emotion, memory, perception).

The concept of the feeling-toned complex was among the first of the theories to be developed by Jung. The theories of complexity and dynamical systems subsequently developed in the physical sciences did not exist at the time. I take a new look at the feeling-toned complex as a basin of attraction which competes for consciousness against other complexes to determine behaviour. This is a view Jung might have taken if the theories had been available to him.

The importance of the link between emotion and the complex in both the establishment of consciousness and the determination of self-esteem is also investigated, making the work relevant to therapeutic practice, albeit without specifically developing these ideas.

An area in Jung's original theory which I think needs reinforcing and to be more explicitly emphasised, is the role played by future goals in the context of the constellation of the complex.

Since most complexes can be classified into certain distinct categories it has been proposed that they result from universal human conditions. These could be evolutionary, in the sense that human brains function in certain ways (Jung 1909/1949 para. 728), and/or they could result from basic needs, such as the need for food, protection and love that a new-born expects its parents to meet. Archetypes, which are associated with each of these categories, can be viewed as self-organising elements of the psyche according to the definition of self-organisation in complexity theory and dynamical systems modelling.

The constellation of an archetype is a second way in which ideas can become conscious. This is also looked at in terms of emergence, and the macro- and micro-levels of the phenomenon are investigated in terms of their neuroscientific components.

The interactions between the archetype and the complex, both at the times of the formation and the constellation of the complex, are examined, and their theoretical implications are looked at in detail.

Several researchers in the neurosciences have produced remarkable works explaining their areas of expertise, while in other areas the scientific justification of theories of mind is still scattered in scientific papers that are difficult for non-specialists in those disciplines to understand and interpret. Some of the models being used to understand brain functioning are highly mathematical and thus not readily accessible.

For this valuable research to benefit people in their everyday lives, it has to be placed in the context of its relevance to behaviour and the meaning of one's life. Jungian psychology is not limited to the treatment of the mentally ill. It is applicable to the behaviour of people in all life situations because it offers a generalised model for the functioning of the psyche. By drawing parallels between current ideas in neuroscience and Jung's theories, I place modern research in a context which shows its relevance for both psychotherapy and everyday life. I extend systems theory and apply it to the continual flux of complexes in their competition for control of the conscious psyche.

The interplay between science and philosophy inherent in Jung's writings has not been adequately maintained in post-Jungian and modern Jungian writing. Although there are a handful of Jungians interested in the relation of his work to empirical findings and to the recent findings in the neurosciences, the majority of work done by Jungian authors has been in the philosophical, symbolic and spiritual domains. This work is important, but it is also important that the plausibility of Jung's theories with regard to current neurological findings, cognitive sciences and philosophies of mind be investigated.

One definition of science is the systematic acquisition of knowledge based on experimentation and/or observation. The generally accepted scientific method stipulates that one's research is designed around a hypothesis, which is either proven or disproven. The findings are to be universally reproducible under identical conditions. Science was originally used for the study of natural phenomena. It has been extended to the social sciences, which includes such areas as education, history, sociology and psychology. Experimental psychology, which was just beginning when Jung started working as a psychiatrist and was involved in his work with the Word Association Experiment, clearly falls into this category. It is more questionable whether the appellation 'scientific' or even 'empirical' can be applied to his later theories based on his psychoanalytic experience.

Jung considered himself to be a scientist and his theories to be based on his observed findings in work with his clients. He considered this experience to be empirical, giving him a wide overview of society. This experience may have led to his hypotheses, which could have been tested scientifically, but it does not, in itself, constitute scientific proof in the positivistic meaning of that term. His clients were not randomly selected, there was no comparison with a control group and the results were not subject to verification by repetition. These are all required characteristics of the scientific method.

No one has ever seen an electron or a field. Their existence is postulated from the effects they have on other objects, for example a bubble chamber or iron filings. Likewise, Jung postulated the existence of archetypes based on the constellation of autonomous complexes he witnessed in his clients. If complexes seem to fall into certain identifiable categories, as claimed by Saunders and Skar (2001), then Jung would argue that archetypes are responsible for this. This form of extrapolation of cause from effect is consistent with scientific method.

It is often debated whether his methods may be classified as scientific in the post-positivist sense of the term. I could ask 'What is in a name?' The corpus of Jung's work is what it is, whether or not it qualifies strictly as 'scientific'. I think it is more important that his theories be investigated in the light of today's scientific theories and in dialogue with ongoing research both within and, importantly, beyond the bounds of Analytical Psychology.

Jung also considered his application of phenomenology to psychological concepts to be scientific. Phenomenology includes a strict methodology, but one which is not identical with that of mainstream science. However, the use of amplification in the case of an archetypal image does come closer to the scientific method as a rigorous analysis of the use of an image, both historically and geographically.

Whether subjective first person experience is scientifically acceptable or not is beyond the limits of this paper. Subjective experiences, as all other phenomena, can be analysed using the scientific method, but what is being investigated is the reported subjective experience and not the physical principles governing that experience. A controlled environment, a clear hypothesis, a large enough sample to be statistically significant and a viable form of quantification are all required. With very few exceptions (Rossi 1977, Prifitera 1981, Shin *et al.* 2005), this has not been attempted within Jungian psychology. Few of Jung's followers have lived up to his claim of being scientific. Each generation needs to review the underlying principles of his theories in the light of the latest findings, not only in neuroscience but in mythology, theology, philosophy, and all of the other fields that underpin the theories of this great polymath.

The word 'science' stems from the Latin word '*scientia*' meaning knowledge. Throughout his career Jung was certainly seeking science, in this broad sense. This applies particularly to his work with synchronicity and the *unus mundus*, an all-encompassing theory that includes both physical and psychic phenomena.

The combined study of mind and brain has, in part, been taken up by the development of cognitive science and the exchanges between it and disciplines such as psychology, the neurosciences, linguistics, philosophy, computer science, anthropology, biology and physics. This has also greatly enlarged the concept of 'science'.

Starting with Copernicus (b.1473–d.1543), and confirmed by the discoveries of Galileo (b.1564–d.1642), there was a radical change in both science and the philosophy of science. The prevailing concept of the world changed from 'a finite, closed, and hierarchically ordered whole', a world based on values, to an 'infinite universe' ordered by 'fundamental components and laws' (Koyré 1957/2008: 8–9). Nicholas of Cusa's (b.1401–d.1464) understanding of God as both the 'center and the circumference' of the world (ibid.: 14), which is so similar to Jung's definition of the Self as both the centre and the totality of the psyche, clearly belonged to the older world view. In this sense, Jung was also a scientist of this old world, the world of the alchemists, a world where value, not measurement, was the determining factor.

Irrespective of the relationship between Jung and science, it is important that contemporary Analytical Psychology define its relation to established scientific theories. This dialectic forms a basis on which our concepts can be revised in the light of new scientific discoveries. If cut off from evolving findings in science, Analytical Psychology becomes alienated and we end up discussing our theories only amongst ourselves. The same is true for its relations to changes in philosophy, literary theory, and academic disciplines in general.

A few Jungian authors have discussed the relation between different aspects of neuroscience and Jungian theory. Margaret Wilkinson (2004) has written from the point of view of the analytic encounter, and Jean Knox (2003, 2011) on the relationship of attachment theory and developmental neuroscience to Jungian concepts. Peter Saunders and Patricia Skar (2001) and George Hogenson (2005) have considered complexes and archetypes in relation to the organisation of large complex systems.

Many people are presently interested in the implications of current research for areas related to Jungian theory, as are almost all psychological schools, but I know of no other in-depth comparison involving almost all of the range of Jungian theory.

Definitions of terms such as consciousness, meaning, symbol, self/ego are given in the context in which they are explored later in this text.

Part I presents introductory material for those who may not have a background in theories of consciousness, the Jungian complex or dynamical systems theory. From these subjects I present only the topics which are relevant to my later argumentation. Readers with previous knowledge in these areas may prefer to begin with Part II.

The central work of Chapters 5 and 6 uses the technique of mapping the psychological state experienced during the constellation of an autonomous complex with the neural and somatic correlates of that experience. This form of mapping between micro- and macro-levels is common in dynamical systems analysis. These chapters map the psychological experience of the constellated autonomous complex to their neural correlates. They investigate how consciousness is generated by this event. The constellation of the complex demonstrates the link between emotion and memory. This same link is activated in the psychoanalytic session when the client tells *good* stories, the ones relating the incidents, good or bad, mainly of their childhood when the emotions can be relived as an adult with an adult's understanding and compassion.

The theory of archetypes is probably the aspect of Jungian theory which has been most interpreted by post-Jungian authors. My interest in archetypes is the psychoid, which by its very bipolar structure of instinct and image implies mapping from a psychological state to an underlying physical state. The constellation of an archetype is one way in which unconscious contents can become conscious. Chapter 7 develops a theory of archetypes based on the psychoid and Chapter 8 investigates the experience and neural correlates of the constellation of the archetype and highlights the differences between this and that of a complex.

Jung took the model of the complex further and went on to define the ego as a complex, with the continual activation of different aspects of the complex generating our underlying feelings of self-esteem. Informed by recent understanding of cerebral development, in Chapter 9 I investigate the extent to which this model of the ego-complex can be used to understand the neurological phenomenon of the self (selfhood). I consider the development of the infant's brain from three months before birth to 24 months postnatal in detail, particularly its implications for the development of the ego-complex. In Chapter 10 I present a tool for illustrating the psychic landscape which includes the ego-complex, autonomous complexes and persona roles. This can be used in conjunction with the Word Association Experiment in a clinical setting to help clients to visualise what is happening when a complex constellates, and thus perhaps why it does so.

Finally, Chapter 11 brings together the various concepts of consciousness investigated, relating them to Jung's theories and the neural correlates of coming into consciousness in these three differing ways of functioning; the constellation of the autonomous complex, that of the archetype and the ego-complex

Note

1 Throughout this book I refer to Jung's concept of the Self with a capital 'S' and the self, as in myself, with a small 's'. I do this to make it easier for the reader to understand which concept I am referring to.

Part I

Introductory material

Chapter 2

Investigation of consciousness

A major problem in the investigation of consciousness is the differing understanding of what consciousness is in the various disciplines. Philosophy has tried to define its characteristics such as monist versus dualist, subjectivity, selfhood and attention. Neuroscience tries to define the neural correlates of consciousness, in other words what is required for its experience, and to measure changes in the state of consciousness. Psychology concentrates more on the effects of consciousness, on what it feels like.

Since my approach is multi-disciplinary these differences afford a multitude of viewpoints from which to investigate the experience of consciousness. My principal areas of study are:

- the relationship of psychic structures defined in Jungian psychology – the complex, the ego-complex and the archetype – to consciousness
- positioning emergence within the philosophy of mind
- the neuroscientific correlates of the phenomena of consciousness

I begin with four topics: attention, the self, language and symbolisation, and meaning, which I have found to be essential to my investigation of consciousness, and which I will use as benchmarks which must be explained in order to more closely investigate the emergence of consciousness from the physical brain and body.

I will consider consciousness to be a process (William James 1890/1950) of neural interactions (Edelman and Tononi 2000a: 146). It is a series of events which, over a space of time, produces a change. It is no longer considered to be binary, that either you have it or you don't. Rather, there is now believed to be a continuum of conscious states, from a basic awareness to a more advanced form of consciousness involving autobiographical memory (Damasio 1999a, Edelman and Tononi 2000a).

Benchmarks for the experience of consciousness

Attention

Attention is so closely related to consciousness that it is often confused with it. However, selective attention can be controlled by will, whereas consciousness cannot. Attention limits the amount of information received. Out of the many simultaneous sensory inputs and the multitude of unconscious processes occurring at any one time in the brain, one or at most a few of these are selected to become conscious. Consciousness has completely different functions from attention. Its main functions are to categorise information, which is related to language and symbolisation as discussed below, and to improve decision-making by, among other things, relating past experience to the present situation to make long-term plans (Damasio 1999a: 201, with regard to decision-making only).

Consciousness has *unity and cohesion*. It cannot be taken apart. Image, emotion and memory form a whole. Although we can attend to one aspect or another, we can never separate the different elements from the whole experience. The scientific method includes taking things apart and investigating them. This cannot be done with consciousness, for relationship is integral to its nature.

There is a continual flow or *stream of consciousness*. Images and experiences pass like episodes in a story book. Both its contents and the intensity of the experience are constantly changing. At some times we are more conscious than at others. Even during periods of wakefulness our state of consciousness varies. When we attend closely to a subject our consciousness appears to be acute and focussed. At other times our concentration wanders; we day-dream and our consciousness seems shallow and diffuse.

Consciousness is usually defined as occurring in the *waking state*. People who are asleep are not usually considered to be conscious. However, some classifications (Austin 1999: 300–1) consider at least two sleeping conscious states: dream sleep and deep sleep without dreams. Medical consideration of consciousness using neuroimaging technologies includes classifications of what would usually be considered unconscious states.

Self

Closely related to consciousness is the concept of the self. The self is the actor, the one who experiences his or her actions and perceptions. Consciousness consists of an actor and an object or, more precisely, the actor's awareness of him/herself and the actor's awareness of the object. The two are linked together to form the experience.

When speaking of consciousness, we are usually referring to *self-consciousness* or *self-awareness*. This includes the idea of sentience, i.e. of being capable of sensing and responding to external stimulation, of being aware of one's response. It involves not only direct interaction with the environment, but a higher-order awareness of that interaction. I am not referring to self-referential emotions like shame (these will be investigated in the sections on emotion), but to the extent that one is aware of oneself as a conscious being. Expressed most concisely, consciousness is being aware that I am aware.

The content of consciousness, or what is being attended to, is the *relationship between an organism and an object*. By object I mean either an external object (or, more precisely, the internal image of an external object) or a thought. One must be conscious of something. Consciousness includes the knowledge or awareness of that interaction.

The self as subjective experience must not be confused with the self as object. Emotions, thoughts, and images are the *contents* of consciousness. The *subject* of the *experience* of consciousness, and of the unconscious, is the self.

Modern authors (Young-Eisendrath *et al.* 1987) have established a number of characteristics of the self which seem to be universal:

- **Agency**: The self is the originating cause, author or intent of an action.
- **Coherence**: There is an experience of unity and of a 'core self'. One has a discrete body and psychical boundaries.
- **Continuity**: A feeling of being the same over time through nonverbal and verbal narrative which gives me a feeling of connecting the present with the past and carrying it on into the future.
- **Emotional consistency**: There are relatively fixed instinctual patterns of emotions which are evoked in interpersonal relationships.

While these factors appear to be universal, the course of each individual life is unique and depends on a number of variables including family, society and culture as well as personal character and health.

Four characteristics of the experience of the self are essential (Blasi and Oresick 1987: 75–6):

- **Initiator/agent**: the awareness that the action results from myself as agent. Some part of me is the initiator of this experience. This does not mean the initiator of the associated bodily movements, but of the motivating force for the action.
- **Distinctness from oneself**: the understanding that the self as agent is the same as the self which is aware of the action, but that there is also a separation between the two. This separation must exist since I can reflect on both.
- **Unity**: the experience that myself as actor, myself as agent, myself as reflecting on the experience are all the same self.
- **Separateness from others**: the experience is my personal experience. It cannot be shared. I can never really feel the entire experience of another. My self is separate from everything else in the experience, and from all other people.

In any intentional action, the experience of the self includes that of a motivating force, conceiving the action; of myself as experiencing the entirety of that action and as separate from everything else that is not me in that action. I have a sense of identity with myself. I am conscious of myself both as subject and object of the action. I can reflect on my actions. I am responsible for my actions, for no outside agent is controlling my body or my mind. I am aware of different parts of myself and can reflect on them separately or globally. At times these separate parts are not in unity with one another, they have different 'minds', so to speak (ibid.).

I may also be aware that I am experiencing a certain emotional state, e.g. I may feel happy or angry. I have a certain feeling about myself which varies in different circumstances.

Language and symbolisation

Language appears to be unique to humans. Other animals use sounds or other forms of communication, but this seems to be limited to identifying objects, usually predators – at least as far as we can judge from our perspective. When referring to language as 'symbolic', researchers do not mean it in the Jungian sense of the term. Symbolic here means the linking of a sound and an object, emotion or event, etc. We also use our body as reference to immaterial objects or processes, e.g. we *explore* a problem or *feel on top of the world*. A similar process is the use of metaphor, in which two otherwise dissimilar things are linked together by a common aspect. It has been argued that all speech which is not a direct retelling of something that happened is metaphoric. Terrence Deacon (1997) calls this form of speech categorical, expressing the beginning of consciousness. Objects are not identified individually, but common characteristics are identified and abstracted, and the objects are placed into categories. An image or symbol can then be used to reference the category and, indirectly, any objects in that category. This has the advantage that larger quantities of information can be manipulated and decisions can be made based on broader concepts. However, it has the disadvantage that the richness and diversity of the original object or experience is lost. Jung reserved the use of the word 'symbol' for those images or objects which retain the richness of this lost diversity.

Meaning

Meaning needs to be distinguished from information. Information results from the ordering of data which in turn generates knowledge. Information has been defined precisely in a number of different mathematical disciplines. It has been broadly compared to a pattern and may, or may not, convey meaning.

Meaning exists only within a given context and does not exist independently of that subject-object relationship. It induces a change in the cognitive state of the subject. 'What was a mere phenomenon before becomes something that in association with other phenomena has meaning, that has a definite role to play, serves certain ends, and exerts meaningful effects' (Jung 1922/1928: para. 121).

'The sky is grey' conveys information about the colour of the sky. Placed in the context of someone's life situation and the emotions expressed it may convey the meaning that the person is sad or depressed. Meaning is created by putting the statement in an emotional setting and in context with what is already known about the person's life situation. If the intent which the person had is understood, meaning is communicated. Understanding then goes one step beyond the literal information to reception of the meaning content of the communication.

Meaning also conveys completeness. Things fit together; they are coherent with past experience. If something does not accord with our past experience, we are suddenly aroused, questioning if what we experienced is correct or if we have misinterpreted the event. When we understand the meaning we are again at ease; our sense of stability has been recovered.

I consider the establishment of meaning to be the final step in the process of creating consciousness. Once meaning emerges, an idea crystallises from a vague image or impression and becomes conscious.

The physical model of brain functioning

My primary source of scientific analysis of the creation of consciousness is the work of Antonio Damasio (1994, 1999a, 1999b, 2000) and Gerald Edelman and Giulio Tononi (Edelman and Tononi 2000a, 2000b). Both propose similar models, the principal difference between them being that Damasio emphasises the role played by emotions whereas Edelman stresses changes in the external environment. Since both emotion and perception are involved in the constellation of a complex, I will combine the two models and then show how this leads to consciousness.

Joseph LeDoux (1996, 2002) is another 'hard' scientist who has written readable works on his own research and the current state of neuroscientific understanding. In *The emotional brain* (1996) he explores the neural processes underpinning the generation and experience of emotions, principally fear, and their importance for survival. He concurs with Damasio that although emotions are not themselves conscious, they are central to our becoming conscious. His works have been referenced extensively by Jungian authors, notably Tresan (1996), Ekstrom (2004), Knox (2003, 2011) and Wilkinson (2006).

Global workspace theory (GW)

The global workspace theory, a concept within the philosophy of mind, complements the models of consciousness presented by Damasio and Edelman. GW divides the brain functions into a number of sub-processes. As long as only a small number of these sub-processes are involved in responding to a problem or stimulation, the event remains unconscious. If co-ordination between a larger number of sub-processes is required, the event becomes conscious (Dehaene and Naccache 2001). This theory is similar to some theories in biology. It is supported by brain imaging which shows that conscious cognition is associated with large-scale coherence of neural processing (Baars 2005 and Edelman 2004). It has also been supported by EEG and ERP mapping studies of global microstates of the brain lasting generally under 100ms (Lehmann 1989).

GW theory was formulated in *A cognitive theory of consciousness* by Bernard Baars (1988). It builds on the concept of modularity which, in its current versions, stems from Jerry Alan Fodor's work *Modularity of Mind* (1983). It is also supported by Dennett in his book *Consciousness explained* (1991). This model contests the Cartesian Theatre and the idea of a homunculus controlling consciousness. Consciousness in Dennett's theory, called the 'Multiple Drafts Model', has many parallel streams which are not 'viewed' in any one central place in the brain. There is no stage; there is no audience. The experience of a continuum of events happens when attention 'probes' one stream or another (also Dennett and Kinsbourn 1992).

GW is one of the major current theories on consciousness. Baar's original work (1988) has been acclaimed by Bruce Mangan (1995) as 'In my opinion the most important single book on consciousness since William James' *Principles of Psychology*'. It has also been criticised. Bruce Bridgeman calls it 'a thoroughly mechanistic, neurological idea' (Bridgeman 1996). David Chalmers criticises GW theory for being reductive and not acknowledging a direct physical correlation between consciousness and awareness (Chalmers 1995). Antti Revonsuo (2000: 64) criticises the lack in GW of a description of phenomenal consciousness, a point which Baars had already dealt with (Baars 1997b).

Jung's concept of consciousness

Jung, as one of the principal founders of depth psychology, was more interested in the unconscious than in consciousness. That is not to say that he considered consciousness unimportant. He called the differentiation of consciousness 'the most important task of human biology' (1942/1953: para. 291) and the act of being conscious 'the second cosmogony' (1961/1963: 371). 'Through consciousness man completes God's act of creation, because without consciousness the hundreds of millions of years of senseless birth and death have no meaning' (ibid.: 285). But he was concerned about the excessive emphasis being placed on it. He referred to the 'hypertrophy of consciousness' (Jung 1940/1954: para. 442) to the detriment of the archetypal forms and symbols of the unconscious (see also Jung 1953: para. 60).

When Jung speaks of individual consciousness and a person becoming conscious, he is usually not referring to a scientific definition of the conscious state, but principally of becoming aware. It is through the process of differentiation and the broadening of consciousness that one is freed from the 'claim of the other' (Jung 1921/1971: para. 179), the collective. It enables one to live out one's own free will, to engage in the process of individuation. Differentiation and the discernment of meaning is, however, a slow, deliberate process in comparison with the emergence of meaning discussed above. The 'meaning' here is in context of one's whole life rather than the immediate 'meaning' of the conscious moment.

By stressing differentiation, intellectualisation, awareness and free will, Jung is positioning himself as a dualist. The mind is something different from the brain and body. It is an intellectual, at times spiritual, quality. It is something we have that separates us from other species. It would be surprising, given the time and the culture that he grew up in, if he did not have a dualist perspective.

I will be considering three elements in the psyche in relation to consciousness: the ego-complex, the autonomous complex, and the archetype.

Ego-complex

Jung related consciousness closely with the ego: 'By consciousness I understand the relation of psychic contents to the ego, in so far as this relation is perceived as such by the ego. Relations to the ego that are not perceived as such are unconscious' (Jung 1921/1971: para. 700). He also often uses words such as 'awareness', 'directed', 'outward' and 'rational' as synonyms for consciousness.

The essential function of consciousness for Jung is discrimination (Jung 1921/1971: para. 179, also Jung 1916/1953: para. 329). As long as something is unconscious it is undifferentiated, i.e. internally undefined and fused together with other objects (Jung 1921/1971: para. 705). This act of differentiation begins with the separation of object and subject. Jung borrowed the term '*participation mystique*' from the anthropologist Levy-Buhl to mean the fusion of subject and object imagos. Their separation releases the psychic energy which is trapped in the unconscious relationship and makes it available to consciousness. This is why Jung said that the contents of the unconscious lack the energy to become conscious (Jung 1955–6: para. 152). He also relates the same process in terms of projection, and its withdrawal, to the widening of consciousness.

The ego is central to the concept of consciousness, which begins as an awareness of one's body and existence (Jung 1935a: para. 18) at the age of three or four (Jung 1988: 939). To this first body awareness Jung adds memories of past experiences which give one a feeling of continuity over time and impressions from outside (Jung 1935a: para. 18).

It is this form of consciousness, in relation to the ego-complex, that is being investigated scientifically and in the philosophy of mind: the ego-complex corresponds to what is colloquially called the 'self', 'attention' is that of everyday, and 'meaning' is in the context of one's everyday life.

Jung often used the metaphor of consciousness as enlightening or illuminating (Jung 1945/1954: para. 335), and thus the ego, as hero, increases consciousness by overcoming darkness. 'His [the hero's] ascent signifies a renewal of the light and hence a rebirth of consciousness from the darkness, i.e. from regression to the unconscious' (Jung 1912/1956, quoted in Frey-Rohn 1974: 117. My explanation added).

The autonomous complex and the archetype

However, Jung also wrote that 'unconscious complexes possess a certain luminosity, a kind of consciousness' (Jung 1955–6: para. 502) and described their coming into consciousness as the realisation of new insight. The ego-complex is, symbolically, the light of the sun, but there are 'other luminaries besides the sun' (ibid.), i.e. the autonomous complexes. Jung used the term 'splinter psyche' (1934/1948: para. 203–4) to describe the complex which, as Sandner and Beebe note, suggests 'each carrying a splinter of consciousness of its own' (Sandner and Beebe 1982: 298, quoted in Knox 2003: 91). Indeed, Jung even goes so far as to say that: 'The possibility that unconscious complexes possess a certain luminosity, a kind of consciousness, cannot be dismissed out of hand' (Jung 1955–6: para. 502, quoted in Shalit 2002: 76). This implies that consciousness is linked to the complex *per se* and not necessarily to the ego-complex alone. The constellation of a complex, or an archetype, brings with it the possibility to modify the existing position of the ego-complex. Attention is taken away from everyday activities, normal consciousness is disturbed, and one sees oneself and one's situation in a new light. The immediate meaning of the situation may be felt in terms of an instinctive reaction. However, the long-term meaning of the experience may contribute to the further development of the person, although it may only be fully understood, if at all, some time afterward when the ego-complex is back in control and the process of integration of the complex into the ego can take place.

In this respect the constellation of an archetype is different, for in this case the meaning is immediately apparent. In fact it seems to be the meaning which dominates the experience.

So although consciousness is usually associated with the ego-complex, the constellation of an autonomous complex or an archetype can lead to increased consciousness, i.e. increased understanding and freedom from unconscious domination.

The psyche

It was with the concept of the psyche that Jung left the traditional dualist position. He considered consciousness to be only a small part of the psyche. He envisaged the psyche as a continuum extending from consciousness through the personal unconscious and memories, and then through the emotions and the collective unconscious, to the instincts and ultimately to what he called the psychoid layers of the psyche where the mental passes into the physical body

(Jung 1958b: para. 780, Jung 1958c: para. 852). In several places he stresses this dependence of the ego, as the seat of consciousness, on the brain, particularly the neocortex, and ultimately on the physical body. However, he admits that he does not know what the psyche is, or where it comes from. 'At this point all science ends' (Jung 1937/1940: para. 33).

According to Jung, then, consciousness is not something given to humans from some higher power, as is usually believed by dualists, but arises from the brain and the body. Ultimately, Jung makes no distinction between the body and the psyche.

> The difference we make between the psyche and the body is artificial. It is done for the sake of a better understanding. In reality, there is nothing but a living body. That is the fact; and psyche is as much a living body as body is living psyche: it is just the same. (Jung, 1988: 396)

By linking consciousness with the body, Jung is stressing a phenomenological model of consciousness over an abstract, theoretical, dualist model. Because of its first-person investigation, phenomenology is much closer to the body in the mind-body continuum than are the more traditional scientific approaches. Indeed, phenomenology's close relation to the body and its link with the Kantian concept of transcendental idealism which Husserl introduced into phenomenology bringing in the concept of meaning (Woodruff Smith and Thomasson 2005: 10) positions it close to Jungian thought, as has been argued by some modern analytical psychologists (Brooke 1991a).

Jungians on consciousness

In classical Jungian theory, increased consciousness is seen as the goal of the Hero's journey. It is equated with enlightenment, light versus the darkness of the unconscious (Edinger 1984, Neumann 1954, Jaffé 1970/1984). However, Roger Brooke's analysis of Jung's views on consciousness (1991a: 120–35) is much closer to what I am proposing here. Brooke argues that, through Jung's work with complexes and their relation to the body, as with the Word Association Experiment, Jung is moving beyond the classical psychoanalytic distinction between conscious and unconscious (ibid.: 128). Starting, like Brooke, from Jung's theory of complexes, I explore how closely this matches current scientific understanding of consciousness.

Chapter 3

A theory of complexes

My aim in this section is to give an overview of what is considered in Jungian theory to be the feeling-toned complex and to emphasise those areas which I feel are important in the study of consciousness. It is necessary to separate the complex as a psychological structure from the experience of the constellation of an autonomous complex. I look at the two principal components of the complex from Jung's original definition and begin investigating their neural correlates. These will then be dealt with in greater detail in later chapters.

Jung was not alone in attempting to identify the psychological structures underpinning ways of reacting. I will compare some approaches from psychology and other fields with his complex theory.

Complexes and the body – why psychology started from here

My initial topic of interest in investigating complexes is the immediate, bodily experience. When one experiences a complex, one reacts to the bodily sensations and the disturbed ideation when one is taken by the constellation of an autonomous complex. It is not abstract. This was probably why psychology started from the complex.

Théodor Ziehen, professor at the University of Jena, (1898), first used the term 'complex' or 'gefühlsbetonter Vorstellungskomplex' (emotionally charged complex of representations).

Eugen Bleuler, Jung's supervisor at the Burghölzli, initiated the Word Association Experiment (WAE) which were designed to identify and measure complexes.

Working at the same time in France, Pierre Janet labelled the same phenomena with the term 'fixed ideas' which are characterised by the 'formation of new spheres of consciousness around memories of intensely arousing experiences, which … organise cognitive, affective and visceral elements of the trauma while simultaneously keeping them out of conscious awareness' (van der Kolk and van der Hart 1979: 1532, cited in Moskowitz 2005). Fixed ideas are 'thoughts or mental images which take on exaggerated proportions, have a high emotional charge, and, in hysterical patients, become isolated from the habitual personality, or personal consciousness' (van der Hart and Friedman 1989: 8, cited in Moskowitz 2005).

It was from Jung's initial training and experience as a psychiatrist at the Burghölzli in Zurich that the direct link between body and mind became evident to him. He realised the importance of the body while treating the mind. This is not something that once discovered he then abandoned; it runs like a thread through his entire work, even in his more esoteric themes of alchemy and the God image. His interest in alchemy was motivated by what he saw as a too one-sided concentration of western religions on spirituality and their exclusion of the physical body (von Franz 1982). In *Answer to Job* he speaks of the coming into consciousness of the God image through incarnation, i.e. manifesting as body. And in 1935, in the Zarathustra seminar he wrote: 'So it comes home to us that the body is the ultimate reason of everything which can be represented in and by consciousness. ... The body is extremely important, at the bottom of the whole business' (Jung 1988: 349–50).

Jung's early work on the complex as it manifests in the Word Association Experiment was heavily dependent on somatic measurements, as the titles of his works at that time indicate: 'On the psychophysical relations of the association experiment' (Jung 1907), 'Psychophysical investigations with the galvanometer and pneumograph in normal and insane individuals' (Peterson and Jung 1907) and 'Further investigations on the galvanic phenomenon and respiration in normal and insane individuals' (Jung 1907–8).

That the mind and body are closely linked can hardly be doubted today. The classical studies of brain anatomy investigated the result of brain lesions on the mind as well as on the body. Since the development of imaging techniques, the simultaneous effect of changes of both the mind and the brain can be observed. The widespread use of psychopharmacology is based on the effect that chemicals can have on mind phenomena such as mood and psychotic delusions.

Bipolar complexes, splinter psyches, sub-personalities and other Martians

Once the initial formulation of the theory was established, the complex did not inspire much further investigation and elaboration of the theory. Development eventually came in two areas: how complexes are related to one another, and the splitting off of part-personalities.

The first major development of the theory came from John Weir Perry (1970) with the concept of the bipolar complex, i.e. that complexes form in pairs such as father-son, authority-rebel or hero-cripple. Part of the complex is ego-systonic; it supports the ego and is ego-aligned. The other part is ego-projected, and thus part of the unconscious. Donald Sandner and John Beebe (1982) further developed this idea. Expanding from a pair to a network, Gustav Bovensiepen (2006) developed the concept of complexes related in a network structure, which is demonstrated in the illustration of the complex landscape revealed in the Word Association Experiment (Kast 1980, Vezzoli *et al.* 2007). Verena Kast also supports the bipolar nature of the complex (1990/1992: 47–8) as well as Bovensiepen's network, which she refers to as a 'landscape' (ibid.: 33). Kast also links complexes with episodic memory (Kast 1997: 41, cited in Jacoby 1999: 93), thus placing them in explicit, conscious memory. However, as I explain below, I generally position them in implicit, or unconscious, memory, thereby also contradicting Jacoby's association of them with RIGs[2] (ibid.).

Hans Dieckmann (1991/1999) stays very close to Jung's definition of the structure of the complex with the core and the related associations. He uses Jung's device of the four octahedrons assembled on top of one another in the analysis of complexes. He states that all complexes originate from the father and mother complexes, and uses Oedipus as an example to investigate parental complexes. Erel Shalit (2002) also uses Oedipus, along with other mythological and dream figures, in a very archetypal interpretation of complexes.

Joseph Redfearn (1994) developed the concept of the not-I as a sub-personality with relation to the body, but he did not mention complexes or splinter psyches. Nor do the body-oriented Jungians, such as Woodman and Sidoli, elaborate the complex in relation to body sensation or awareness.

My approach is closest to that of Anthony Stevens (Stevens and Price 1996: 26–7), who relates them to emotional schemata, and to Jerry Fodor's (1983) concept of modules.

Characteristics of the complex

There are two attributes of the complex which Jung identified that characterise his complex theory: the tendency of the psyche to split and the autonomous nature of the resulting 'splinter psyches'.

Splitting

Jung saw the psyche as highly dissociable, consisting of splinter sub-personalities (the complexes) which can be highly independent of the central ego. He was working at the time in close cooperation with Eugene Bleuler, who wrote: 'In every case, we are confronted with a more or less clear-cut splitting of the psychic functions. If the disease is marked, the personality loses its unity; at different times different psychic complexes seem to represent the personality … one set of complexes dominates the personality for a time, while other groups of ideas or drives are "split off" and seem either partly or completely impotent' (Bleuler 1911/1950: 9. Quotes in the original).

Originally the cause of the split was attributed to a traumatic event (Jung 1934/1948: para. 204). Although we still accept that a complex can form from a traumatic event, it is now more common to attribute the formation of complexes to a slow, repeated, pattern of mis-attunement, usually early in life.

Autonomous

Jung took up the term 'complex' in a much broader way by emphasising its relative independence from conscious control by calling it 'autonomous' or 'independent'. He believed splitting to be a normal process. It is the degree to which the splinters are disconnected from the ego which defines the pathology: a neurosis is a relative dissociation that allows for continued existence of the ego, whereas a psychosis is a total fragmentation of the ego (Jung 1939a: para. 516).

A complex is separate from the ego, except for the milder complexes which make up the ego complex itself. Other complexes are positioned with regard to their relation to the ego. According to later theory (Perry 1970), ego-aligned complexes are in relationship with the ego. Ego-projected ones are, like all projections, unconscious, and take energy away from the ego and break the original wholeness of the psyche.

Structure of a complex

Jung stated that the complex has a 'nuclear element and a large number of secondarily constellated associations' (see Figure 3.1). The nuclear element itself consists of two components. One of these is determined by experience, i.e. the life history of the person, especially his or her relations with parents and significant others. The other component in the nucleus of the autonomous complex is 'innate in the individual's character and determined by his disposition'. Around the outside are the cultural associations shaping the expected behaviour. What holds these all together, according to Jung, in effect the 'glue', is the emotional experience (all references from Jung 1928/1948: para. 18).

This structure is depicted in Figure 3.1.

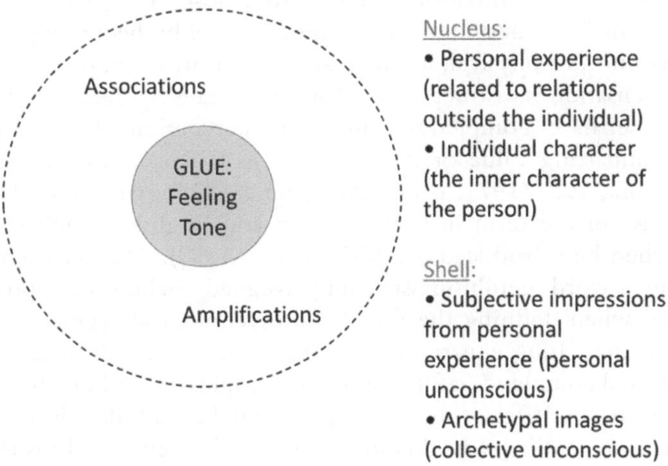

Figure 3.1 Structure of a complex

Jung most often spoke of the 'feeling-toned complex', stressing the central role played by emotion in holding together on the one hand personal memories, experiences, associations etc., and on the other archetypal associations.

Emotion

Neuroscientists differentiate between feelings and emotion. Emotions manifest as certain chemical states in the body, while feelings are the conscious awareness of those states (LeDoux 1996, Damasio 1999a: 42, 282). Feelings are what emotions feel like. To the extent that they are conscious they can enter into the evaluation and determination of future action. However, to the extent that they differ from the emotional experience, they fail to fully represent that experience. A part of that experience then remains unconscious and inaccessible to conscious forms of expression.

The scientific distinction between the phenomenal experience as feelings and the physical underpinning of that experience as emotions is no different from that between the experience of a sensory perception and the mechanism underlying that experience (e.g. a perceived sound as distinct from the ear and auditory primary and association cortices).

Jung also distinguished between emotions and feelings, although somewhat differently. For him emotion, as in today's neuroscience, is the physiological condition. It can be measured by such things as heart rate and chemical reactions. What neuroscientists call 'feeling', Jung labelled 'sensation' ('Empfindung' in German). 'Sensation is the psychological function that mediates the perception of a physical stimulus' (Jung 1921/1971: para. 792). This approaches what is meant by 'wahrnehmen' in German (Jung 1971: para. 787), which is a wonderful word that we don't have in English; the closest translation would be to 'realise' or 'actualise'. It means literally to make something real, genuine or true by becoming conscious of it. It connotes a physical, bodily reaction to a situation; one is physically present. Sensation is distinct from what Jung means by 'feeling' ('Gefühl'), which he separates completely from bodily perceptions. He uses it in the sense of imparting value or judgement (e.g. I like or dislike, it is good or bad) (Jung 1921/1971: para. 723–5, Jung 1935b: para. 45). This is an unusual use of the term in both German and English, which was questioned when he introduced it (1935c: para. 44–59). This does agree with the German word 'gefühlsmassig'. Jung assigned 'feeling' in opposition to 'thinking' when defining the four basic psychological types. To confuse matters further, Jung equates affect with emotion, which means that the feeling-toned complex ('gefühlsbetonter Komplex') should really be called the emotion- or 'affect-toned' complex, but he had already established the expression 'feeling-toned complex' before he developed his theory of psychological types.

In American English 'feelings' may also be called 'affects'. During the constellation of the complex, they 'affect' us; the sympathetic nervous system accelerates, heart rate and blood pressure increases, perception may be affected, and so forth.

Henceforth I will use the terms 'feelings', 'emotions' and 'affects' as defined by neuroscientists rather than Jung.

There are many different classifications of emotions, even though the existence of a set of basic emotions has been seriously contested (Ortony and Turner 1990). Most systems identify five to eight basic emotional response patterns (LeDoux 1996: 112–14). They all include some form of anger, joy, sadness, fear and disgust.

Charles Darwin in *The expression of the emotions in man and animals* (1872) identifies eight basic emotions (joy, surprise, interest, fear, distress, anger, contempt and shame). Each one of these has an innate bodily and facial expression which makes it readily identifiable by other people. The work of Sylvan Tomkins (1962, 1963, 1991) reinforced and extended the original work of Darwin.

Jaak Panksepp, in his investigation of the neural basis of emotional development (Panksepp *et al.* 1998), identifies three emotions, each linked with what he terms a corresponding 'basic emotional behaviour' (ibid.) which, I believe, correspond to what used to be called 'instincts': desire (seeking), anger (attack), and fear (freezing and flight).

More recently others, including cognitive psychologists (Kim and Hamann 2007, Plutchik 1994 for example), have developed similar classification schemas. Most of these are, however, abstract classifications which separate feeling from both the life situation in which it occurs and the emotional disposition of the subject, whereas Jung considered these to be of equal importance to the physical stimulus (Jung 1934/1948: para. 200).

In keeping with the importance of goal orientation in appraisal theory (see below), Richard Lazarus (1991) distinguishes between goal-incongruent (negative) emotions: anger, fright-anxiety, guilt-shame, sadness, envy-jealousy and disgust, and goal-congruent (positive) emotions: happiness-joy, pride, love-affection and relief.

Louis Stewart (1987), a Jungian analyst, has linked a set of seven basic emotions, which are very similar to those given by Darwin and Tomkins, to instinctive life-preserving situations. Stewart eliminates 'love' from their list, and combines shame and contempt by considering contempt to be the result of shame. To Stewart's list I have added 'caring' as a basic affect, manifesting at first the infant's self-caring expressed by actions such as thumb-sucking, and later developing into caring for others.

The Table 3.1 includes my modifications to Stewart's classification of the basic emotions and the life situations in which they are encountered.

Table 3.1 Affect and the life situation

Affect	*Life situation*
Engaging in the world	
Ecstasy (joy)	Encountering the familiar
Excitement (interest)	Encountering something novel, intriguing
Caring	Encountering others
Desire (sexual attraction)	Founding a family
Existential threats to life (self preservation)	
Terror (fear)	Confronting the unknown
Anguish (sadness)	Experiencing loss
Rage (anger)	Being restricted or controlled
Disgust (contempt)	Rejecting someone or something
Shame (humiliation)	Being exposed, defenceless
Centring attention	
Surprise	Sudden confrontation with the unexpected

It has been established that several of these, the 'negative' emotions, are present at birth. From these basic emotions others can appear in various combinations and intensities. Each expression is nuanced by many other factors. For example, even the potential euphoria of desire can be mixed with the fear of losing the desired object. This makes the neurological study of emotions imprecise, as shown by the following list of synonyms and associations.

- **Ecstasy/joy**: happiness, joy, relief, contentment, bliss, gaiety, delight, gladness, amusement, pride, sensual pleasure, thrill, rapture, gratification, satisfaction, euphoria, whimsy, ecstasy and, taken to extreme, mania.
- **Excitement/interest**: curiosity, fascination, attention, intrigue, mystery, fascination, cathexis.
- **Caring**: concern, acceptance, trust, kindness, affinity, friendliness, devotion, adoration, love, *agape*, desire.
- **Desire/sexual attraction**: wish, want, long for, crave, zeal, envy, lust, passion, ambition, aspiration, obsession, avarice, greed, gluttony.
- **Terror/fear**: anxiety, apprehension, nervousness, concern, consternation, misgiving, wariness, qualm, edginess, dread, fright, terror; as a psychopathology, phobia and panic.
- **Anguish/sadness**: grief, sorrow, cheerlessness, gloom, melancholy, self-pity, loneliness, dejection, despair, hurt and, when pathological, severe depression.

- **Rage/anger**: fury, outrage, resentment, wrath, exasperation, frustration, indignation, vexation, acrimony, animosity, annoyance, irritability, hostility and, perhaps at the extreme, pathological hatred and violence.
- **Disgust/contempt**: disdain, scorn, abhorrence, aversion, distaste, revulsion, contempt when directed outward.
- **Shame/humiliation**: guilt, embarrassment, chagrin, remorse, regret, mortification and contrition when directed inward.
- **Surprise**: shock, astonishment, amazement, wonder.

Joseph LeDoux states that, due to the great diversity in the neural basis of specific emotions, it is doubtful that a single, general-purpose system of emotion will be found. If such a system is envisioned, it will most likely involve synthesising across the findings for specific emotions (LeDoux 1995: 210).

Memory

Using the definition quoted above (Jung 1928/1948: para. 18) that the complex consists of:

1 a nuclear element, which itself is comprised of
  a life experiences and
  b the innate disposition of the person
2 secondary cultural associations

It can be seen that memory is involved in the complex as both memory of personal experiences, the life situation (1a) and memory of cultural associations (2). At one point Jung even spoke of the 'memory-complex' (Jung 1917/1953: para. 130).

Complexes involve the activation of memories, but not necessarily their recall, and sometimes not even their conscious recognition. The mechanism and consequences of such an unconscious activation have not yet been thoroughly studied scientifically. For this reason the relationship between complexes and memory storage and retrieval/activation in the brain is an area where Jungian theory could lead to interesting research in autobiographical memory and the level of consciousness.

Complexes may form because of a single traumatic incident, in which case the memory would be considered episodic (explicit). This would be the result of a discrete experience, which can be placed in a context of what happened before and after it even if, as in many cases, the actual traumatic incident is not always consciously remembered.

The more common case is when the complex forms because of repetitive experiences which run together in memory so that individual events are not remembered. In this case the memories would be classified as semantic. In severe cases of abuse, a person may dissociate during the incident and not consciously experience what is happening. Alternatively, the incidents contributing to the complex may have taken place before an infant was able to form explicit memories. These types of memories would then be classified as implicit.

In all of these cases, however, I propose that the trigger which sets off the constellation of the complex is a form of perceptual memory related usually to visual memory, but which can relate to any sensorial experience. It is, therefore, much closer to the bodily reaction. These memories are stored in the limbic system, principally in the amygdala, and are implicit (Dubuc 2002).

The second way in which memory is involved in the complex is through cultural associations stored as semantic memories laid down very early in life. Semantic memory begets meaning. Once we can tell a story a thread begins to run through our lives, connecting events. From this thread of events patterns can be discerned and categories appear around which we organise our perception of the world.

The infant learns ways of regulating emotions from the primary caregiver who is central in enabling, modulating and restricting experience and stimulation (Schore 1994: 12–13). The infant's developing neurobiology interacts with the caregiver's role of affect regulator (ibid.: 7). These early experiences are pre-symbolic and form part of the nonverbal, image-based memory system described by Pillemer and White (1989). Beebe and Lachmann concur with earlier research which indicates that these pre-symbolic representations of interaction will 'later constitute largely unconscious organising structures or memory structures in the child or adult' (Beebe and Lachmann 2002: 79). What is important here is that these memory traces are unconscious and nonverbal. They are stored before the development of the orbitofrontal cortex, which takes place during the second period of cortical development during the second year of life, and its role in the regulation of emotion (Schore 1994: 226).

The way that the caregiver interacts with the infant, her or his reactions to the child's emotional outbreaks and subtle gender cues all form part of these early memories and are largely culturally dependent (Leichtman, Wang and Pillemer 2003). They are similar to procedural memory and as such are stored in the putamen and the cerebellum, and as deeply ingrained habits in the caudate nucleus (Carter 1998: 162–3). This agrees with the research cited by Schore (1994) that they are pre-cortical, hence laid down before the control mechanism of the corticolimbic-orbitofrontal cortex is in place.

To this initial core of cultural memories are added the images imagined during exposure to fairy tales, religious rituals and other forms of cultural assimilation. They are the sort of things that one just picks up from one's surroundings and converts into memory traces of the way things 'should' be. Implicit memory is unconscious in the sense that one does not remember when it was learned. It includes culturally learned ways of reacting. These may not be in accord with a person's natural disposition, which is the second element in the nucleus of the complex as defined by Jung (Jung 1928/1948: para. 18), thereby causing feelings of not fitting in, of being an outsider.

Other theories similar to Jung's theory of complexes

Psychological theories

A number of psychological theories have developed in an attempt to define the structural organisation of the mind. No claim is made for corresponding physical structures in the brain. These theories are ways of conceiving how the mind structures relations with important people and events. It is not my intention to give a complete explanation of these theories, only to furnish enough information to be able, at the end of this section, to compare them with Jung's theory complexes.

Internal object and internal working model

Internal objects form from repeated caregiver-infant interactions. They are introjected images of important people in the life of the infant into its ego. They can be used to replace the real object when it is not present, but they include neither emotion nor interaction. The concept of the formation of negative and positive internal objects developed from this.

Internal working models include both the affective and cognitive representations of relationships (Bowlby 1973, cited in Schore 1994: 179; Main, Kaplan and Cassidy 1985) used by the infant in developing strategies to regulate affect (Kobak and Sceery 1988, cited in Schore ibid.). Schore elaborates the mechanism of such an internal working model in controlling emotion in the infant at approximately one year of age (ibid.: 192–6).

Both the internal object and the internal working model are formed before explicit memories can form, so they are implicit.

Schemas

One of the earliest and most widely discussed theories developed to address the broad category of semantic, autobiographical memory, more specifically to describe the mechanism of how memories are stored and subsequently retrieved, are schemas, scripts and memory organisation packets (Anderson and Conway 1997: 228–34, Baddeley *et al.* 2009: 128–34). The schema is based on both lived experiences and cultural norms.

The concept of schema approaches that of complexes in that it creates expectations that the scene being lived will end in a predetermined manner. Schrank (1982, referenced in Anderson and Conway 1997), in his formulation of the theory, specifically included the function of the achievement of a specific goal as an element in the schema. Similarly Bovensiepen (2006: 458) stresses the important role of the non-fulfilment of expectations, saved as implicit memories, in conjunction with inner working models and affects, in the constellation of a complex and the rupture of relationship which may follow. Personal expectations are also implicit in the formation of RIGs[1] (Stern 1985), which are considered to be the forerunners of complexes (Jacoby 1999: 56). What happened before is expected by the infant to happen again. The process by which the lived experience is transferred to fit the expected situation, as well as the expectations forming the lived experience, could lead to an interesting area of study.

As helpful as the original theory of schemas was as one of the first attempts to describe memory, in my opinion it fell short of explaining the emotional and unconscious nature of the complex. As Ekstrom (2004) notes, Schrank's revision of his earlier theory (1999) allows for unconscious knowledge gained from experience which is used without one's being able to explicitly state it, e.g. the knowledge behind split-second decisions, or knowledge of subtle body-language. This knowledge may be learned at a very young age. The theory still falls short because it overlooks the central role played by highly emotional content; this is made explicit in the theory of the feeling-toned complex.

Maladaptive or emotional schemas

A later version of schema theory, called maladaptive schemas, addressed these shortcomings by including emotion and both emotional (unconscious) and cognitive (conscious) memories (Young *et al.* 2003: 1–62). Although the 'triggering' of a schema sounds similar to the constellation of a complex, other ways in which the schema is described give the impression of a more generalised response pattern, i.e. a sort of coping mechanism, than an autonomous complex. The language used to explain schemas is both more in line with cognitive psychology and more descriptive of an emotional situation being played out – abandonment, mistrust, emotional deprivation, social isolation, and so forth (ibid.: 14). Complex theory would benefit from using this clearer form of naming the complexes in addition to 'classical' names such as mother and father complex.

On the other hand, from a clinical perspective, people suffering from, for example, early abuse exhibit several maladaptive schemas and a finer analysis of their emotional and behavioural patterns is needed.

Appraisals

Based on an evaluation of the current situation within the life history of the individual, appraisal theory includes both the personal history and the external situation. However, going beyond complexes, it also formally identifies future life goals as an element within the model of what is being played out at those moments when a complex constellates or an appraisal is made (Lazarus 1991: 133–52). This is of course implied in complex theory as an element in the formation of the meaning which emerges, but it is not explicitly elaborated by Jung in his formulation of the theory.

Appraisal theory also clearly identifies emotion as a central player. This link was reinforced by the more recent work of Marc Lewis which recognised appraisals as involving non-linear, self-organising processes incorporating both emotions and meaning (Lewis 2005: 173). The development of an appraisal is conceived as evolving from a two-phase process: a fast emotional path and a slower analysis resulting from cognition (ibid.: 172).

Jean Knox (Knox 2003: 14) acknowledges the similarity of emotional appraisals, as defined by Richard Lazarus (1991), to the feeling-toned complex.

Comparison

The following table summarises the information given above. Jung's theory of complexes is the only theory to incorporate an explicit awareness of the body's reaction during the experience and of a relation with the instinctive and/or collective unconscious. It is also the only theory which sees the autonomous complex as being outside of the ego's sphere of influence.

Table 3.2 Comparison of psychological theories

	Internal object	*Internal working model*	*Emotional schema*	*Appraisals*	*Complex*
Implicit memory	X	X	X	X	X
Explicit memory			X	X	X
Emotion		X	X	X	X
Internal image	X	X			X
Self in interaction		X	X	X	X
Meaning				X	X
Archetypal, instinctual core					X
Awareness of body reaction					X
Relation to ego	In ego	In ego	In ego	In ego	Separate

Other theories

The dual memory system

Pillemer and White (1989) developed a memory classification by dividing it into two large, functionally independent systems: a nonverbal image-based system and what they called a 'socially accessible system'. This division corresponds basically to that between semantic and episodic memory, with the additional specification that the nonverbal image-based system is present from birth and addressed by situational, affective cues. These memories are expressed through behaviour and emotion, as opposed to the verbal, narrative based, socially accessible system which develops during pre-school and early school childhood. The nonverbal image based system remains in place and underlies the later developed verbal system.

The primitive, nonverbal system comes close to Jung's concept underlying the feeling-toned complex; it is present from birth and uses emotion to encode and retrieve memories. Unfortunately Pillemer and White are known more for their work on the recall of childhood memories rather than the nonverbal, image-based memory system. They made one interesting finding, which is relevant for therapeutic work with people suffering from early wounding: although the development of the verbal ability to share memory is viewed as positive, it shapes how and what is eventually remembered (Reviere 1996: 58–9), and consequently what is forgotten, or what remains unconscious. With the beginnings of speech, a split occurs between the infant's direct personal experience and the retelling of it. A space is opened and 'it is exactly across this space that the connections and associations that constitute neurotic behavior may form' (Stern 1985: 182).

Table 3.3 The dual memory system (taken from Johnston 1997)

Dual memory system	
Nonverbal image-based system	*Socially accessible system*
• primitive • present from birth • addressable by situational or affective cues • contains fragmentary information • memories expressed through images, behaviours or emotions • learned routines • generalised past experiences not linked to specific events • accessed through reinstatement	• emerges slowly throughout the preschool years • addressable through intentional retrieval efforts • personally experienced events • encoded in narrative form • actively thought about or processed • can be accessed and recounted in response to social demands • contains information specific to time and places • develops with the acquisition of language

> This is the danger of narrative smoothing (semantic memory, referring here to the socially accessible system) – it not only supplies a simplified description for a more complex happening, but in many cases, the description, or covering narrative, take the place of the original happening and makes it impossible ever to see it clearly again. (Spence 1987: 137)

It is by bridging this divide that psychoanalysis can have an effect. It is by retelling the story of the original incident in the analytic session, reliving the emotion experienced, that the client can experience the same event, but this time as an adult, with an adult understanding of the event. This also opens the possibilities for using fantasy and psycho-drama type activities in analysis to change the emotional content of the memories. Dreams or memories can be played with by the analyst asking the client to imagine how he or she would have liked the experience or dream to have ended. If it could be changed, what could be imagined. Active imagination also bridges the gap between the language left and the image right brain, creating a global workspace involving emotion and cognition, and strengthening the ego.

Distributed processing models

Sophisticated connectionist theories in IT based on parallel processing models in distributed electronic information systems (McClelland and Rumelhart 1985) come closer to dealing with the complexity and flexibility of human autobiographical memory. These theories include inhibitory as well as excitatory signals and interactions. While applying this to a theory of mind does not explain unconscious memories, it at least elicits ideas of repression as an unconscious defence mechanism. Retrieval of memories involves the reinstating of activation patterns which arose previously from the external stimulus. This activation does not necessarily mirror the original input, thus allowing for a variation between the original event and the memory. Distributed processing models allow for variations in the importance of connections between the various memories, thereby explaining changes which can occur with the re-experiencing of memories.

As an aside, after working for about 40 years in a number of different positions within IT, I do not believe that machines, including sophisticated information systems, will ever be conscious in the same way that humans are. There may eventually, if they become complex enough, emerge some state which is as yet unknown to us. It would be useless to try to speculate what that state would be, but it would not be consciousness, which is based on a physical brain and body. We can, however, learn a lot by simulating consciousness using machines and by drawing analogies from our understanding of them.

Conditioning

It may be interesting to consider the behaviour resulting from a complex as the result of operant or learned conditioning, for there are a number of similarities between the two. The types of implicit memory involved in complexes activate the basal ganglia and, in particular, the caudate nucleus. These areas are also involved in conditioning, particularly the memory of associations and stimulus-response reactions. Conditioning also involves emotion, whether fear evoked by negative experiences or pleasure from positive, rewarding experiences. Complexes are more complicated than simple Pavlonian conditioning, but I question whether the underlying processes in the brain might be similar. In contrast with most other areas in cognitive psychology, the role of emotion in forming the connection between the conditioned stimulus and the resulting conditioned response is recognised. Some element in the context of the originating situation could act as the stimulus, just as the stimulus word is used in the Word Association Experiment to evoke the complex.

In the original Pavlonian conditioning, the conditioned response was very physical. This is also the case in conditioning a fearful reaction, which produces the same galvanic skin response which Jung used in 1906 and subsequent tests of the word association. Jung did not appear to be aware of Pavlov or his work. It is not mentioned in the collected works and there is only one reference to 'reflexology' in a letter to N. Kostyleff in 1952 (Jung 1976: 56). This is surprising because Pavlov's major work was done at the end of the nineteenth and beginning of the twentieth century at the time of Jung's own work with complexes and the Word Association Experiment, and before the Russian revolution and Stalinism closed the door to Russian and western scientific exchange.

Current, neuroscientific investigation of conditioning has demonstrated the existence in the amygdala of prepared, prewired connections to other cells that control emotional response. In this way certain responses are more easily evoked and conditioned than others (LeDoux 1996: 254). The existence of innate neural pathways supports what has been termed a fear-instinct.

Although fear conditioning is a form of unconscious implicit memory, phobia victims also have explicit memory of their fear reactions during previous exposure to the fear stimulus.

Work with people suffering from panic attacks has shown that these are similar to other fear conditioned responses, except that the stimulus, such as increased blood pressure or increased level of carbon dioxide in the blood, is internal (LeDoux 1996: 259). This could be similar to the many forms of inferiority complexes and social phobias where a combination of external and internal stimuli elicit the constellation of the complex.

Memory processing

Jung identified emotion as the glue which held together the memories making up the complex. The neuroscientific investigation of the link between these two areas goes back to Papez's discovery of the circuit linking the limbic system (emotion) with the hippocampus (the storage, retrieval and evaluation of memories) (Papez 1937, LeDoux 1995: 87–90). A larger circuit has more recently been discovered, establishing the role of the prefrontal cortex in the learned control of emotion (Schore 1994, 1999).

Types of memory

Yuko Munakata (2004) argues that types of memory having greatly divergent functions rely on different areas of the brain. She has linked three areas of the brain to three types of memory:

- working memory – prefrontal cortical regions
- episodic memory – hippocampal regions
- semantic memory – posterior cortical regions

Although there is general correlation of these three memory types with brain areas, the relationship is not simply one-to-one. Each of the memory types also depends on other cerebral functions, for example the temporal lobe also plays a crucial role in semantic memory, and each of the brain areas is also involved in other activities. In Munakata's analysis of the posterior cortical regions involved in semantic memory, which corresponds most closely to complexes, she relies in part on the works of McClelland and Rumelhart (1985, cited above with reference to distributed processing models) on parallel distributed information systems.

The pattern of neural connections which participate in the encoding and retrieval of a specific memory, called an *engram*, are not restricted to a single area but are distributed over many functionally different areas of the cortex (Bruce 2001: 308). Engrams were first proposed by Karl Spencer Lashley in 1950 (Lashley 1950). Recent research supports this theory that memories reside in specific, distributed brain cells and can be recalled by artificially stimulating these cells (Liu *et al*. 2012). What is also interesting about this research is that it is using fear conditioning in rats, thus integrating emotion and memory, the principal elements of the complex.

The following section reviews research on memory which I relate to the complex. It is based on the traditional classification of the memory process into stages comprising attentional arousal, initial encoding of the memory, a period of consolidation and storage, and finally retrieval.

Attention

As cited above, Louis Stewart (1987) as well as Darwin (1872) and Tomkins (1962) identified startle as the emotion which gets our attention. It starts the constellation of a complex by identifying the trigger which will set off the emotional reaction.

Although implicit and explicit memory systems have been shown, through behavioural studies based on lesions and brain damage and through neural imaging techniques, to differ, Turk-Browne and his colleagues have concluded that attention focussing is identical in implicit and explicit memory. Attention activates representational processing in the association cortices of the sense involved, which can then be used in either explicit or implicit memory processes (Turk-Browne *et al.* 2006: 923–4).

During encoding of memories, focussing attention on emotionally salient features of the experience ensures that these elements are retained, conferring an advantage for future retrieval (LaBar and Cabeza 2006: 55). Attention accentuates certain elements of an experience which are judged particularly dangerous, and which might then be used as a trigger to the constellation of a complex.

During the formation of a complex, certain signals are noted as being of particular importance and are then linked with what follows. These then serve as a warning. Studies in the reinstatement of extinguished conditional fear have shown that this contextual information, dependent on the hippocampus, is an important element in the reconditioning of a fearful response (LaBar and Cabeza 2006: 61). By the same logic it would appear that contextual cues add to the activation of a complex.

Initial encoding

The encoding of emotional and neutral experiences has been found to activate different parahippocampal areas: emotional memories are activated in the anterior, and neutral memories in the posterior, parahippocampal region (LaBar and Cabeza 2006: 57).

Episodic (explicit) memory is largely cognitive, and there is widespread agreement that it is predominately related to the hippocampus where context – the connection of the event with time and space – is added (Austin 1999: 182–4).

The relation between emotion and memory has been studied particularly with regard to fear and anxiety because of their importance in pathology, and to understand the effect of psycho-pharmaceuticals, particularly anxiolytics, on memory performance (Allain *et al.* 1999: 82). The central role of the amygdala in processing fear reactions and memories makes it a special case within the study of emotion and memory. It would appear probable, given the importance of fear for survival, that a special, fast-path mechanism for processing, evaluating and reacting to fearful situations has evolved. A large number of neurochemical substances are involved in the memory of anxious/fearful situations. All of these substances are found in both the amygdala and the hippocampus and are involved in both the evaluation of stressful situations and the storage of memories of these situations (ibid.).

Given the importance of immediate reaction to fearful situations, the creation of an imprint of the fearful situation in the form of a feeling-toned complex would bring an evolutionary advantage. Since nature has a way of repeating solutions which work in one situation, the formation of a complex might bring an advantage for survival not only in identical situations but also in similar, dangerous situations. Fear is rarely experienced without other emotions, and can thus be combined in unlimited ways with other emotions around which complexes can form.

Memory consolidation

Memory consolidation takes place at two timescales: synaptic consolidation within minutes extending to hours after the event, and system consolidation, the process by which memories are no longer dependent on the hippocampus for their retrieval, taking weeks, months, or years.

Three interconnected areas are involved in the consolidation of declarative memories (semantic and episodic): the medial temporal lobes including the hippocampal complex, the diencephalon and the basal forebrain. The hippocampus plays a central role in the encoding and retrieval of declarative memories until the memories have become 'long-term memories', this term denoting a state and not a location of memory storage. Less well known than the role of the hippocampus in memory retrieval, areas of the thalamus and the hypothalamus are also involved with memory retrieval, principally the voluntary retrieval of episodic memories. Interesting for us is the role played by the basal forebrain, closely associated with both the limbic structures and the orbitofrontal cortex and its role in the parasympathetic nervous system. The Papez circuit, involving the hippocampus, areas in the hypothalamus, the thalamus and the cingulate gyrus, originally conceived as a major circuit for emotional processing, is now primarily associated with memory (Zillmer *et al.* 2008: 229–31). This relationship of memory and emotion reflects the structure of the complex.

After a period of several years, episodic memories no longer need the hippocampus for their retrieval. It has been proposed that at this point they become semantic memories (Cohen and Squire 1980, cited in LeDoux 1996: 197). As a general rule, after about two years memories have become so distributed, stabilised and consolidated by being interconnected with other memories that damage to any one area of the brain will not destroy them (Austin 1999: 186).

The engagement of mild stress hormones, linked with the amygdala, during memory consolidation processes result in more explicit long-term memory for emotional than for neutral events (LeDoux 1996: 243–4). This is true for memory formation in the medial temporal lobe that has to do with emotional contextual situations and conditioning. The opposite is true for working memory and autobiographical memory centred in the prefrontal cortex which are impaired by stress hormones (LaBar and Cabeza 2006: 56). This may explain why the emotional elements of a complex are so readily activated while the cognitive information is difficult for one to consciously recall when placed in a similar situation. After the stressful situation has passed, the memories come back and one wonders why he or she didn't react more appropriately at the time.

Memories are the re-firing of neurons that fired together when the sensation, thought or experience first occurred. In the memory of sensory perceptions, the same neurons in the association cortices, which fired when the sense object was first encountered, fire again. Since memories are scattered over the various association cortices, some control agency is needed to see that they fire together again when the memory is invoked. For the first two or three years after the event this control agency is the hippocampus. After that the neurons are so used to firing together that they do it automatically and the hippocampus is no longer needed. Much of the replaying of memories during this two to three year period is done during dreaming (Carter 1998: 165). 'Information acquired during active behavior is thus re-expressed in hippocampal circuits during sleep' (Wilson and McNaughton 1994: 676). Jung considered complexes to be not only similar psychic formations to dreams (Jung 1937/1940: para. 37), but also the 'architect of dreams' (Jung 1934/1948: para. 210). To investigate dreams is to investigate complexes. In this process of memory consolidation we observe the reinforcing of the links between events and emotions which constitute the complex. In the dream series we are watching the evolution of the neuronal links as they become progressively integrated with other memories.

Retrieval

During the constellation of a complex, memories of what caused the complex are not usually activated. The memories retrieved are usually more implicit, or correspond more to familiarity than actual recollection. Andrew Yonelinas and his colleagues demonstrated that the patterns of neural activity generated during recollection and familiarity are qualitatively different across a number of brain regions including the prefrontal and parietal cortices. The hippocampus is involved in both, but in inverse relationship to the degree of confidence of recognition during familiarity. They were, however, unable to identify concretely what was happening in the regions specific to familiarity (Yonelinas *et al.* 2005).

Nicholas Turk-Browne and his colleagues concluded that implicit memory retrieval involved the activation of existing perceptual representations, and hence is more sense and body related than explicit memory retrieval, which relies on conscious reflection and elaboration of ideas, and is therefore more cognitive oriented (Turk-Browne 2006: 924). This corresponds with the bodily reactions experienced in relation to complexes.

In general it was found that retrieval of memories of emotionally charged images was clearer than that of neutral images, and that this could be predicted by measuring the activity between the amygdala and the medio temperal lobe, during both encoding and retrieval (LaBar and Cabeza 2006: 59). Viewing this data on the psychological level and applying the idea of psychic energy to these findings, these experiments suggest that the act of retrieval of the memory into consciousness releases the psychic energy associated with the memory when it was encoded. This psychic energy is related to the emotional charge of the memory and independent of the amount of cognitive recall involved. According to Jung an autonomous complex 'remains subliminal until its energy-charge is sufficient to carry it over the threshold into consciousness' (Jung 1922/1928: para. 122). For contents that are not remembered or are only familiar, this energy is not released and remains in the unconscious where it is then available to be used in the formation of a symbol which will eventually bring the content into consciousness.

Support for Jung's theory of memories being linked by emotion has come from mood-dependent memory studies. There is an innate bias to recall memories which match one's current mood, e.g. one remembers sad events if one is depressed (Blaney 1986, cited in Baddeley *et al.* 2009: 178). This tendency is recognised in cognitive treatment for depression in which the client is encouraged to resist the negative downward spiral of a depressed mood bringing to mind depressive thoughts which in turn reinforce the mood.

Note

1 Representations of Interactions that have been Generalised (Stern 1985).

Chapter 4

Dynamic systems theory (DST)

Complexity has been observed at all levels in living systems; within single organisms, between individuals in community, and in coevolving eco-systems. Within the individual, organised complexity is observable, to point out only a few instances, within the genomic system, the immune system, and the neural systems (Kauffman 1993: 173). In this section I apply the theories of complexity and dynamical systems to Jung's concept of the feeling-toned complex.

The application of nonlinear dynamics to complexes

Hermann Haken, founder of synergetics and Professor Emeritus of theoretical physics at the University of Stuttgart, started his career studying and formulating laser theory. The conception of the laser as a manifestation of self-organisation led to his further development of the theories of non-linear, non-equilibrium dynamical systems. He is the author of many books and articles, including those on synergetics (1983), chaos theory, cybernetics (1988/2000), physics and quantum mechanics, and brain functioning (1996). His theories are important for my discussion of the emergence of consciousness, and differ from those of other researchers in that he considers 'enslavement' – the emergence of an order parameter[1] which in turn locks the system into a new, emergent state – to be an example of 'circular causality'. This is a more rigorous application of the theory than simple emergence. I propose that this is the role played by symbolisation and meaning during the constellation of an autonomous complex.

Complexity is about patterns, particularly patterns which exhibit self-similarity across scale. Patterns emerge; they also evolve. The system is not fixed. Complexes too are about patterns of feeling and behaviour, patterns which form again in different, but similar, situations with predictable results, but in which variations also occur.

Within a basin of attraction, a complex system will always fall into a predetermined pattern. Once it is in the proximity of a complex, the psyche will tend to react as it has done many times before. This reaction may be very sudden. It could be described as nonlinear, as Jung measured with the Word Association Experiment. Suddenly consciousness is taken away from the normal functioning of the ego. Normal thought patterns are interrupted. The brain/psyche system enters into a period of instability and a new pattern emerges from within the system itself and forms around the new dominant emotion.

Enslavement by the order parameter is carried out by feedback. Both Damasio (1999a) and Edelman (2000a) have stressed the importance of feedback loops in the creation of consciousness.

Complexity deals with problems that cannot be solved using normal scientific methods: fluid mechanics, lasers, weather and open systems in general. It analyses systems, not by reducing them to their constituent parts, which is how science usually proceeds, but by observing the emergent characteristics of the system as a whole. As previously discussed, it is now believed that the brain functions as a global workspace (Baars 2005, Edelman and Tononi 2000a, 2000b). In investigating consciousness we are no longer interested in individual neurons, but in the emergent properties generated by their coordinated actions; about values, feelings, consciousness.

The following is my interpretation of how the autonomous and the ego-complexes could be viewed from DST. There are major differences between an autonomous complex and the ego-complex. The psychological state experienced as a complex correlates with a physiological configuration in the brain and the body. The autonomous complex is a single pronounced attractor state (i.e. a state into which the system settles after a long enough period of time), whereas the ego-complex is a set of less well-defined attractors which are activated routinely and which are usually formed during childhood. An autonomous complex may also be integrated into this basin of attractors, thereby losing its independent character in the ego-complex.

An autonomous complex is usually a total-body, defensive reaction to a perceived threat, either physical or psychological. Complexes reflect our evolutionary history and are present in all animals. The complex forms around, or can be identified ultimately with, an interpretation/meaning/evaluation which is archetypal in origin. It may or may not be conscious and may or may not be formulated in words or an image, but if it is, this grounding of the meaning in a concrete image or word helps the integration into the ego-complex. The emergence of the meaning or interpretation of the complex is the order parameter which synchronises the other sub-systems and constellates the complex.

The constellation of an autonomous complex is a sudden, nonlinear change, or state transition, involving an exaggerated emotional reaction. Changes within the ego-complex are more gradual and gentler.

The constellation of an autonomous complex is usually triggered by something happening outside the organism and first perceived by the sense organs. In some cases it may also be caused by the memory of a previous incident, but in this case the memory is playing the same role as the external event. Neurologically the memory of an object forms the same pattern in the neocortex as the actual perception of the object, minus the actual decoding in the primary sensorial cortex associated with the initial image. Changes within the ego-complex can additionally be triggered by the will, hence coming from inside as well as outside the organism.

The phenomenon of consciousness is related to complexes, either autonomous complexes or the ego-complex. The constellation of an autonomous complex usurps consciousness from the ego-complex. I propose that consciousness arises as a result of the synchronised integration of subsystems in the brain coordinating perception, attention, emotion and cognition in order to handle situations in the environment which cannot be dealt with automatically (unconsciously).

Consciousness, and hence the complex, is a result of the global coordination of many subsystems within the brain and emerges from their synchronised functioning.

Scientific arguments for the application of dynamical systems theory to consciousness

The mind as emergent

Roger Sperry was the first scientist to consider consciousness as an emergent quality of cerebral functioning. This realisation resulted from his work in the 1960s and 1970s with patients who had had their corpus callosum surgically severed, along with the division of the smaller anterior and hippocampal commissures, in an attempt to control extremely violent and potentially life-threatening epileptic seizures.

Subsequent tests revealed what appeared to be 'two independent streams of conscious awareness' (Sperry 1968: 724) split along the now well-known division between processing by the left, or dominant, cerebral hemisphere relating to language and logical analysis, and the right cerebral hemisphere relating to visual and auditory stimulation, spatial coordination and artistic ability. Each hemisphere appeared to function independently from the other, but also, depending on the task, simultaneously with it. Sperry concluded from this that consciousness emerged from a large area of the brain functioning as a single unit.

Although he conceived of the mind as being inevitably linked with the living brain, he did not reduce it to a material phenomenon. He placed his theories midway between dualism and materialism. He speaks of a 'mutual interdependence' existing between the physical and chemical processes occurring in the brain and emerging consciousness (Sperry 1968: 534). Jung expressed this same link of mind and brain when he wrote:

> Since psyche and matter are contained in one and the same world, and moreover are in continuous contact with one another and ultimately rest on irrepresentable, transcendental factors, it is not only possible but fairly probable, even, that psyche and matter are two different aspects of the same thing.
>
> (Jung 1946/1954: para. 418)

Sperry not only saw the mind arising from the brain, but saw consciousness exerting an encompassing control over the brain's functioning in the same way that Haken (1983) spoke of the order parameter enslaving a dynamical system. In other words, the mind emerging from the brain controls it. This hypothesis was highly contested when Sperry presented it in the 1960s and 1970s; it is much less so now that complexity has been scientifically and mathematically developed. That higher order macro-properties can enslave and affect lower-order micro-properties is a fundamental principle of emergence. Sperry calls this 'emergent mentalism' (Begley 2008: 136) or 'emergent causation' (Erdmann and Stover 1991: 50ff). In the same way I argue that it is the meaning/interpretation, and hence a cognitive product of the emerging system, which enslaves the constellation of a complex.

Although not explicitly claiming that consciousness is an emergent function of neural activity, Gerald Edelman links consciousness with the level of neural complexity evident in information processing: 'And it is only after such a level of complexity has been achieved that an adult brain, even when relatively isolated as in dreaming, can generate integrated neural processes of sufficient complexity to sustain conscious experience' (Edelman and Tononi 2000a: 138).

The question of causality is central to viewing consciousness or mind as an emergent property of the physical brain. However, the causality which is evident in emergence is not linear causality, but the circular causality of self-organisation which Haken calls enslavement. The combined action of neurons, neuro-chemicals and sensory inputs form a pattern of activity which in turn constrains the activities of these same neurons and neuro-chemicals (Freeman 1999: 180). The combined micro-level activity generates the macro-level state which in turn 'causes' or enslaves the same subsystems which generated it. A complete explanation of the mechanism involved does not yet exist, but at some later time may be explained by many-body field theory[2] (Freeman and Vitiello 2005). Neural networks cultivated *in vitro* have repeatedly been found to self-organise into hierarchical structures of spontaneous dynamical activity (Robinson *et al.*, 1993; Nakanishi and Kukita, 1998; van Pelt *et al.*, 2004; earlier references are cited in: Beggs and Plenz, 2003, 2004; all references cited in Werner 2010: 9). What is clear is that consciousness emerges from the coordinated, synchronous functioning of the brain, which is what happens when a complex constellates.

Emergence resulting from the global workspace

There is much scientific evidence in support of both functionalism and the global workspace theories of consciousness. Functionalism supports the view that multiple parallel conscious and unconscious processes occur simultaneously in the brain. Theories differ in the extent to which this compartmentalisation is believed to take place. In Jerry Fodor's original work (1983) he delineated nine domains. Others working along similar ideas of functional specialisation, including Dennett (1984), Tooby and Cosmides (1992), Pinker (1997) and Barette and Kurzban (2006), differ with regard to the extent of modularity, the level of automation involved, and the amount of decision-making autonomy a functional domain may exhibit, however the central idea of the division of labour remains. The global workspace adds to this the idea that, in order for higher-level consciousness to occur, several concurrent processes must be interconnected and in inter-communication to create within the brain a so-called 'global workspace'. Micro-states, mapped as EEG landscapes and lasting from milliseconds to under a second, attesting to a momentary, global functional state support the concept of this global workspace (Lehmann 1989).

The idea of a global workspace integrating these various areas to generate consciousness is hardly contested today. 'Most psycho-physiologists agree that, whatever form it takes, widespread coordination must occur' (Freeman 1999: 148).

This idea is in accord with a long history of attempts to create a hierarchical organisation of high-level conscious functions resting on low-level unconscious and automatic tasks (Dehaene and Changeux 2004: 5). It is in agreement with Fodor's concept of the co-existence of relatively independent functional modules, for handling such tasks as perception and linguistic processing, with a coordinating function (Fodor 1983). It builds directly on the work of Bernard Baars (1988, 1997a) defining a global workspace which is required to coordinate the various unconscious, specialised functions.

The global workspace does not define a fixed hard-wired area of the brain, but rather a flexible, dynamic assembly of functions needed for the immediate exchange of information and which changes from one instant to the next. These changes are activated by impulses originating from the limbic system (emotions) and modulated by the anterior cingulate cortex, the orbitofrontal cortex, and neuro-chemical balances. These impulses may arise from either internal or external sources (Dehaene and Changeux 2004: 10). This theory then goes beyond the search for the neural correlates of consciousness, for it claims that there is no single, fixed area necessary for consciousness to happen, but a flexible assemblage of differing modules involving processes of recurring and re-entrant stimulation. The correlation is not between particular individual neurons or even groups of neurons, but between distributed neural processes (Edelman and Tononi 2000a: 140). Edelman calls these linked processes the 'dynamic core' and uses the metaphor of a tangle of coiled springs under tension – any movement is rapidly transmitted to all the individual springs and has repercussions throughout the system (ibid.: 172).

The difference between the global workspace investigated by Dehaene and Changeux and the dynamic core proposed by Edelman and his colleagues is that the global workspace has more of a hierarchical, supervisory nature with a 'key role given to connections with the prefrontal cortex' (Dehaene and Changeux 2004: 24), while the dynamic core is more open. Both models stress re-entrant interactions within the thalamocortical system.

Numerous experiments have been conducted requiring subjects to respond once conscious recognition of a stimulus has been established. These verify that the subject is only conscious of the image once global synchronisation has been attained. Although this shows that synchronisation is necessary for consciousness, it does not show that it is sufficient, or that synchronisation at gamma frequencies is synonymous with consciousness. However, if there is synchrony, it must have an important function because there is a cost in energy and design to generate it.

Additional testing has shown that consciousness is associated with the activation of a widely distributed cortical network involving areas in all lobes and occurring simultaneously in both hemispheres. 'This observation fits with the hypotheses that conscious access is associated with a breakdown of local 'modular' processing and the broadcasting of accessed information to many bilateral cortical regions through long-distance cortico-cortical connections including those of the corpus callosum' (Del Cul *et al.* 2007: 12).

What these studies have also shown is that there is a considerable amount of unconscious processing taking place before consciousness is attained. Even at extremely short exposure times (16 ms) to a visual stimulus, activity was reported in the occipital cortex, and under 33 ms activity was also measured in the contralateral occipital, parietal and temporal areas, suggesting that even at such short time intervals effects are measurable at a 'peripheral or *subcortical* level' (ibid., emphasis added). Hence within a very short time the processing of a visual image has spread over a large portion of the brain. Del Cul and colleagues conclude that consciousness is not instantaneous, and that the data collected prior to its onset reflect a 'progressive process of conscious access' (ibid. 2007: 10–2).

Separation of consciousness from cognitive functions

Victor Lamme (2006), a dissenting voice, argues that our concept of consciousness should be separated from the cognitive functions (speech, movement, and learning) which are used in these tests to report it. Thus he seriously questions research based on the subject's response to visual stimuli which claims to supply evidence of the global workspace.

> You cannot *know* whether you have a conscious experience without resorting to cognitive functions such as attention, memory or inner speech. This problem lies at the heart of the seemingly unsolvable debate on the existence of 'non-accessible' or phenomenal (P-) consciousness.
>
> (Lamme 2006: 499)

At what point should one draw the line between conscious and unconscious? Lamme draws it at the level of processing between different areas within the association cortex. '... recurrent interactions between cortical neurons are the crucial feature of consciousness' (Lamme 2006: 499). He dissociates consciousness from emotion and even from what are usually considered cognitive functions required for consciousness such as attention, learning and working memory. Instead, he is stating that an image is conscious even before the person is aware of it, has responded to it or even paid attention to it. This agrees with the concept of a continuum of conscious states (Damasio 1999a, Edelman and Tononi 2000a) and the association of core or basic consciousness with awareness. One could say that rapid processing within the sensory cortex corresponds to a first level of awareness, whereas extended consciousness involves cognitive processing of that first level of awareness and corresponds to the global workspace. We are here at the dividing point between mind and brain.

Hierarchal dynamical systems

Dynamic causal modelling, which is the study of the interrelationships between dynamical systems, has revealed that a causal hierarchical architecture often exists between systems. They exhibit a bottom-up, rather than a top-down, control mechanism (Marreiros *et al.* 2010). A dynamical hierarchy is a system consisting of multiple levels exhibiting dynamical systems organisation within and between levels. Each emergent level can have properties exhibiting different functional characteristics. This is a characteristic of all emergent systems. Dynamical hierarchies have been found to be 'ubiquitous in living systems and fundamental to concepts of self-organization ...' (Lenaerts *et al.* 2005: 403). They have been identified in the building of protein molecules from amino acids and in protein-protein interactions, i.e. the very foundation of life as we know it.

Self-organisation has been identified at several anatomical levels of the brain, thereby defining a dynamical hierarchy. It has been studied in the sensory primary and association cortex of the olfactory (Freeman 1999), visual, auditory, and somatosensory systems; at the level of the primary motor and premotor cortex concerned with the coordination of sensory input with motor output, e.g. hand-eye coordination; at the rostral anterior cingulate cortex in the production of basic concepts required for decision-making; in the lateral prefrontal cortex and the control of emotions; and in the orbitofrontal cortex where emotion and expected future outcomes are combined in the making of decisions (Kiebel *et al.* 2008: Section 1).

Based on their investigation of timescales in brain functions, Stefan Kiebel (2008) and his colleagues propose that the brain adapts to the environment via a hierarchy of dynamical systems operating in a bottom-up direction over time intervals ranging from

- the fastest (millisecond to hundreds of milliseconds) neural connections operating in the sensory and association cortices
- tens of milliseconds response in the primary motor and premotor cortex

- tenths of seconds (100s of ms) to longer periods in the rostral anterior cingulate cortex, which involve decision making and action prediction
- similar time spans in the lateral prefrontal cortex involved in controlling emotion.

These same systems will be investigated in the discussion of the constellation of the autonomous complex.

Kiebel (Kiebel *et al.* 2008: 2–3) also supports the free energy principle, proposed by Karl Friston and his colleagues (Friston *et al.* 2006), which states that agents such as brains, which need to respond to the environment, function so as to minimise the uncertainty about sensory input. This would explain the tendency for the autonomous complex to perform as an attractor where the output from the second- or third-level systems forming preliminary decisions feeds back into the faster sensory cortices, interpreting current experience according to prior experience and thereby reinforcing the tendency to re-experience the sensation of the autonomous complex. On an unconscious level, the emerging pattern is interpreted as identical to one experienced before, and so confirms this same interpretation.

In the study by Del Cul and his colleagues, consciousness was identified by the correlation of objective measurements, based on EEG readings and subjective reports. Both measurements showed that the onset of consciousness is significantly nonlinear, a 'major transition in processing occurs' (Del Cul *et al.* 2007: 3). Their results showed that there appears to be a cumulative effect leading to conscious access of information, and that at a given point a nonlinear bifurcation occurs which produces the binary state of conscious or not-conscious. This supports the findings of Walter Freeman cited earlier.

Mapping psychological to neural state spaces

Harald Atmanspacher (Atmanspacher and beim Graben 2007, Allefeld *et al.* 2008), has applied dynamical systems theories to the emergence of consciousness. As well as specifying scientific criteria for the discussion of reductionism, emergence and supervenience, he and his colleagues determined the mathematical criteria (Allefeld *et al.* 2008) which must be met to prove emergence. After applying these criteria to human EEG readings, they were able to establish the presence of macro-states corresponding to the physical data (micro-states) in a patient suffering from petit-mal epilepsy. This enabled them to accurately differentiate when the patient was medically 'conscious' from times when he was not. I have followed this method of matching macro- to micro-states in my analysis of the constellation of the autonomous complex and the archetype.

The application of dynamical systems theory implies the correlation of two state spaces, one at the micro-level and one at the macro-level. In the case of an autonomous feeling-toned complex, the micro-level consists of the neural environment, and the macro-level is the phenomenological experience of the complex. I will be applying similar reasoning to that used to investigate the neural correlates of consciousness. Juergen Fell has used a state space analysis based on dynamical systems to investigate one of the constituents of consciousness, namely phenomenal awareness (Fell 2004). Marc Lewis relies on dynamical systems theory to 'bridge emotion theory and neurobiology' (Lewis 2005). Walter Freeman sees examples of self-organisation at all levels of the nervous system, and recommends the correlation of neural populations with perception, cognition and consciousness (Freeman 2000a).

Jung himself implied this method in a late article when he speculated that the neurological correlate of the archetype lay in the brain stem:

> I have long thought that, if there is any analogy between psychic and physiological processes, the organizing system of the brain must lie subcortically in the brain stem. This conjecture arose out of considering the psychology of an archetype of central importance and universal distribution represented in mandala symbols. … The reason that led me to conjecture a localization of a physiological basis for this archetype in the brain-stem was the psychological fact that besides being specifically characterized by the ordering and orienting role its uniting properties are predominantly affective. I would conjecture that such a subcortical system might somehow reflect characteristics of the archetypal form of the unconscious.
>
> (Jung 1958a: para. 582).

The application of dynamical systems theory to Jungian psychology views the neural environment as the micro-level. I'm using 'neural' to refer to the entire composition and activity of the brain, including neuro-chemicals and electromagnetic interactions, as well as the groupings of neurons themselves. This extends, through the endocrine system, to the entire body state, i.e. heart rate, respiration, levels of adrenaline, etc.. The macro-level is the psychological configuration as defined by Jung's theories of feeling-toned complexes. I shall be using the term 'attribute' to describe the characteristics which identify a psychological state, i.e. properties, which can take on differing values for different states and which are thus characteristic of them (for example, the degree of dissociation experienced, or the nature and intensity of emotion generated by a complex). For each of the attributes of the psychological state, there is a configuration of physical processes on the micro-level which correlates with it. Each attribute constitutes a separate dynamical system with its own attractor states. During normal ego-consciousness, in which no autonomous complex is activated, each system operates more or less within the normal limits defining its attractor state. There is a certain level of coordination between the states since the psychological states share some of the neural correlates with the systems of the other attributes. With the constellation of an autonomous complex, the separate systems coalesce to form a global, coordinated, higher level macro-state. This macro attractor state is characterised by what I believe to be the 'meaning' of the complex.

There then exists a correlation between the neural state (the micro-level) and the psychic state (the macro-level), experienced as either the ego- or an autonomous complex. This is not surprising; psychopharmacology is based on the premise that there is a correlation between the brain and psychological, phenomenological states. Once a conscious state has emerged it can no longer be equated or 'reduced' to the component parts any more than water can be reduced to hydrogen and oxygen.

Complexes and DST

Once triggered by an outside event, a complex dynamical system exhibits self-organisation, a phenomenon whereby the structure or form of a system results from internal constraints. It is often a characteristic of self-organising systems that, once the initial conditions are met, the resulting change in the macro-level state happens very rapidly. It may appear to be almost instantaneous. This radical change is not predictable from the observable initial characteristics of the system. In dynamical systems the old structure suddenly becomes unstable. Close to the transition point, the old control parameter (in the case of the constellation of an autonomous complex, this is the original emotional state) becomes enslaved by the new destabilising parameter (the predominant emotion associated with the complex) which will then determine the macro-level behaviour of the system (Haken 1983).

The reaction is not the result of linear, but of circular, causality. There is often an initial emotional reaction to something perceived. The new emotion affects the body which, in turn, affects perception and, at the same time, memories are activated. These both then modify the emotional state. Self-amplification in the form of positive feedback, a very fast spiralling of cause and effect between the limbic system, brain stem, body and neocortex, takes place until a new mental state (the constellated complex) is reached.

Marc D. Lewis, professor of human development and applied psychology at the University of Toronto, cites extensive research showing that non-linear dynamic interaction involving bi-directional feedback and circular causality must be applied in order to accurately model the integrated character of the emotion/appraisal psychological system (Lewis 2005). He used dense-array EEG/ERP (event-related potential) methods to tap the electrical activity of medial-frontal cortical regions. He then applied nonlinear dynamical systems modelling to traditional, causality-based cognitive theories of emotion. He argues that the theories of emergent order, bi-directional feedback and circular causality need to be applied in order to integrate emotional and appraisal psychological systems in a functional unity constituting a higher order motivational loop affecting conscious behaviour (Lewis 2005).

Chaotic complexity, characterised by power-law scaling, self-similarity, and self-organised criticality, has been identified at all levels of neuronal structures and processes (Werner 2010: 2; Toib *et al.* 1998 cited in Werner 2010: 7) from the micro-level – ion channels controlling the firing pattern of neurons (Anderson 2000: 203–4), neurotransmitter release in synaptic gaps (ibid.: 205–6), the branching patterns of dendritic trees (Caserta *et al.* 1990, cited in Werner 2010) – through the meso-level to the macro-level of neural organisation.

Power-law scaling, self-similarity, and criticality have been found at various levels connected with *perception*: the fractal dendrite branching structure in the visual cortex (Zietsch and Elston 2005, cited in Werner 2010: 5), the cutaneous afferent nerve fibers (Werner and Mountcastle 1963, 1964 cited in Werner 2010: 6), and the olfactory bulb (Freeman 1999). David Gilden showed that what had been attributed to random neuronal firing in the cerebral cortex was in fact a 1/f fluctuation (also called power law scaling) attributable to a form of representational *memory* (Gilden 1997, 2001, cited in Werner 2010: 22). *Energy levels* are also reflected through the transmission of the neural impulse at the neuromuscular junction (del Castillo and Katz 1954 cited in Werner 2010: 6). These three systems; *perception*, *memory* and *energy levels*, are all attributes involved in the constellation of the autonomous complex.

Much of what was one time considered to be merely noise, i.e. random background neuronal pulses, has now been identified as exhibiting a power-law spectrum. This has been interpreted as evidence of self-organisation on a cognitive level, coordinating the activity via hierarchical timescales. Researchers differ in considering whether 1/f scaling is a cause or a result of self-organised criticality (Van Orden *et al.* 2003, cited in Werner 2010: 23; Wagenmakers *et al.* 2005) but the presence of complexity is not questioned.

Power-law scaling has been identified not only in numerous physical systems such as coast lines, cloud formations, tree branches etc., but also in cognitive processes such as language. Zipf's law (Costa *et al.* 2009).) identifies a power-law probability distribution in the frequency with which a word is used. George Hogenson proposes that this can be extrapolated to symbolic systems in general (Hogenson 2005).

Self-organised fractal neural burst patterns have been documented in foetal REM sleep, which are believed to be associated with long and short range coordination in the development of lungs, muscle control, the brain stem and cerebellum (Anderson 2000: 195). These are all fully developed by birth (Eliot 1999), showing that complexity is instrumental even before birth and plays a major role in our development. Analysis of fMRI scans has revealed self-similar time scale fluctuations in the temporal lobes, brain stem and cerebellum (Anderson 2000: 195), and hence in the cortical and subcortical regions. These fluctuations may combine, thereby 'creating the functional unity of consciousness' (ibid.: 196).

What is needed is research, either imaging or EEG, conducted at the moment a complex constellates, i.e. when sudden, pervasive emotion is triggered, to show clearly the detailed sequence of events which follow.

Research supporting the global workspace

Werner (2010: 13) gives two guiding considerations for neuroscientific research with regard to dynamical/chaotic systems: the network structure of cortical connectivity, and the presence of macro-level attractor states (i.e. the attractor state of the constellated complex) due to complexity of its underlying components (the brain and body system involved in that constellation). 'There is considerable evidence that *anatomical* and *functional* connections between different cortical areas possess an intricate organization … forming clusters of nearby cortical areas with short links, which in turn have long-range connections to other structures' (ibid., citing Watts and Strogatz 1998; Hilgetag and Kaiser, 2004; Sporns and Zwi, 2004; Sporns *et al.* 2004; Stam 2004; Stam and Reijneveld 2007, emphasis mine). It is believed to be this hierarchical modular structure which guarantees the stability and diversity of functions (Kaiser *et al.* 2007, cited in Werner 2010: 14). This structure has been found to be conducive to synchronisation across the network (Zhou *et al.* 2007, cited in Werner 2010: 15), to conserve energy, and to lead to optimal problem-solving (Anderson 2000: 207).

Advances in imaging techniques over the last decade, indeed in the last couple of years (Buckner 2010), have verified the presence of resilient, small-world, functional networks between the cortical and subcortical regions, some including the paralimbic and limbic regions, although these were more peripheral (Achard *et al.* 2006). The formation of a global neuronal workspace was validated during cognitive performance testing involving working memory at differing levels of difficulty (Kitzbichler *et al.* 2011). Mark Kramer and colleagues studied the evolution of functional networks with a core set of connections which constellated frequently and concurrently, thereby forming a stable cortical network structure. They observed that from this stable platform intermittent activity patterns form and dissipate (Kramer *et al.* 2011).

Although I would like to claim that the global workspace model has been definitively proven, I must admit that the concept has not been adequately validated because of the lack of substantiated evidence of cortical-limbic integration. More research linking cognitive and affective processes needs to be carried out. Most of the research cited above involves cortical to cortical connections. Another omission from this research is the concept of the self, which is considered to be centred in the cortical and precortical structures close to the limbic system, and investigation into how that is integrated with other, principally cortical, areas functionally involving perception and movement. Although a number of the articles cited, and others, speak of 'cognition', none affirms *consciousness*. I believe that this will be done, but that at this time this research is insufficient to completely validate the global workspace model and its role in determining consciousness.

Complex as attractor

Self-organising criticality is the tendency of a dynamical system to settle into an attractor state at certain, critical points in the state space. Critical activity patterns in the brain were proposed as early as 1950 by Alan Turing (1950) and have been documented by Haken *et al.* (1985) and Kelso (1995). These examples, and more recent ones (Varela *et al.* 2001 and Le Van Quyen 2003, cited in Werner 2010: 15), are limited to motor behaviour and do not include the cognitive-affective coordination that I propose is involved in the constellation of a complex.

The phase transition at a critical point (as happens during the constellation of either a complex within the ego-complex or an autonomous complex) transforms local into global functional connections which coordinate over widely dispersed functional and special areas (Perez-Mercader 2004 and Penrose 1986, cited in Werner 2010: 25). This synchrony over various functional areas is believed to lead to the experience of consciousness.

The set of all of the possible attractors constitutes all of the possible long-term behaviours of the system (Kauffman 1993: 177). Likewise, the set of all of the complexes constitutes all of the possible states that the psyche can be in. Because the brain is an open system and people can always learn, new complexes, and hence new attractors, can form.

The fact that the psyche can move about from one attractor, or one complex, to another implies that there is some form of psychic energy which is the driving force. Jung postulated the existence of such a form of energy on the psychic level which, when added to the complex, would push it over into consciousness (Jung 1922/1928). Criticality, the ability of dynamical systems to change attractor states, is observed in non-equilibrium open systems having many degrees of freedom, and therefore always functioning, approaching conditions causing constant shifting within a fluctuating state space.

A system which is in an attractor state may be more or less stable against outside perturbations (Kauffman 1993: 177). The degree of stability can be measured for physical systems, so the same should be true of complexes. Some complexes seem more entrenched, in which case the person has a harder time getting out of them and back to a normal state than from others; some also last longer and are more resistant to integration into the ego complex.

The autonomous complex as a point attractor

The simplest form of attractor is a point attractor. Figure 4.1 could represent any damped physical system (the grey ball) coming to rest at the bottom of the curve indicating that there is only one possible state that the system can take. This is an example of a state space diagram.

Figure 4.1 Complex as a point attractor

An autonomous complex corresponds to a point attractor in a psychic state space. In this case the ball represents the psyche, and the line all of the psychological states that could be experienced around a single complex. This illustrates my hypothesis that the complex is an attractor, a point or state in the space where the system of the psyche stays for a relatively long period of time.

Bipolar complexes as a set of two point attractors

J.W. Perry (1970) proposed that some complexes have two modes of constellating, for example the rebel-authority complex. Such bipolar complexes correspond to a set of two point attractors in a psychic state space (Figure 4.2).

The system can be in only one of the two states when this complex is fully constellated. The person is acting as either the rebel or the authority figure. They are limited to stay in only one of these two roles (states) depending on the parameters of the system.

The ego-complex as an attractor network

An attractor network is a set of attractors which are recurrently connected and, with time, settle into a stable pattern. Theoretical neuroscience has associated cognitive functions, such as memory and behaviour, with attractor networks (Eliasmith 2007).

The ego-complex described by Jung (Jung 1946/1954: para. 387) as a set of complexes corresponds to an attractor network.

George Hogenson claims that the Self is the set of all attractor states in a state space in which 'a process of self-organising emergence can take place' (Hogenson 2004: 76), analogous to defining 'an individual's life pattern' (ibid.: 77). He is equating here the archetype with the attractor state of *the complex* (although he doesn't state this explicitly, it is clear from the Saunders and Skar article (2001) that he references). Careful attention must be paid to exactly what state space is being addressed. Within the system he is proposing the archetype is emergent and consequently, on the macro-level, the state space would comprise all the archetypes which can emerge. As the Self is the sum of all archetypes, his logic is consistent (see Figure 4.2).

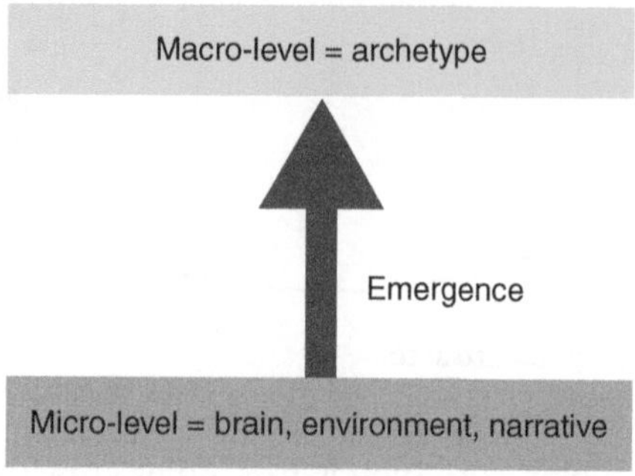

Figure 4.2 Archetype as emergent property (Hogenson)

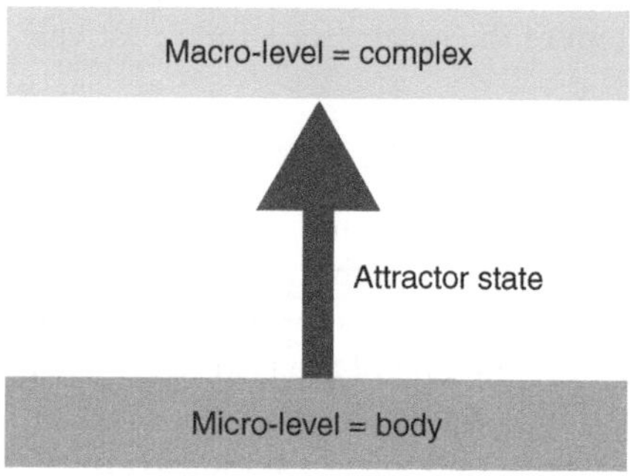

Figure 4.3 Complex in relation to the body (my model)

I contend that brain (including the body), environment (through perception and awareness) and narrative (including memory, both cultural and personal) are constantly combining to form or modify complexes, either the ego-complex or an autonomous complex.

I will start from the more tangible position of the body and how the psyche is physically experienced, as I find it much more informative to view the complex as emergent from the body (see Figure 4.3).

Both models are correct depending on one's viewpoint. Dynamical systems are hierarchical, so one must just be clear what level is being described.

It remains for me to explain the archetype in the context of my model. Jung most often described the archetype as a *pattern of behaviour* or a *pattern of action* (1957/1959: para. 549–50; 1912/1956: para. 224; 1919: para. 270, 274, 398; 1946/1954: para. 398 and others). The pattern in a self-organising system is fractal. A fractal is generated by a node or pattern which is repeated when the scale of reference is changed. It can also be seen as defining the form of the curve in the state space, the states that the system can be in. In Hogenson's example of the Self as the 'differential equation' of the line defining the state space (Hogenson 2005: 77), the differential equation defines how the system changes over time. The pattern in Hogenson's model would show the pattern of archetypes in a person's life, and this could be called the Self. In my model this would be the pattern of complexes as they constellate. In everyday life, this is the attractor network defining the ego-complex. Allowing for the autonomous complexes, this represents the psychic landscape of states which are regularly experienced.

I argue that it is consciousness which emerges from the complex (Figure 4.4). The archetypal image and, by putting it in the context of an individual's life, the interpretation or meaning it has for the person, is the order parameter which enslaves the dynamical system of body and psyche, thereby leading to the emergence of consciousness. The revelation of the archetypal, symbolical image and its associated meaning is the final step in a hierarchal dynamical process of emergence (see Chapter 6).

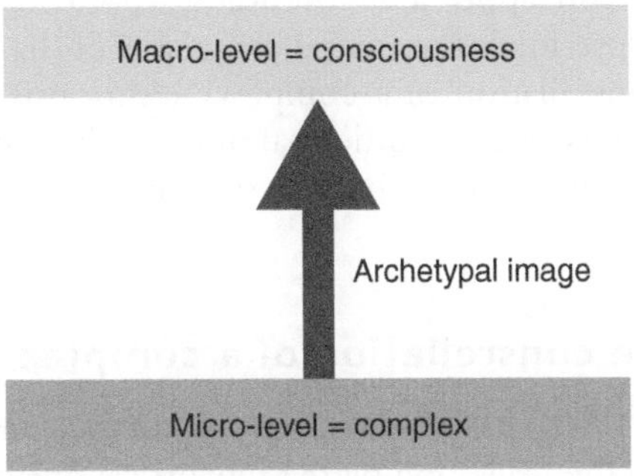

Figure 4.4 The emergence of consciousness

Notes

1 An order parameter is an element in the system (it may be a single variable or something more complicated like a field) which emerges from the system and which, in turn, determines the resulting phase transition. For example, in the case of water boiling, the order parameter is the water density, when it reaches a certain point the liquid change to gas.

2 Many-body field theory, also called quantum field theory, is the study within physics of extremely complex, interacting systems (e.g. fluid mechanics).

Chapter 5

Constellation of a complex

In this chapter I will apply a methodology used in dynamical systems theory (DST) to determine the neural correlates of the psychological phenomena of the constellation of a complex. Using this method, I identify six control parameters and one order parameter which determine the reaction of the psychological and physical systems as self-organising into an attractor state.

A model of the constellation of a complex

Antonio Damasio (1999a) has proposed a model of the generation of core consciousness based on the realisation by the subcortical organs of a change in the body state. With the addition of the self in the form of autobiographic memory this becomes extended consciousness, the state we recognise as consciousness. I propose that the constellation of an autonomous complex is a similar process. In this case the memories bring with them a strong emotional charge which floods the limbic system. The body reacts accordingly and, in the best of cases, the neocortex is able to sort out what is happening and correctly evaluates the situation. It sends dampening messages to the limbic system to calm down, and things eventually return to their normal state. If the memory images are too strong, or if the dampening mechanism is not functioning optimally, then inaccurate, overly emotional images are sent to the neocortex for evaluation, resulting in the activation of a complex.

The constellation of a complex is an overall reaction to a situation. Most of it occurs in the unconscious. Based on the logic of Damasio (1999a), and supported by Edelman and Tononi (2000a), it seems that only after the body has reacted can the conscious mind become aware of the reaction and recognise the constellation, if at all.

In the reactivation of old memories associated with the complex, Jung also discovered the feedback loop Damasio and Edelman identified as necessary for consciousness. Using fright as the central affect, Jung gave the example that the awareness of the threatening situation:

is followed by bodily excitations of the sympathetic nervous system. The perception has thus found the way to somatic innervation and thereby helped the complex associated with it to gain the upper hand. Through the fright, countless body sensations become altered, and in turn alter most of the sensations on which the normal ego is based. Consequently the normal ego loses its attention tone ...

(Jung 1907/1960: para. 86)

Jung's model of psychic energy as related to the constellation of a complex

Jung used an extension of the libido theory, what he conceived of as psychic energy, which was in vogue at the time with other psychoanalytical schools as well as in philosophy, to describe what happens during the constellation of a complex. According to his model, in the normal state energy flows constantly between various complexes associated with the ego complex. Once something triggers the constellation of an autonomous complex, energy is taken away from other psychological complexes, which thereby become impoverished, and flows to the constellating complex (Jung 1907/1960: para. 103, Jung 1922/1928: para. 123).

The vestiges of the theory of psychic energy can be seen in the evaluation of glucose consumption in brain imaging techniques. It is the basis for fMRI and PET imaging. The brain actually requires enormous amounts of energy in comparison to its proportion of body weight. Much of this energy is used for the transformation of amino acids into the neurotransmitters which are important in the generation and regulation of emotions (Benton *et al.* 1996). Since the constellation of a complex generates emotions, it must be associated with an increase in glucose consumption and hence psychic energy.

The original experiments

Jung's original experiments were conducted between about 1902 and 1909 (Read *et al.* 1973: v-vii). Although he tested electrical conductivity, measuring effectively moisture on the skin, and respiration rate, the pneumographic test results were inconsistent (Peterson and Jung 1907: para. 1062) and only the galvanic tests results were retained as significant and passed into history. Jung related the reaction to the intensity of the 'feeling-tone' elicited by the stimulus word (Jung 1907: para. 1015), and physically to the sympathetic nervous system (Jung 1926/1960: para. 642).

The sympathetic nervous system, originating in the spinal column, controls not only the sweat glands and heart rate, but also blood pressure, pupil dilation, breathing, and digestion. (Zillmer *et al.* 2008). It is believed to have evolved because of its contribution to species survival (Ornstein 1992). This tends to support Jung's view of the evolutionary background of complexes.

Mapping between psychological and physical state spaces

I will attempt to map the neural correlates underpinning the constellation of a complex. The method of mapping has been used since the first attempts to define the neural correlates of a psychological state; indeed it goes back to the earliest attempts to investigate the capacity for thought in artificial intelligence (Browne et al 1997: 1304). It has been used by Atmanspacher and his colleagues to investigate the emergence of mental representations from neural assemblies (Atmanspacher and beim Graben 2007, Allefeld *et al.* 2009).

This method describes the correspondence of what happens on a physical level to what is experienced on the psychological level. First, the attributes of the psychological state space must be identified. These are the parameters of the system, in other words what needs to be described in order to uniquely distinguish that state from all others, thus defining the variables which must be specified in order to identify a particular phenomenological experience. A similar method is used in object-oriented systems analysis as defined in information technology. Here they are called the attributes of the object. In mathematics, these correspond to the components of the state vector. In dynamical systems theory, they are the degrees of freedom of the system.

Jung intuitively felt this same link between the physical and psychic levels: 'It is extremely difficult, if not impossible, to think of a psychic function as independent of its organ, although in actual fact we experience the psychic process apart from its relation to the organic substrate' (Jung 1946/1954: para. 368).

Second, the possible values of each attribute or parameter must be specified. Not all physical or conceivable values are possible, so some values can be excluded.

Third, a correlation between the states in the psychological environment (the constellated complex) and the states in the neural environment must be established, and an explanation given for the corresponding interrelationship. I base this mapping on already existing scientific research.

Parameters of the constellation of an autonomous complex

The following is my own classification of the parameters or attributes of the constellation of an autonomous complex. The complex itself was discussed above. The physiological and psychological changes that can take place when a complex constellates are listed below. Apart from Jung's initial work I could find no other attempts by Jungian authors to define what is meant physically when a complex constellates. Hillman comes close to defining the same attributes when he writes on emotion:

> Each emotion has: its own pattern of behaviour and quality of experience which is always a total attitude of the whole psyche; its own distribution and intensity of energy; its own symbolic stimulus which is partly conscious and partly not presented to consciousness; its own achieved transformation which has some survival value and is some improvement compared with non-emotional states.
>
> (Hillman 1962: 286 quoted in Stewart 1987: 32 and Cope 2006: 24)

Both Hillman's specifications and mine refer to the level of energy generated and the symbol involved. While Hillman refers to the value for survival of emotion, I go back to Jung's reference to the constellated instinct, which also often has implications for survival.

Jung proposed that complexes are part of an evolutionary system which predates self-consciousness (Jung 1930/1950: para. 152). In his early studies he stated that complexes regulate an organism's reactions in situations of danger and within a social setting. These situations have been similar throughout evolutionary history, and the mechanisms involved have strong corollaries with those operating in other animals (LeDoux 1996: 17). Thus much of what happens on the physical level is independent of conscious awareness.

Because the emotion generated during the constellation of a complex is such a central and characteristic phenomenon, much of what has been written about emotion and feelings applies also to complexes. Much of the scientific investigation of various emotions is the basis for the mapping of psychological to physical state spaces which follows. However, the constellation of a complex also involves the activation of implicit and explicit memories of the experience and the feeling of having been in similar situations, as well as those memories related to the cultural and archetypal images. It culminates in a meaning, interpretation, or evaluation for the individual in a social context.

Jung linked sense perception, intellectual components (ideas, memory, judgements, etc.) with a distinctive feeling to form a functional unit which he called the complex (Jung 1907/1960: para. 79). To these I have added the physical and psychological effects resulting as the complex constellates: the change in the level of awareness, the energy generated, and the emergent symbolic image and meaning.

Therefore I identify the following parameters of the constellation of the autonomous complex:

- perception
- level of awareness/attention
- emotion and instinct
- energy generated and somatic metrics
- memory
- symbolic image
- interpretation/meaning

Perception

Autonomous complexes are most often triggered by something perceived. Something in the outside world, experienced by one or more of the senses, suddenly upsets the current state of the psyche, causing a phase transition away from the normal ego-complex into a new psychic state.

Research with trauma victims has shown that they 'over-focus on trauma cues' and 'show hypersensitivity and enhanced perceptual priming to traumatic or threatening stimuli' (Paz-Alonso *et al.* 2009: 213). This suggests that less and less stimulation is needed to trigger each subsequent constellation of a complex. Each time a situation is encountered that is similar to those related to the complex, the body reacts with increased sensitivity.

Level of awareness/attention

The phenomenal awareness of oneself and one's surroundings is altered during the constellation of a complex. One can have the experience of being in a fog with sense perception diminished, or the opposite, hyperconscious of every sound, every smell, every sense perception. In addition to the relation of the ego to consciousness, dissociation (and, I suggest, over sensitivity) also interrupts normal ego functions, such as memory, identity and perception (DSM-IV-TR 2000: 519), so that normal processing may become distorted or temporarily interrupted, thereby affecting memory and future interpretation of the event.

Awareness is often confused with consciousness. We can say that a person is 'conscious' of something, meaning that he or she is aware of it, but that does not mean that awareness and consciousness are identical. Awareness is related to attention. Both involve the relation between a subject and object, but awareness is more centred in the body, whereas attention is more cognitive. Moreover, attention may involve an element of directed will, a voluntary act of paying attention to something. Awareness is more something that happens to one, a state in which one is aware of something. Nonetheless, the two are definitely similar.

Citing numerous experimental results involving attention under stressful conditions, Easterbrook (1959: 191) concurs with the conclusion that the resulting narrowing of attention under such conditions has the effect of rendering the central object more important. Sven-Ake Christianson (1992) proposes that we are predisposed by evolution to attend more to a negative stimulus so as to avoid it in the future (both Easterbrook and Christianson are cited in Paz-Alonso *et al.* 2009). If so, the constellation of a complex could be related to an evolutionary mechanism that makes one aware in certain dangerous situations.

Jung saw attention as the central coordinator of consciousness: 'Attention is that infinitely complicated mechanism which by countless threads links the associative process with all other phenomena of the psychic and physical domain in consciousness' (Jung and Riklin 1904/1919: para. 4).

Emotion and instinct

Perhaps the most remarkable and distinguishing parameter of the constellation of a complex is the sudden, overwhelming feeling associated with it. Jung considered emotion to be the central element which linked the memories and associations of the complex together (Jung 1928/1948: para. 18). Therefore each time the same emotion is activated, the same memories and associations are brought to mind and the same complex constellates. A list of basic emotions was discussed above. I argue, when discussing instinct with regard to the psychoid archetype, that much of that which has been considered instinct is closely related to emotion. What was often considered as 'instinctive' in Jung's time is now explained as an innate, emotional reaction. To the table presented earlier (Table 3.1) of affects and the life situation, I have added a column for the corresponding instinct.

I reiterate that these emotions are never discrete but always manifest in subtly nuanced combinations. It has been proposed that the discrete emotions themselves interact to form a dynamical system (Izard *et al.* 2000: 18). Izard *et al.* also link emotion together with an image or thought to form what they call an 'affective-cognitive structure' (ibid.).

Table 5.1 Instinct, affect and the life situation

Instinct	*Affect*	*Life situation*
Engaging in the world		
To play	Ecstasy (joy)	Encountering the familiar
To learn	Excitement (interest)	Encountering something novel intriguing
To protect	Caring	Encountering others
To procreate	Desire (sexual attraction)	Founding a family
Existential threats to life (self preservation)		
To flee	Terror (fear)	Confronting the unknown
To submit	Anguish (sadness)	Experiencing loss
To fight	Rage (anger)	Being restricted or controlled
To avoid	Disgust (contempt)	Rejecting someone or something
To freeze	Shame (humiliation)	Being exposed, defenceless
Centring attention		
To startle	Surprise	Sudden confrontation with the unexpected

Joseph Cambray identifies the experience of a change in feeling as signalling 'an emergent process associated with a phase transition in the brain's body mapping' (Cambray 2006: 8–9), referring to Damasio's (2003: 112–13, also 1999a: 169ff) distinction between the actual state of the body and how it is represented in the brain. Since experience implies a conscious state, Cambray's assertion appears to be consistent with the hypothesis that consciousness is emergent and dependent on emotion.

Physical energy generated

The constellation of a complex may prepare the organism for a fight or flight response: the heart rate accelerates, blood pressure increases and adrenalin is released. These are all regulated by the sympathetic nervous system. One hears one's heart pounding in one's ears. On the other hand, the constellation of other complexes may prepare the organism for a freeze response in the form of submission or collapse through depression, depersonalisation or dissociation. The complex does not only happen in the mind or refer to the past. It is an all-body defensive reaction to a perceived current danger. In addition to internal changes there may also be definite, and sometimes characteristic, changes to body posture, overt gestures and facial expressions.

All of these body reactions make it impossible for someone to ignore what is happening. The situation must be dealt with, for better or worse.

Memory

During the constellation of a complex, personal memories of similar experiences or emotions, even if not actually conscious, may become active and reinforce the emotions originally triggered by the current perception. Also included are memories of previous occasions when the same complex constellated.

The question of unremembered memories is interesting. What is actually remembered? This is an area which has so far been ignored by scientific research. Referring back to the concept of psychic energy, it is as if the memory did not have enough energy to actually become conscious, but still enough to evoke the emotions associated with it. If and how these unconscious memories affect conscious reactions and decision-making could be investigated.

Symbolic image

It is through the symbolic image that the archetype is most clearly expressed (Figure 5.1). People describe their experiences of the constellation of a complex with expressions such as 'I saw red' or 'It felt like I was beating my head against a brick wall'. By symbolic image here I don't necessarily mean anything more sophisticated than this, although it can be.

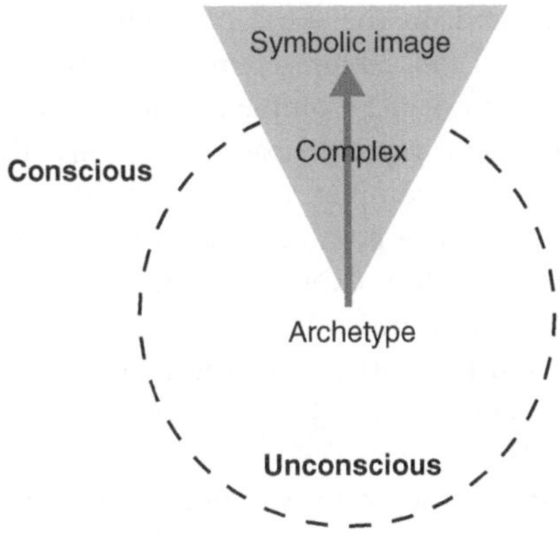

Figure 5.1 Constellation of a complex

As the complex constellates, the symbol carries into consciousness the emotional charge, which has been trapped in the unconscious. Sometimes it is this image that can finally bring the memory of past experiences into consciousness.

Jung elaborated the strong link between the symbolic image and the meaning buried in the complex. (Although he used the term 'primordial image' before 1919 to mean the archetype, I believe he was then referring to the image pole of the archetype rather than to both poles of the instinct-image psychoid archetype):

> The primordial image is thus a condensation of the living process. It gives a co-ordinating and coherent meaning both to sensuous and to inner perceptions, which at first appear without order or connection and in this way frees psychic energy from its bondage to sheer uncomprehended perception. At the same time, it links the energies released by the perception of stimuli to a definite meaning, which then guides action along paths corresponding to this meaning. It releases unavailable dammed up energy by leading the mind back to nature and canalizing sheer instinct into mental forms.
>
> (Jung 1921/1971: para. 749)

Evaluation-Interpretation-meaning

The complex forms around an interpretation/image of the situation, which carries meaning. This interpretation may or may not be conscious. It may or may not be formulated in words. Jung refers to the constellation of the archetype as 'self-activating' (Jung 1921/1971: para. 734), hence self-organising. The same can be said about the constellation of a complex. A complex is the emergence of the meaning or interpretation of an archetype in the context of an individual life. This meaning is the order parameter which synchronises the other sub-systems and, in the sense of circular causality as explained by Hermann Haken (1983, 1988/2000), secures the constellation of the complex. While a single constellation of a complex centres around the meaning for a person at that moment, the repeated pattern of constellations over a lifetime shows the relevance of the complex to their self-identity. At the next larger scale of analysis, the pattern of constellations throughout a population reveals an evolutionary, cultural pattern expressed in the archetypal image.

The trigger for constellation is in the present situation, but the images evoked use symbols and memories from the past to express both the current experience and future anticipation (Jung 1913/1955: para. 365, para. 373 referenced in Brooke 1991b: 513).

On the relationship of analytical psychology to poetry and art, Jung said:

> We must interpret, we must find meanings in things. Otherwise we would be unable to think about them. We have to break down life and events, which are self-contained processes, into meanings, images, concepts, well knowing that in doing so we are getting further away from the living mystery.
>
> (Jung 1922/1928: para. 121)

The complex is only one way in which images are formed by the psyche, thereby bridging the gap between the unconscious and consciousness, and leading to possible interpretation and the deciphering of meaning; others include art, mythology, fairy tales, dreams and spiritual experience.

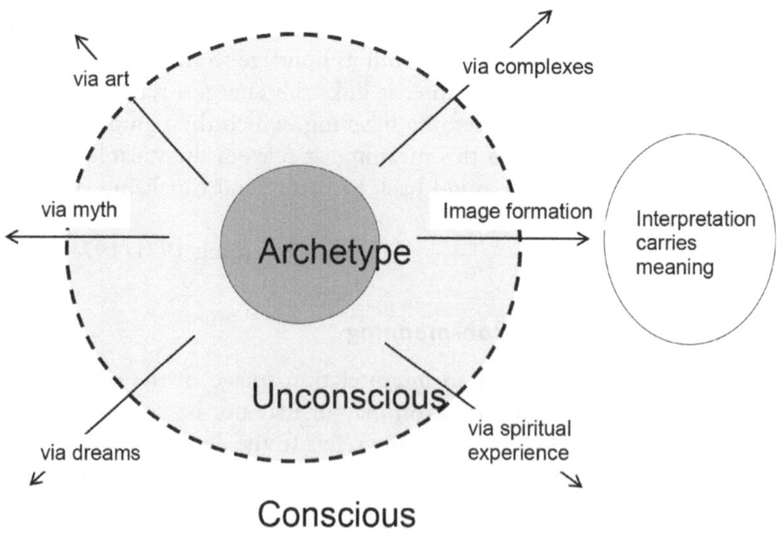

Figure 5.2 Possible ways the archetype may manifest

On attractor states

Attractors of individual parameters

Each of the individual parameters proposed above can be viewed as a separate dynamical system with its own attractor states. Daniel Amit (1989: 81–3) presented a phase state diagram similar to the one in Figure 5.3 as a representation of memory states, but it can be viewed as a generalised abstract representation of any of the individual parameters.

Points P1, P2 and P3 represent point attractors in the dynamical system represented. They could be psychic state 1, 2 and 3 combining memories, emotions and energy levels. An event perceived at point A causes the psyche, represented by the 'o', to fall into the attractor P1, thereby eliciting the specific memories, emotions and energy levels associated with it. From this it can be observed that a number of different events can evoke the same psychic, or attractor, state. Also the sides of some attractors are steeper than others causing the psyche to fall quicker into these states than into others. Eventually every event will cause the system to be in one attractor state or another, i.e. some combination of memory, emotion, attention and energy will be experienced.

In addition to the three major attractor states (P1, P2 and P3) two additional temporary states (T1 and T2) are also indicated. These represent states which are less stable than P1, P2 and P3. They are areas where changes in the system (psychic growth) can occur.

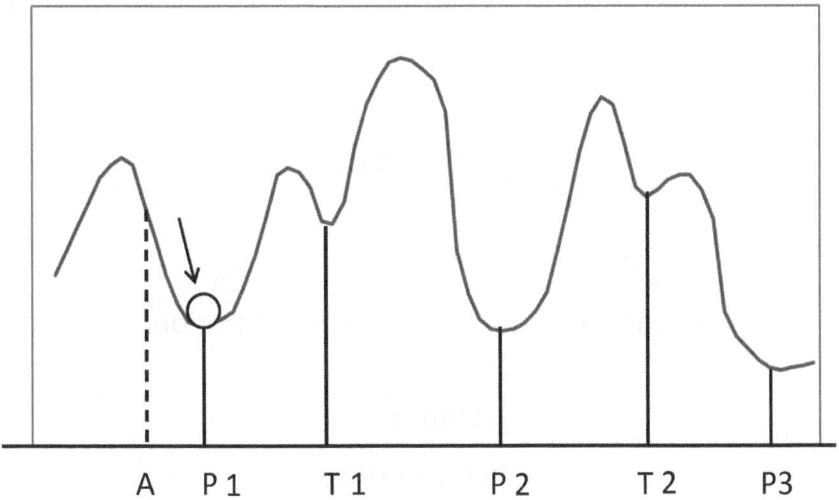

Figure 5.3 Attractors in state space (adapted from Amit 1989: Figure 2.10.)

Of course in the real psyche each system is not independent of the others, and thus events happening in one system will influence the trajectory in the other systems.

A dynamical hierarchy

Although a dynamical system is not in itself hierarchical, such a system may be an element in a so called 'higher order' dynamical system, thereby forming a hierarchy of dynamical systems. I propose that this is how different areas within the brain coordinate during the constellation of a complex and, ultimately, in the creation of a global workspace.

Based on Stefan Kiebel's study of the hierarchy of timescales in brain functioning (Kiebel *et al.* 2008), I propose that the constellation of the autonomous complex takes place in three major temporal groups.

The first level of dynamical interaction involves the triggering perception, the almost instinctive reaction to this and the related emotions arising from it. Complexity has been identified within the visual primary and association cortex, as can be readily demonstrated by the Necker cube experiment (Haken 1996: 60) and the olfactory bulb (Freeman 1999: 115–18). This agrees with the analysis presented by Damasio (2000). This reaction is happening on a timescale of a few to a couple of hundred milliseconds. It is unconscious and principally subcortical. This interaction settles the psyche into a first level attractor state (Figure 5.4).

This attractor State 1 then engenders changes in the body, preparing it for a fight or flight reaction to the situation, which is reflected in the energy

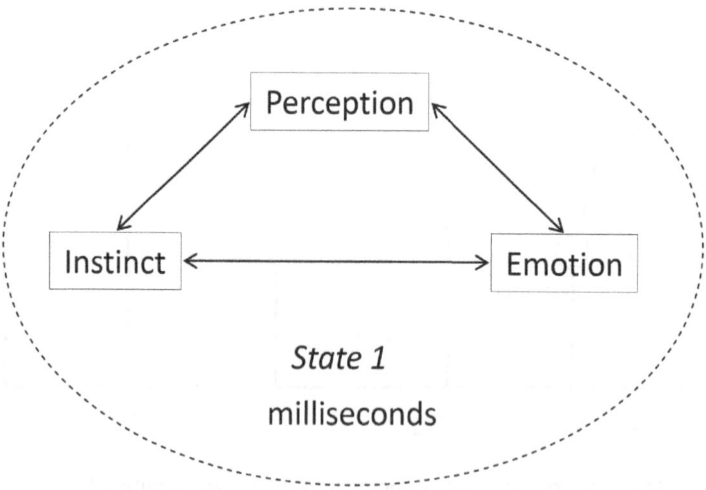

Figure 5.4 First level of emergence

level and which in turn affects the level of awareness of what is taking place (Figure 5.5). Memories of similar situations, perhaps unconscious, are stimulated. Changes in the energy level and awareness are the result of changes in the body and are very fast, although the awareness of these changes as feedback will take on the order of hundreds of milliseconds. The activation of memories involves the association cortices and will also be of the order of a few hundred milliseconds. I have labelled this attractor 'state 2'. However, state 2 is not independent of state 1 and will feed back and influence perception and affect the nature and intensity of the emotion. Conscious awareness of the situation takes about half a second. The emergence of a symbolic image (represented in state 3) takes from seconds to tens of seconds.

As a result of the interaction between attractor states 1 and 2, a symbolic image forms which is very closely related to the evaluation-interpretation-meaning (Figure 5.6).

This evaluation-interpretation-meaning then enslaves the lower level dynamical systems and locks in the constellation of the autonomous complex (Figure 5.7). Care must be given not to equate the cortex with consciousness. It can be seen from this explanation that areas of the cortex are involved long before (100s of milliseconds) one is conscious of what is happening.

Examples of specific complexes

The table below gives five examples of complexes (inferiority complex, road rage, jealousy, adventure complex and protective situation). It then specifies what might be reasonable for each of the parameters explained below.

- **Perception**: What the person is seeing or experiencing which triggers the onset of the complex
- **Level of awareness/attention**: Whether the constellation of the complex reduces or exaggerates awareness.
- **Emotions**: Which of the ten basic emotions are activated
- **Instinct**: Which basic instinct underpins the emotion
- **Physical energy generated**: Whether energy is generated or depleted during the experience.
- **Personal memories**: Conscious or unconscious memories which are activated by the complex.
- **Symbolic image**: The symbolic or cultural image which epitomises the complex.
- **Evaluation-interpretation-meaning**: A sentence, conscious or unconscious, which expresses what the ultimate meaning is for the person.

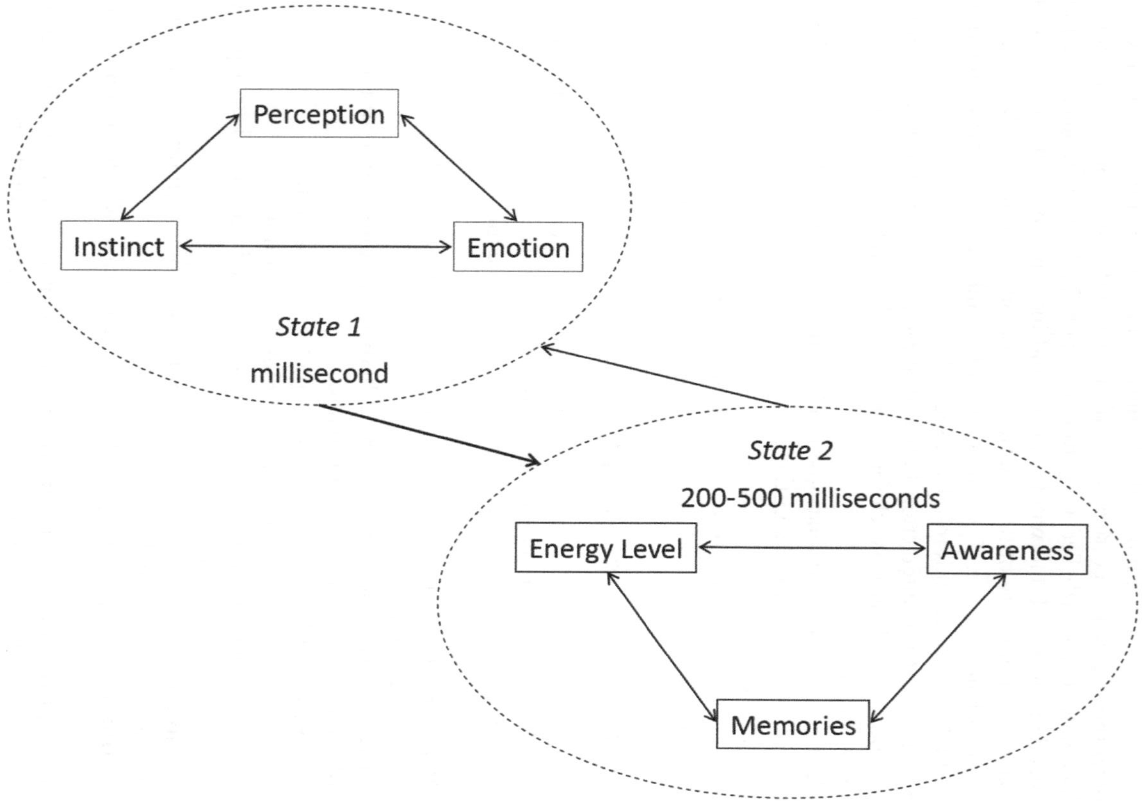

Figure 5.5 Second level of emergence

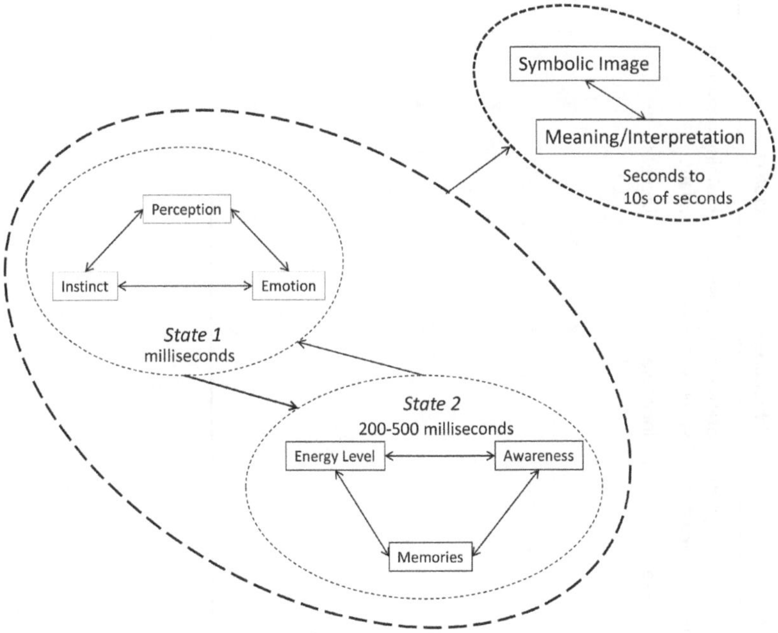

Figure 5.6 Third level of emergence

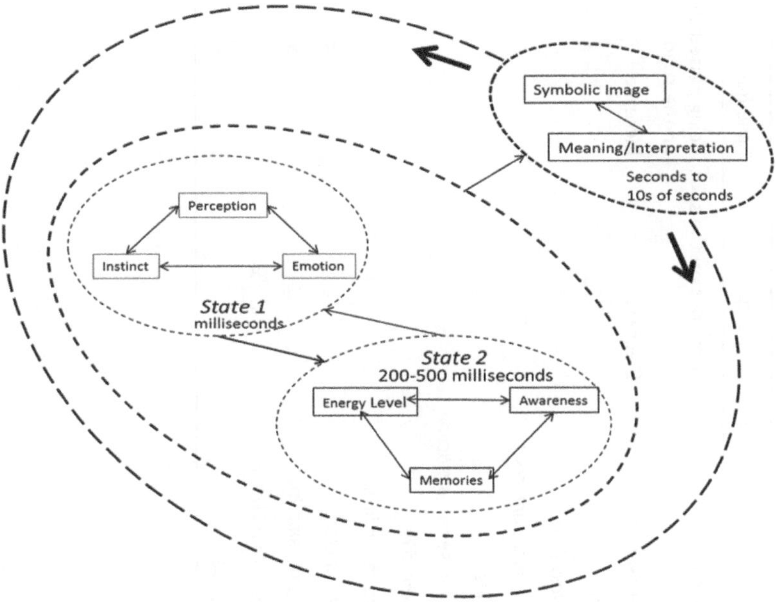

Figure 5.7 Enslavement of the dynamical hierarchy

Table 5.2 Examples of specific complexes

Complex	*Inferiority*	*Road Rage*	*Jealousy*	*Adventure*	*Protection*
Perception	Being put on the spot	Being passed suddenly on the road	Partner talking with other man/woman	Standing on edge of virgin snow slope	Holding newborn infant
Level of awareness	Decrease	Increase	Decrease	Increase	Increase
Emotions					
Ecstasy (joy)				x	x
Excitement (interest)			x	x	
Caring					x
Desire (sexual attraction)			x		
Terror (fear)	x	x	x	x	x
Anguish (sadness)			x		
Rage (anger)		x			
Disgust (contempt)		x	x		
Shame (humiliation)	x		x		
Surprise		x		x	

Complex	*Inferiority*	*Road Rage*	*Jealousy*	*Adventure*	*Protection*
Instinct	Self-defence	Aggression	Attachment	Play	Maternal care
Energy	Depleted	Increased	Depleted	Increased	Increased
Memory	Of failure and ridicule	Of being passed up, overlooked, treated unfairly	Of betrayal	Of challenge and excitement	Of having been helped by others
Symbolic image	Orphan	Avenger	Loser	Hero	Protective mother
Evaluation-interpretation-meaning	'You can't do this. Don't even try.'	'Who does he think he is, cutting in front of me?'	'She loves him more than me. I'll be left alone and have no one.'	'This is going to be fun.'	'This helpless person needs me.'

Part II

Application to analytical psychology

Chapter 6

Neural correlates of the constellated complex

Each neural structure supporting brain functions has its own attractors, i.e. the set of states into which the system settles after a long enough period of time, states which are often experienced. It is the coalescing of the individual subsystems which generates the global state space and leads to the final evaluation-interpretation-meaning. I will consider two alternative modes of functioning. In the first, each subsystem is functioning more or less on its own, going from attractor to attractor in its own state space and generating a background feeling of diffused attention which may, if appropriate, be consciously focussed. This is the ego complex and will be dealt with in Chapter 9. The second mode is when something perceived causes attention to be involuntarily focussed and a state transition occurs, coordinating the subsystems into a single workspace. Consciousness is taken away from the ego-complex and the impact of the constellated autonomous complex is experienced.

There is an innate tendency for certain states to become attractors. This is due in part to instinct and in part to need. The need carries with it an image of its expected fulfilment. Past experience makes one sensitive to certain inner feelings and external events. The creation of attractor states is reinforced by experience. It has been established that once neurons have fired together, their potential for doing so again in the future is increased (Hebb 1949). This is important for the activation of a complex, and explains the tendency to identify similar inputs and to repeat previous responses. An evaluation/interpretation of the situation emerges which then locks the system in what is experienced as the constellated complex.

First level of the dynamical hierarchy: perception, instinct, emotion

As stated above, the first level of the dynamical hierarchy involves perception, an instinctive reaction and an associated emotion.

I shall be discussing primarily the visual image as it is perceived, but the other senses function in a similar manner. The image transmitted by the optical tract takes two paths, which result in two different timescales in their reactions;

the faster passes directly to the superior colliculus in the midbrain which is involved in instinctive reactions. The superior colliculus can cause the head to turn and orient the eyes in the direction of the stimulus. There is also a direct connection between it and the motor areas of the neocortex, which can further coordinate a responsive movement.

A second path taken by the optic nerve is to the thalamus, which will in turn trigger an activation of various emotions in the limbic system. A second output from the thalamus will transmit the image to the primary sensory cortex. This is a much slower comparison with stored memories in the sensorial association cortices and involves the recognition of the perceived object. This will be dealt with later under perceptual memory.

One of the few modern researchers still referring to instincts is James Austin, who identifies instinctual drives including sexual longing, hunger, thirst, fear, anger and aggression, and argues that their initiation is 'hardwired' into the brain and brain stem (Austin 1999: 189). Of these, hunger, thirst, pain and startle responses can be initiated by stimulation of the lateral hypothalamus (ibid.: 192). Instinctual responses are almost instantaneous. Stimulation of this area of the hypothalamus of monkeys will activate nerve cells in the motor cortex within three milliseconds (ibid.: 190). Austin associates self-preservation, the most basic of the instincts, with the amygdala, the hypothalamus and the central grey (at the top of the brain stem) (ibid.: 658).

Although he does not explicitly speak of instincts, LeDoux (1996: 254) proposes the existence in the amygdala of prepared, prewired connections to other cells that control emotional response. In this way certain responses are more easily evoked and conditioned than other responses.

The activation of instincts is related to the evolutionary nature of the complex and links our reactions with those of our pre-human ancestors. What is inherited is a predisposition to behave/feel in a certain way, not a hardwired behavioural response pattern (Jung 1946/1954: para. 398). This can vary slightly from person to person, which contradicts Jung's position that instincts are phylogenetically determined and universal, and it can be modified by environmental factors (from the fertilised egg onwards).

Instincts are not identical with bodily functions such as sleep or digestion, therefore I object to the Freudian use of the term 'death-instinct'. Death is not mentioned in any scientific listing of instincts.

The various emotions have evolved for different reasons, and not all are associated with the same distinct area in the brain. Rather than associating them only with the limbic system as a single unified functional system, emotions should also be associated with various brain networks, arising from different evolutionary challenges, which coordinate perception, action and memory to solve immediate environmental problems (LeDoux 1996: 105–6, 126, Lewis 2005: 170). An emotion such as fear, which protects us when we are in danger, is part of a different all-body system from that used, for example, to procreate. It has, therefore, different origins and different functions from love or sexual attraction (LeDoux 1996: 16). Likewise, the various complexes form from individual emotional-cognitive-somatic reactions, each serving a different defensive purpose.

Emotions, like complexes, constellate in patterns. One emotion may stimulate or inhibit another. Indeed the attempt to define 'pure' emotions has been abandoned. An entire subset of emotions can emerge as an identifiable whole, which has motivational consequences for the organism. Again, due to Hebbian reaction, the excitation of one emotion may consistently also activate others. Thus self-organising sets of emotions, such as anger-disgust-contempt and anger-fear, which often manifest together, have been postulated (Izard *et al.* 2000: 18–20). From his research and experience, Jaak Panksepp (2000) argues that dynamical systems form for varying periods of time, based on emotional value systems, establishing self-organised stable states, and becoming increasingly complex and recursive with cognitive processes (Panksepp 2000: 253).

Long, fast neurons connect the limbic system directly with the neocortex. Together with slow-firing return connections, these serve to synchronise different areas within the brain (LeDoux 1996). Synchronisation is required for the emergence of a unified field over non-contiguous areas of the brain. This supports the philosophical concept of the global workspace. Synchronisation has been confirmed by Marc D. Lewis (Lewis 2005) who monitored the electrical activity of medial-frontal cortical regions. He then applied non-linear dynamical systems modelling to traditional causal cognitive theories of emotion. He argues that theories of emergent order, bi-directional feedback and circular causality need to be applied in order to integrate the emotional and appraisal psychological system into a functional unity constituting a higher order motivational loop affecting conscious behaviour. Looking at the relation between emotion-appraisal systems affecting levels of self-esteem and large-scale cortico-limbic self-organisational patterns he concludes that 'Emotional and cognitive processes influence each other continuously during an emotional episode from the first neural changes induced by a triggering event to the synchronization of the entire nervous system in a coherent mode of thinking, feeling, and acting' (ibid.: 193). This gives strong, scientific support for the global workspace theory. The hypothesised interaction of the two systems was supported by the research of Walter J. Freeman (2000b) supplying evidence from EEG readings of how hemispheric chaos can explain actual behaviour in times of emotional upset.

State space configurations are determined by the constellation of self-organising emotional systems which dictate cognitive attentiveness initiated by emotion-specific stimulation. '... these primal state spaces, generated early in development by the arousal of emotional value states, interact dynamically in increasingly complex and recursive ways with all the higher cognitive mechanisms. These interactions are self-organising' (Panksepp 2000: 253). This is analogous to Jung's postulation of the instinctive archetypal image conveying value and ultimately meaning for the organism.

Control of emotions is exercised predominately by the right orbitofrontal cortex. This mechanism develops in the infant at about the end of the first year through socio-affective interaction with the principal caregiver, which strengthens the dampening effect of the parasympathetic nervous system (Schore 1994). Research has also shown that the orbitofrontal region is involved not only in the regulation and adjustment of emotional and motivational states in the body, but also in social interactions (Damasio and Tranel 1988, de Briun 1990, Kolb and Whishaw 1990) and in attachment behaviour (Steklis and Kling 1985). (All references in this paragraph are taken from Schore 1994.)

Voluntary regulation of both positive and negative emotion was found to activate areas in the prefrontal and anterior cingulate regions, and to increase or decrease activity of the amygdala associated with the experience of fear (Kim and Hamann 2007: 776).

Andrzej Nowak and his colleagues, in their report on the mathematical modelling of complex systems, state that: '…although positive information is more prevalent than negative information in cognitive structures, negative information tends to be more salient than positive information' (Nowak *et al.* 2000: 47). This might explain why it seems that complexes tend to be built around negative, rather than positive emotions.

There is as yet no failsafe means to evaluate the neural correlates of distinct emotional states. Although modern imaging methods, notably PET and fMRI, can clarify certain aspects, their application is limited and they lack precision in identifying ensembles of neurons in real time. EEG and MEG are imprecise in measuring subcortical activity (emotions) because the readings are influenced by cortical processing (Panksepp 2000: 239–40).

Alexandre Schaefer *et al.* (2003) investigated the neural correlates of what they termed 'hot' and 'cold' emotional processing. 'Hot' emotional responses correspond to those involved in the activation of an autonomous complex and are characterised by sudden, automatic, overwhelming emotional reactions, whereas 'cold' responses are under the control of cognitive processes (reasoning, rationalisation, etc.) They place hot responses in the context of a schematic system integrating sensory, perceptual and semantic information. This is therefore similar to what we are considering as an autonomous complex. They investigated the emotions of anger, happiness, sadness and affection in both hot and cold situations. All reactions in the hot context were rated by the participants as more intense. The specific neural correlates are given in the summary table below. These results agree with other studies that they referenced (Luan Phan *et al.*, cited in Schaefer).

Analysis of the data presented in Table 6.1 on page 80 gives the following generalities:

- Fear (both the immediate experience of fear and fearful memories) involves the amygdala.

- Sexual arousal is also related to the amygdala (so we have in the amygdala the old pairing of sex and aggression).
- Integration of sensory information takes place around the thalamus.
- Emotional behaviour, learning and motivation are associated with activity in other areas of the limbic system, notably the hypothalamus.
- Positive emotions result from stimulation of the frontal lobe (ecstasy, joy, excitement, interest) rather than the limbic system. (But it cannot be absolutely ruled out that areas of the limbic system, including the amygdala, are not minimally involved in what are usually termed the positive emotions.)
- Excitement is more of a sustained body reaction, with increased heart rate and respiration, which could be in preparation for a fight or flight tactic taking over from the initial surprise.
- Maternal caring is primarily hormonal.
- Based on imaging alone, it is difficult to separate the reported experience of an emotion from attempts in the frontal lobe to control it.

Because several of the emotions investigated originate in quite different areas of the brain with differing reaction times, we may be lumping together under the heading 'emotion' things which are really quite different from a neurological point of view.

Neural correlates of the basic emotions

I present here the experimental data on the neural correlates of the primary emotional states identified by Louis Stewart (1987). The data are summarised in table format in Table 6.1 on page 80.

Engaging in the world

ECSTASY (JOY)

Stimulation of the frontal lobes produces positive emotions in test subjects: feelings of wellbeing and euphoria, and smiling. There can be abrupt changes of positive and negative feeling, but these are followed by a sudden and complete experience of satisfaction (Austin 1999: 256–7). Laughter is often accompanied by an element of surprise and an increase in energy.

Stimulation near the midline on the under-surface of the frontal lobe can yield pleasurable and relaxing experiences. Negative feelings of anxiety and irritation can result from stimulation more to the sides. Stimulation around the hypothalamus causes more vigorous reactions, either positive or negative. In some cases stimulation around the midbrain causes euphoria (ibid.: 387).

EXCITEMENT (INTEREST)

Surprise is registered in the prefrontal cortex, an indication that perhaps pre-cortical mechanisms are already at work preparing the way for a decision on a future response, whereas sustained interest, such as waiting for an event, activates areas further back in the parietal area (ibid.: 286).

Excitement, as stated above, is more of a sustained body reaction, increased heart rate, respiration in preparation for a fight or flight tactic, than the initial surprise.

CARING (AT FIRST SELF-CARING, LATER CARING FOR OTHERS)

Panksepp (2000) cites research which relates maternal care for rat pups principally to increased hormonal production, especially of oxytocin but also progesterone and oestrogen (ibid: 61). Endogenous opioids have been identified for some time in the mother allowing permissive behaviour of the pups and increasing social contact between her and the pups which enhances bonding (ibid.).

Existential threats to life

TERROR (FEAR)

LeDoux measured the somatic metrics of the fear reaction in rats and the results were consistent with those found for other species (LeDoux 1996: 141–9). His results are summarised in the table at the end of this section.

Fear directly affects vision and hearing, and thus 'increases excitability in the midbrain reticular formation in the cortex' (Austin 1999: 161). Both learned and primal fear have been linked with the amygdala. Incoming signals come in contact with the amygdala, which reacts instantly to certain instinctive or learned stimuli creating a feeling of primal fear (ibid.: 177–9). Activation of the posterior hypothalamus elicits feelings of extreme horror (ibid.: 192–3).

RAGE (ANGER)

The existence of two diametrically opposed defence systems has been postulated. Their functioning has been associated with changes in the brain stem. Fight (aggression) is associated with the sympathetic nervous system and catabolic changes and flight (fear) with parasympathetic activity and anabolic changes (Schore 1994: 328).

Going beyond the neural correlates of the actual experience of anger, Krämer *et al.* (2008) recorded higher activation of the prefrontal cortex in the suppression of aggressive behaviour in test subjects with highly aggressive tendencies than for less aggressive test subjects. This higher prefrontal activity was attributed to the decision processes involved in determining a response.

Aggressive behaviour initiated by induced sexual jealousy in male macaques was correlated with larger increases of plasma testosterone and greater activation in the central grey area of the midbrain than under control conditions (Rilling *et al.* 2004).

A significant positive correlation between the volume of the anterior cingulate cortex and aggressive, antisocial behaviour in boys was established. A similar, although non-significant, correlation was found in girls. Although similar results were expected for the ventromedial prefrontal cortex, no significant correlation was found (Boes *et al.* 2008).

DISGUST/HUMILIATION (SHAME/CONTEMPT)

Shame, like disgust and sadness, exhibits a sudden change from sympathetic to a parasympathetic functioning, from hyper- to hypo-arousal. Shame is also associated with distinctive body reactions, such as averted gaze and blushing (Schore 1994: 204). Early forms of the so-called self-referential emotions of shame, pride and guilt were found to develop very early in infants and to contribute to the development of their concept of self (Zinck 2008: 496). A distinction is made between physical disgust/revulsion at the thought of eating rotting or infested food, which is universal (and either prevents people from eating contaminated food or saves them by causing vomiting), and moral disgust at socially unacceptable practices such as mixed or homosexual marriage, which is considered repugnant in some societies and not in others. Although both cause a drop in heart rate and activate areas in the lateral and medial orbitofrontal cortex, in the posterior orbitofrontal cortex only moral disgust activates the evolutionarily more recent anterior regions linked with abstract emotional reasoning (Jones 2007: 769). Disgust and contempt are usually considered self-reflective emotions. They show a distinctive pattern of activation involving the insula, which correlates with the insula's relation to concepts of the self.

Sexual arousal has been correlated with activation of the right amygdala, the right anterior temporal pole and the hypothalamus. Attempted inhibition of sexual arousal has been correlated with activation of the right superior frontal gyrus and right anterior cingulate gyrus, but not with activation in the limbic areas (Beauregard *et al.* 2001).

Summary table

Table 6.1 summarises the data presented above.

Table 6.1 Summary of research findings with regard to emotion

Emotion	*Neural correlate*	*Somatic reaction*	*Source*
Engaging in the world			
play	periaqueductal grey, medial thalamic, anterior cingulate		Panksepp (2000)
happiness	left ventral pallidum of the ventromedial prefrontal cortex	heart rate increases ++	Schaefer *et al.* (2003)
wellbeing and euphoria	stimulation of the frontal lobes	smiling	Austin (1999: 256–7)
pleasure and relaxation	stimulation near the midline on the under-surface of the frontal lobe		Austin (1999: 387)
seeking	periaqueductal grey, hypothalamus, amygdala, basal ganglia, frontal cortical areas		Panksepp (2000)
affection	ventromedial prefrontal cortex	heart rate decreases –	Schaefer *et al.* (2003)
maternal care	periaqueductal grey, hypothalamus, amygdala, basal ganglia, frontal cortical areas		Panksepp (2000)

Emotion	*Neural correlate*	*Somatic reaction*	*Source*
Existential threats to life			
fear	amygdala central nucleus	heart rate increases	LeDoux (1996: 141–9)
	central grey	freeze reaction	
	reticulopontis caudalis	startle reaction	
	lateral hypothalamus	blood pressure increases	
	paraventricular hypothalamus	stress hormones increase	
		pain suppression	
		reflex reactions increase	
	reticular formation and amygdala		Austin (1998: 161, 177–9)
	geniculate nuclei concerned with vision and hearing		Austin (1999)
	parasympathetic activity and anabolic changes		Schore (1994: 328)
	periaqueductal grey, hypothalamus, amygdala, basal ganglia, frontal cortical areas		Panksepp (2000)
anxiety and irritation	stimulation near the sides on the under-surface of the frontal lobe		Austin (1999)
panic	periaqueductal grey, medial thalamic, anterior cingulate		Panksepp (2000)
sadness	ventromedial prefrontal cortex	heart rate increases	Schaefer *et al.* (2003)

Continued

Table 6.1 Continued

Emotion	*Neural correlate*	*Somatic reaction*	*Source*
	parasympathetic functioning and hypo-arousal		Schore (1994: 204)
anger	left ventral pallidum of the ventromedial prefrontal cortex	heart rate increases	Schaefer et al. (2003)
rage	periaqueductal grey, hypothalamus, amygdala, basal ganglia, frontal cortical areas		Panksepp (2000)
aggression	sympathetic nervous system and catabolic metabolic changes		Schore (1994: 328)
suppression of aggressive behaviour	prefrontal cortex		Krämer *et al.* (2008)
shame	parasympathetic functioning and hypo-arousal		Schore (1994: 204)
disgust	parasympathetic functioning and hypo-arousal		Schore (1994: 204)
	orbitofrontal cortex particularly the lateral and medial areas, which are closely associated with the amygdala	reduced heart rate, vomiting	Jones (2007: 769)
Centring attention			
surprise	frontal lobes	laughter and increased energy	Austin (1999: 256–7)
startle	frontal lobes	instantaneous involuntary movement	Austin (1999: 286)

Second level of the dynamical hierarchy: energy level, awareness, memories

The second level of the hierarchy involves the bodily reaction and the level of awareness which results from the reaction of the first level of the hierarchy, and includes memories from the past related to these. The result of this process, particularly the recognition or recall of memories of previous situations, can feed back into the first level of the dynamical hierarchy, focussing attention and directing perception. Shin and his colleagues demonstrated this to be the case by showing that implicit memory affected attention when working with the Word Association Experiment (Shin *et al.* 2005). These reactions take 200 to 500 milliseconds.

Physical energy generated and measurable physiological parameters

The hypothalamus acts as a bridge from the limbic system, brain stem and forebrain to the pituitary gland, which in turn regulates the body's water and salt balance, temperature and hormones, thereby having a large influence on somatic responses to emotions (Austin 1999: 189).

Electrical stimulation of different areas of the hypothalamus produces a wide range of somatic reactions. This is in part due to its connections to the pituitary gland, as well as to neurochemical reactions. The latter vary, ranging from discharges in the sympathetic nervous system (which may cause the increased blood pressure and heart rate, flushing of the face, perspiration and dilated pupils used currently in lie detector tests evolved from the original Word Association Experiment) to feelings of horror and extreme rage (which may cause energy to be generated for flight or to fight) to, at the other extreme, the dampening of pain and increased sleepiness (an extreme reduction of energy). Body temperature positively correlates with alertness and is lowest in periods of deep sleep. It is also instrumental in regulating wake-sleep patterns (Austin 1999: 192–4).

Other measurable physiological parameters are also greatly affected by hormones controlled in part by the hypothalamus, but are also influenced by other organs in the limbic system: the ventromedial hypothalamus and the amygdala (Austin 1999: 195).

Level of awareness/attention

The formation of neuronal patterns increases when the organism is in an excited state due to threat or physical need. More importantly, each input perceived while the organism is in an excited state from a previous input within the last milliseconds markedly affects the neuronal activity, increasing the output of excitatory or inhibitory neurons to further excite or dampen the system

(Freeman 1991: 77–8). This could explain the sometimes increased, sometimes decreased level of awareness during the constellation of a complex.

Stimulation of the lateral hypothalamus, which happens during instinctual responses, reduces visual messages coming from the outside world to the visual cortex. This is due to inhibition at the level of the thalamus (Austin 1999: 192) and could account for the feeling of dissociation and depersonalisation often accompanying the constellation of a complex.

Arousal is dependent on activity at the top of the brain stem, which is the area where the inputs from the sensory cortices converge (Carter 1998: 186). Artificial stimulation of this area is accompanied by increased activity in several areas in the thalamus. At the same time, activity in the cerebral cortex (thinking) is reduced by slowing the firing of short interneurons (local processing) in favour of long cortical projection neurons outputting to the superior temporal region, the inferior frontal regions and the cingulate gyrus. States of arousal are also greatly influenced by the thalamus and hypothalamus, particularly neurons situated in the area where the posterior hypothalamus and the subthalamus join the midbrain (Austin 1999: 161–3).

Sudden changes in awareness synchronise the various areas of the brain and concentrate global functioning in preparation for an imminent response. They render the system more sensitive to perception, interrupt undirected thinking and alert the body for future action based primarily on evolutionary, physical response patterns.

Memory

Perceptual memory

Perceptual memory includes the formation of a sensorial image of the perceived object and its recognition through comparison with previously stored images. It cannot be understood from the micro-level of the firing of individual neurons, but only by investigating patterns of neuronal activity in the sense organ and the primary and secondary sensorial cortices and their interactions (Freeman 1991). Based on his investigation of the olfactory bulb of the rabbit, Walter J. Freeman (ibid.) concluded that the activity within the olfactory bulb is self-organised. He identified the patterns characteristic of recognisable odours as attractors (Freeman 1999: 84, 107–8). The input stimulus passes from the sensory receptors in the nose to the olfactory bulb (the primary sensory cortex) and the olfactory cortex (the association sensory cortex) (ibid: 131). Contact is then made with the frontal cortex where formal recognition takes place and a decision is made on a suitable response (ibid: 133). The stimulus is identified from the pattern formed in the bulb, not the activation of individual neurons. Recognition of a pattern is based on both instinct and prior experience (ibid: 134).

This also applies to visual perception. When an object is viewed, the first reaction takes place in distinct, localised areas in the back of the brain which distinguish such features as shape, colour, movement and position using perceptual memory. Once an image is established, rapid recurrent processing enables the exchange of information between and within areas of the occipital cortex which leads to image recognition (Lamme 2006).

The establishment of a meaningful pattern, i.e. an attractor state, at the level of the primary and association cortices is evidence of dynamical systems processing (Freeman 1999: 109) and most probably happens with all forms of perception.

Freeman identified the strengthening of the connections between packets of neurons within the olfactory bulb, and between the bulb and the olfactory cortex, during training of the rabbits to recognise certain odours. He called these packets 'nerve cell assemblies' (1999: 182). When a subset within an assembly fires, the entire assembly fires and can, in turn, determine the pattern of the entire bulb. This is an example of self-organisation.

Repeated research with rat pups subjected to mild electric shock while exposed to a characteristic odour shows enhanced olfactory bulb activity and a heightened sensitivity to this odour that was retained into adulthood (Sevelinges *et al.* 2007: 1076, Sullivan and Leon 1986, Coopersmith and Leon 1986, Woo and Leon 1988 referenced in Sevelinges *et al.*). This could be called conditioning, but it could also be seen as a complex. It shows that perception itself can in fact be modified in the long term due to early emotional experiences.

The theory of nerve cell assemblies offers a solution to what has been called the 'binding' problem, i.e. how one can identify a particular figure from a background of other figures. Once a part of the assembly is activated, the entire assembly fires together, forming an identifiable subset within the mass of input data. Such formation of nerve cell assemblies could also explain the unity and repetition of experiences during the constellation of a complex, as the firing of a subset initiates the firing of other previously related groups of neurons.

LeDoux distinguishes between 'natural triggers' and 'learned triggers'. Natural triggers are instinctive and programmed by evolution so that, for example, the sight, smell or sound of a predator is recognised by the prey. Learned triggers are related to some information associated with, to pursue the same example, previous times the predator was encountered, such as the location (LeDoux 1996: 127). Either would be sufficient to initiate the constellation of a complex.

After having passed through the primary and association sensory cortices, the end phase of perception is the mixing of the individual images from the different senses to form a coherent whole. The images converge near the hippocampus and the limbic system in the perirhinal cortex and parahippocampal gyrus (LeDoux 1996: 194), which contains the entorhinal cortex (Freeman 1999: 134–7). From the entorhinal cortex the information passes into the hippocampus where it enters the memory subsystem. All of these areas are subcortical. This goes against traditional theory which proposes that this integration and the analysis of the input data takes place *only* in the neocortex. It is an important change in theory, reinforcing Jungian complex theory which stresses the central role of emotion in human behaviour. It is less well known, but nonetheless important for the establishment of meaning and memory, that the *hippocampus* as well as the neocortex, is greatly enlarged in humans, implying that memories play an increased role in us, perhaps in forming an autobiographic history. The entorhinal cortex functions as the main point of exchange with the hippocampus as well as communicating with all of the sensory cortices. This multisensory convergence, together with the spatial and temporal integration which takes place in the hippocampus, is central in the formation of an image upon which future action is based.

Memories of previous experiences

During the constellation of a complex, memories of past situations, including the feelings associated with those memories, become activated. They may not become conscious but, as noted previously, their activation will affect the global psychic environment.

Daniel Amit (1989) investigated memory as an attractor in a neural network to determine how memory is recalled. He modelled recall triggered by an incoming visual stimulus, which is interesting because it corresponds to the case of the complex being constellated by something perceived. 'The network state [what is being remembered] … is the memory *associatively recalled* by the incoming visual stimulus. The *realization of the recall* is a *pattern of activity* which corresponds to a *fixed* network state' (Amit 1989: 36, emphasis in the original). In other words, a memory is recalled if the incoming neural pattern matches that stored in the (neural) network as an attractor state since '… these special patterns of activity – the fixed point, or other types of attractors – are the nearest we come to having *representations* in this attempt at a description of cognitive processes' (ibid. emphasis in the original). He also states that these pattern 'may be partly innate and partly learnt' (ibid.).

LeDoux refers to this match as a correspondence between the emotional state being experienced and the emotional state of the stored memory. This match 'facilitates the activation of the explicit memory' (LeDoux 1996: 212) implying, as did Jung, that it is the emotion which links the current and past situations.

Amit has also determined that an indication for deciding if there is a match between the incoming and the stored pattern is the length of time the system stays in the attractor state. There is no homunculus which makes this decision. He also proposes that the attractor and this mechanism of decision-making are a 'universal mechanism' of neural functioning and evokes the idea of a dynamical hierarchy of attractor states repeated on successively higher levels of processing (op. cit.: 41). He even goes so far as to propose that such attractors are '*emergent* properties of the network.' (ibid.: 42, emphasis in the original.).

In addition to being retrieved, memories are also laid down during the constellation of a complex. In particular, the explicit, episodic component of the memory is formed, or re-formed, at this time due to the abundance of neurotransmitters, particularly noradrenaline, present in the system (LeDoux 1996: 207–8, 243).

Third level of the dynamical hierarchy: Symbolic image, evaluation/interpretation/meaning

The third level of the hierarchy, the emergence of the symbolic image and the associated evaluation-interpretation-meaning, taking from seconds to tens of seconds, is the point at which consciousness may begin to emerge. This involves the self in relation to the environment and an evaluation of the consequences of this for the individual.

Symbolic image

'Image and meaning are identical: and as the first takes shape, so the latter becomes clear. Actually, the pattern needs no interpretation: it portrays its own meaning' (Jung 1946/1954: para. 402).

I propose that the process of emergence of the symbolic, archetypal image is similar to the activation of the memory of something seen or imagined in the past. Such memories may, for example, be of actual illustrations one saw as a child, or of images one's imagination created on hearing a frightening fairy tale. They could also be images remembered from a prior experience of the constellation of the same complex. Such images would be part of the sensorial memory, forming a mental image in memory. These images are, of course, not limited to visual representations.

In this case the image is formed in the visual association cortex - not in the primary visual cortex, which processes actual sensory input. This would be a process similar to the formation of dream images (Hobson *et al.* 2000). The corresponding sensory association, rather than primary cortices, would be activated for images in other senses. These images are strongly influenced by close interaction with the limbic system.

Such an image would normally remain unconscious. Usually, it would only be through a conscious attempt to work on the complex, to bring the unconscious elements into consciousness, that a clear image may be retrieved and explicitly identified.

Evaluation-interpretation-meaning

Meaning is the result of a process of interaction between the limbic system and the sensory and motor systems (Freeman 1997: 291), hence involving a large part of the global brain. An evaluation-interpretation-meaning of the mental image of the situation, including the self and the outer world, is formed and a plan of action is made. This includes a self-referential concept of the individual including their self-image in a social setting and their goals and expectations for the future. Therefore, it emerges as an order parameter within a larger dynamical system extending beyond the individual and including interpersonal relationships. The system makes an attempt to fit the data into a pattern in order to understand and to evaluate it. This construction involves all of the elements discussed above: the limbic system based on the emotion activated, memories based on experience from the past, and expectations for the future. The anterior cingulate cortex, which plays an important role in the emotional evaluation of possible, sometimes conflicting, outcomes, and in error detection (Lane *et al.* 1998), would play a decisive role in the formation of this evaluation-interpretation-meaning. It may be refined when higher-order cognitive functions, based principally in the frontal cortex, become involved. This evaluation-interpretation-meaning then enslaves the system in a very fast-evolving re-entrant loop, adjusting the body state, memories and emotions in a phase transition to an attractor state.

In the same way that consciousness pulls together the various visual aspects of an object – colour, form, texture, etc. – during the process of forming an image (Lamme 2006), meaning pulls together the various aspects of the complex to form a definite psychic state. Speaking of the relationship of the archetype to meaning, Jung refers to the archetypal image as giving coordination and coherence to 'sensuous and to inner perceptions, which at first appear without order or connection, and in this way frees psychic energy from its bondage to sheer uncomprehended perception' (Jung 1921/1971: para. 749). Thus, once meaning has emerged, it guides the responses which result.

Amit proposes that the experience of meaning results from the rapid convergence of the neural network in an attractor state.

> Accordingly, we classify stimuli entering the ANN [attractor neural network], as *cognitively meaningful* if they lead the network quickly to an attractor. Otherwise, the input is classified as meaningless and ignored. … The specific meaning is in the particular attractor, and it depends, of course, on the level of cognitive processing …
>
> (Amit 1989: 42, emphasis in the original)

What Amit describes metaphorically as 'leading', Hermann Haken defines as an order parameter. Meaning is the key which locks the system into the attractor state.

Dynamical systems processing has formally been identified at different levels of this model, within the perception and limbic systems, and at the level of cognition. *Self-organisation* happens first at the level of the primary sensory cortex during the first organisation of the input stimulus into a coherent pattern (Freeman 1991; Lamme 2006). It happens again at the level of the coordination of the input signals from the various sense organs in the entorhinal cortex (Freeman 1999: 134–7). The constituted image excites basic, instinctive emotions. No single, pure emotion is activated but rather a mixture of interacting, emotional patterns which self-organise (Izard *et al.* 2000: 18). Stimulation of the limbic system has direct consequences in preparing the body for an instinctive response. This bodily reaction can influence the sense organs, which in turn distort, amplify or diminish subsequent sensation and perception. Direct reciprocal interactions between areas in the limbic system and areas in the neocortex allow for synchronisation of distant areas within the brain by the firing of long neurons reaching from the limbic system to various areas in the neocortex. Because of the slower response time for the cognitive system (a minimum of 400 milliseconds as opposed to under 100 for perception and emotion) the formulation of an evaluation-interpretation-meaning only happens after the other systems have initiated the constellation of the complex. The start of a cognitive evaluation can then trigger the coordination of a globally activated environment, enslaving the global system in the *attractor* state of the constellated complex. This agrees with the contemporary research (Damasio 1994, Edelman and Tononi 2000b, Freeman 1999) that consciousness is *emergent* in a global environment based on rapid re-entrant feedback loops between perceptual, emotional, somatic and cognitive systems. Before enslavement by evaluation-interpretation-meaning, many possible interpretations and behaviours are possible, the system exhibits *many degrees of freedom*. It is sensitive to both internal (disposition, mood, prior history) and external conditions. After the phase transition represented by the constellated complex, both the internal state and possible outer behaviour are severely limited.

Circular causality, as defined by Haken (1983: 43), is evidenced in the feedback between the various subsystems. Attention and emotion, and thus the corticolimbic system, continues to remain interconnected once the complex has constellated, rendering the system sensitive to further positive or negative feedback. Control over subsequent behaviour is dependent on the parasympathetic nervous system (Schore 1994).

These processes can be summarised as shown in Table 6.2.

Table 6.2 Sequence of events leading to the establishment of meaning

System/function	*Associated location*	*Psychic/abstract state space*	*Consciousness*
Individual sense	Primary cortex	Identifiable wave pattern	Core
Multimodal sensory experience	Entorhinal cortex	Form/Gestalt	Core
Instinct	Brain stem and limbic system	Archetypal image	Core and extended
Emotion	Limbic system and prefrontal cortex	Feeling	Core and extended
Memory	Association cortices and limbic system	Interpretation/ meaning	Extended

The first column identifies which mental function or system is involved. The five senses are considered, at first individually and then together, followed by emotion, instinct and memory. The second column specifies the principal area of the brain where each function is carried out. The third column describes how each function manifests. Using Antonio Damasio's classification of core and extended consciousness (1999a), the fourth column indicates which type of consciousness is activated. Finally the arrows indicate the inputs to subsequent systems. Thus each individual sense creates an identifiable wave pattern in the primary sensorial cortex. This wave merges with similar waves from other senses in the entorhinal cortex creating a composite form, a multimodal sensory experience. Intimately connected with the entorhinal cortex, a feeling is initiated in the limbic system and the prefrontal cortex. An instinct related to this feeling activates areas in the brain stem, and through this the entire body and the limbic system. This instinct is associated with an archetypal image, as experienced by the individual, which is stored as memory patterns in the neocortex. These all go together to form an interpretation/meaning for the person in relation to their self-concept and their perceived place in their social and/or environmental context.

Since consciousness is costly biologically and slow physically, it has been proposed that the iterative process stops if a decision is reached before consciousness occurs (Grandjean *et al.* 2008: 489). This concurs with the idea that consciousness is a means by which the organism copes with environmental challenges which cannot be handled automatically (Damasio 1999a: 303). Consciousness arises, in part, from the synchronised integration of the perception, attention, emotion and cognition which are required in defence of the organism.

A concrete example: Road rage

It has happened to all of us. You are driving down the road, maybe daydreaming a bit, when suddenly a car passes you very close. Your first reaction is 'startle'. You are yanked out of your reverie. Your heart starts pounding, you might take a gulp of air and then stop breathing; waiting, watching. Then you are flooded with anger, rage. That guy, with his rodeo cowboy ways, could have caused an accident, he could have killed you! That no good punk could really have been the cause of your death. You are boiling over with rage.

The following is a very superficial explanation of what happened during that first second in your brain. The numbers refer to the flows of information in Figure 6.1.

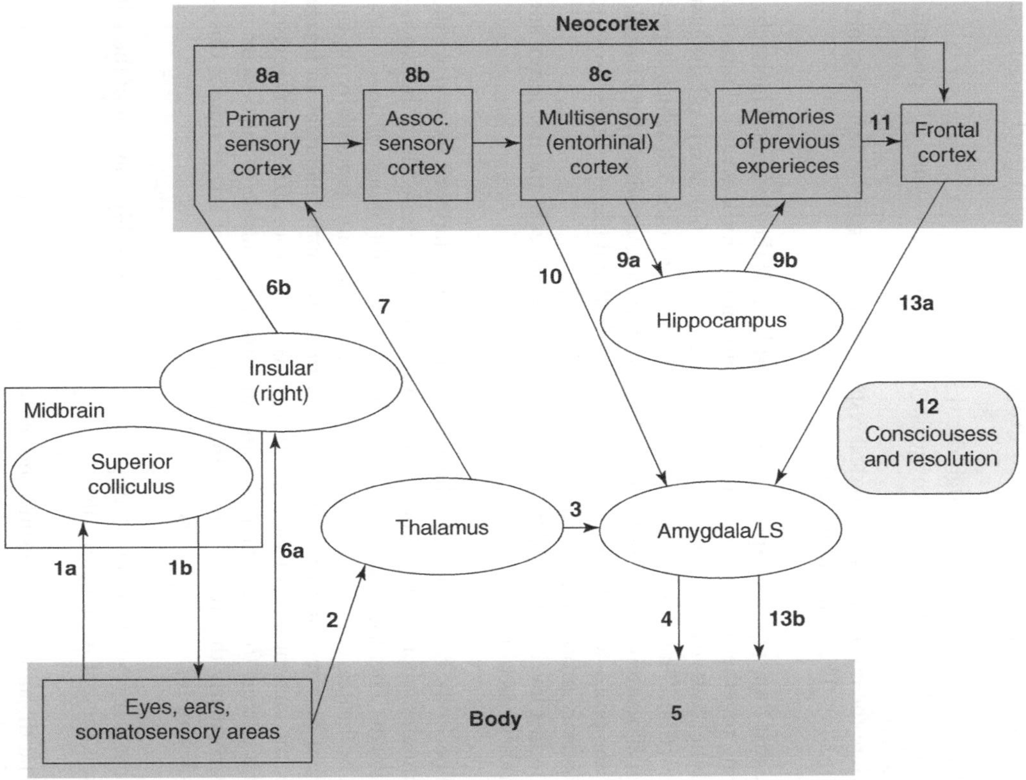

Figure 6.1 The flow of information during the constellation of a complex

1 Directing attention: The visual image of the car passing you travels through the optic nerve. A similar path is taken for the auditory and sensory images. One track the image takes goes to the superior colliculus (1a), in the midbrain, which is involved in reflexive, instinctive reactions. While the upper portions of the colliculi receive input from the senses, the lower portions are able to send commands directly via the cervical spinal cord to turn the head and to control eye movement (1b) (McDougal *et al.* 2013).
2 The image also passes through the thalamus (2).
3 The thalamus warns the amygdala and the limbic system of a potential danger.
4 Here the emotional and physical responses we recognise as fear are generated (4). The lungs fill with air.

These first four steps correspond with the first level of the dynamical hierarchy, bringing together perception, instinct and emotion. This is what LeDoux has called the 'low road to the amygdala' (LeDoux 1996: 164); it sets off the first fear reaction. This process generates a bodily concept of the self which is present in all mammals (Panksepp 2005: 159). It corresponds with what Damasio terms the proto-self (Damasio 1999a) and Northoff and his colleagues associate with sensory processing (Northoff *et al.* 2006: 450).

This first level is followed by the retrieval of memories in the neocortex and the body's reaction.

5 The body reacts (5). The heart rate increases, pumping oxygen to the muscles where it might be needed. Adrenaline is released into the bloodstream. The organism is prepared physically to fight, freeze or flee.
6 The insular cortex, located near the corpus callosum, particularly on the right or non-dominant hemisphere, which constantly maintains an image of the current state of the body (Damasio 1999a: 156, 205–6), will register this change (6a) and will make this information available to the neocortex, particularly the frontal cortex (6b) for recognition at a later time if this is relevant for consciousness.

The first fear reaction is felt. This process generates a bodily concept of the self which is present in all mammals.

7 The thalamus also transmits the sensory impression to the primary cortex of each sense (7).
8 While the body is reacting to the 'fast path' (5) the visual images sent from the thalamus (7) are decrypted (8a) and analysed (8b), and the images from the various sensory cortices are brought together to form a global image of what is happening (8c) in the entorhinal cortex, which is situated as a prolongation of the hippocampus.

9 By way of the hippocampus (9a and 9b) this global image elicits memories from previous experiences (LeDoux 1996: 241). How many times in your life have you been pushed into second place, either physically or socially by someone not necessarily more intelligent or better, but more aggressive, louder, bolder? We have an instinctive, archetypal need for fairness, for having our legitimate place in life being accepted and not overpowered by someone who just pushes in front. What has happened is also an aggressive attack and it is natural to have an instinctive reaction in self defence and/or counter aggression.
10 The multisensory (entorhinal) cortex also reinforces the activation of the amygdala and the limbic system.

The heightened energy level in the body brings with it an increasing awareness that the situation is potentially dangerous. The retrieval of memories of past experiences, although not yet conscious, will increase the fixing of the system in this alert state. The correspondence of the incoming images and emotional reaction (from 6b) with memories of past experiences concentrates the system in a fixed state. This is the point at which the parasympathetic nervous system can kick in, sending dampening signals via the limbic system to calm down. This is depicted as the feedback in Figure 5.5. Or the system, reacting to previous, still unconscious, memories, can lock in the excited, attractor state of the constellated complex. This corresponds with the second level of the dynamical hierarchy.

There is a familiarity associated with this state which identifies a pre-conscious form of the self. The person can recognise what it feels like 'to be me' in this situation, but it is below conscious awareness. Memory retrieval, especially the retrieval of memories related to the self in similar circumstances, would reinforce the feeling of a self existing over time. It is experienced as the coming together of the subject and object of self-referential emotions. Once consciousness emerges one sees oneself as the actor of what one does or feels, but at this pre-conscious stage one is more acted upon by one's emotions than the actor. It is as if the various domains of action controlled by the cortical and subcortical midline structures (Northoff *et al.* 2006: 446–9) – verbal, special, memory, emotional, facial and social – are functioning independently. They have not yet coalesced into a unified, coordinated workspace. It is related to what Damasio calls the 'core self' (Damasio: 1999a).

11 Meanwhile the image of the current situation has been compared to memory images of previous experiences and the information is made available to the frontal cortex.
12 It is at this point that the driver first becomes *conscious* of the change in body state, and his rage at the reckless driver.
13 Upon further reflection he reaches the conclusion that the other is just an idiot driver and it is best to let him go on his way. The prefrontal cortex

sends dampening signals to the amygdala to calm down (13a). There is no danger. The calming message is passed on to the body (13b). In this case the image evoked by past experience is one of the reckless driver vanishing down the road, leaving the way clear for the person to continue on, there is no apparent danger. The complex is *not* constellated.

The image of the current situation, when compared to past experiences in step 11 could lead in two opposite directions. If past experience was negative, indicating that the person was in danger and must fight out against an aggressor, a competitive situation is created leading to, at best, a verbal onslaught against the rodeo cowboy driver, i.e. a safe way of working off the built up energy, or at worst, counter aggression and a chase down the highway. The situation is evaluated as dangerous, either physically or psychologically.

Chapter 7

A theory of archetypes

Below is a selection of quotations from the *Collected Works* which Jung used at one time or another to define what he meant by archetypes. Taken alone none is conclusive, but taken together they give a clearer idea of the breath of what Jung meant and, by their omissions, of what he didn't mean. Given the variety expressed by these quotes it can be seen why it is so difficult to pin him down, and why the subject has led to varying schools of thought within Jungian theory.

Archetypes are:

- instinctive impulses and forms that can be observed in all living creatures (Jung 1958a: para. 565)
- a kind of pre-existent ground plan (Jung 1921/1971: para. 512)
- the inborn mode of psychic apprehension (Jung 1921/1971: para. 624–5)
- symbolic formulae (Jung 1921/1971: para. 625)
- dynamic images (Jung 1917/1953: para. 184)
- *instinct's perception of itself* (Jung 1919: para. 277 italics in original)
- aptitudes (Jung 1927/1931b: para. 339)
- forms or categories (Jung 1927/1931b: para. 342)
- representations of the meaning of the instinct (Jung 1946/1954: para. 398)
- living psychic forces (Jung 1940/1951: para. 266)
- themes (Jung 1946/1954: para. 401)
- 'empirically derived postulates' which 'manifest themselves only through their ability to organise images and ideas, and this is always an unconscious process which cannot be detected until afterwards' (Jung 1946/1954: para. 440)
- formal factors responsible for the organisation of unconscious psychic processes (Jung 1952: para. 841)
- patterns of functioning (Jung 1938/1954: para. 152)
- compared to the axial system of a crystal … the invariable geometric proportions underlying it (Jung 1938/1954: para. 155)
- have an 'invariable nucleus of meaning' (Jung 1938/1954: para. 155)
- a system of readiness for action (Jung 1927/1931a: para. 53)

- an irrepresentable factor, a disposition (Jung 1942/1948: para. 222)
- factors and motifs that arrange the psychic elements into certain images (Jung 1942/1948: para. 222, note 2)
- structural dominants (Jung 1942/1948: para. 222, note 2)

Basic theory of the psychoid

What I consider to be of primary importance in the writings of Jung on the archetypes is the psychoid. With this concept he grounds archetypes in the body. He calls the archetypes the 'hidden foundations of the conscious mind' and compares them to the roots of the psyche in the earth and in the world in general (Jung 1927/1931a: para. 53).

Psychoid processes are distinct from, but lie between, the purely bodily, life-sustaining functions of the brain on the one hand and psychic process on the other. The unconscious continues beyond this into the body (Jung 1946/1954: para. 368). In the concept of the psychoid archetype, Jung has already conceived of the two-way mapping between psychological phenomena and physiological states.

In the same way that humans have two arms, two legs, a heart and a liver, etc., the psyche also exhibits evidence of a common structure. 'The archetypes are, so to speak, organs of the pre-rational psyche.' Jung saw no reason to exclude some of them from existing in animals (Jung 1917/1953: para. 109). They have at first no content: 'Their specific content only appears in the course of the individual's life' (Jung 1935/1953: para. 845). He identified them as being subcortical (Jung 1958a : para. 582–3).

Jung associated psychoid processes with instincts (Jung 1946/1954: para. 380) which are phylogenetic and which establish patterns of behaviour (ibid.: para. 398). We would act solely according to these patterns of behaviour if our actions were not influenced by the conscious mind (ibid.: para. 379). The instinct contains within it a certain image underlying this behaviour (ibid.: para. 398). This image is the goal of the instinct, and determines whether or not the instinctive action is successful. When Jung spoke of the image in relation to the archetype, he did not mean a picture related to a specific vision, but rather an *imago* (Jung 1909/1949: para. 729) which is similar to a figment of fantasy and results from the spontaneous activity of both the conscious and unconscious (Jung 1921/1971: para. 745). This combination of instinct and image is the structure of the archetype.

In my interpretation, Jung's original theories suggest that the archetype is firmly innate in the human embryo, first as the instinct and only later forming the image.

Jolande Jacobi, in her book *The Psychology of C.G. Jung* (1962: 34), depicts the archetype as a metaphor of the magma in the earth welling up in individual lives. The magma in the volcano-like structures represents its universal nature. Beneath the surface it is uniform, but as it wells up into consciousness it takes a different form depending on the specific cultural context. The oldest layers comprising the most basic forms were laid down in our animal ancestors, then those associated with the first humans, ethnic groups and so on up to the individual determine the form the archetype actually takes in each life. This introduces an element of the archetypal image that is less completely innate and is influenced by the cultural environment, although for people in the same family group the underlying layers would be identical.

In Figure 7.1 I depict the psychoid archetype-as-such connecting the two poles of image and instinct. Around the archetypal image, and forming it, are the decreasing influences of family, culture and so on down to our evolutionary ancestors. The instincts are situated in the subcortex and stretch on through the brain stem and the endocrine system into the body.

Only after the archetype-as-such takes a definite form as an image or idea does it enter consciousness. Even then it may be perceived only vaguely as a motif. What is usually called the 'archetype' is an image or set of images like the Mother or the Divine Child, but beyond that is the psychoid archetype-as-such constellating the image. The archetypal image, or what is usually called simply, albeit incorrectly in my opinion, the archetype, is determined at least in part by cultural context. This is why Jung said that the form of the archetype is determined at birth but the content, i.e. what it looks like to any particular person, is determined by the culture and the background of the person (Jung 1909/1949: para. 728).

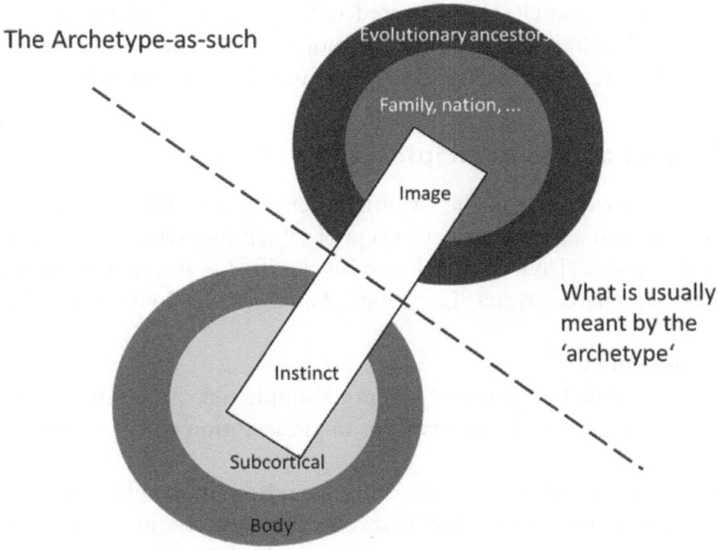

Figure 7.1 The psychoid or archetype-as-such

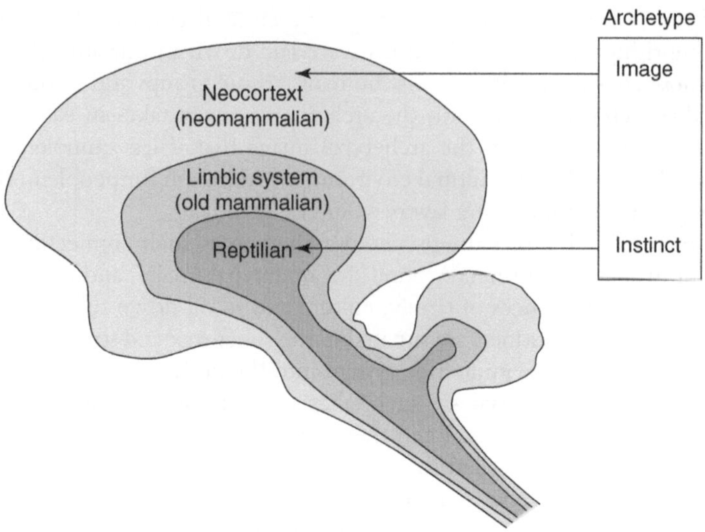

Figure 7.2 The archetype positioned within MacLean's triune brain

In reviewing the Jungian model of the psyche, I associate the psychoid processes with the subcortical structures, while the archetypal image is cortical.

Figure 7.2 relates this to the current concept of the human brain often illustrated as the triune brain depicted by Paul MacLean (1969). The instinctual pole is associated with the oldest part of the brain, sometimes called the reptilian brain, and is also closely associated with the limbic system and emotions. The imaginal pole is derived from memories, fantasies, cultural stories, etc., related to the archetypal image. These are stored in the neocortex.

Instinct as active principle/as process

During the first quarter of the twentieth century a number of attempts were made to establish a list of instincts, none of which met with general agreement (Bernard 1924). Behaviour which can be classified as instinctive has (most of) the following characteristics (Encyclopaedia Britannica 2006 'Instinct'):

- It is inherited.
- It is a patterned sequence of acts not a simple reflex reaction to a stimulus.
- It contributes to self-preservation or preservation of the social group or species.
- When triggered it emerges without rehearsal or planning (although in practice it is often difficult to establish that absolutely no learning is involved).

Spurred by the work of Darwin, the concept of instinct was widely discussed in scientific and psychological circles at the end of the nineteenth and beginning of the twentieth century. It is prevalent in the works of William James (1887, 1890/1950), John B. Watson (1912, 1924), William McDougall (1910) and Konrad Lorenz (1956). The use of the term fell out of favour after World War II; some believed this was because of the misuse of the concept to define behaviour (all references from Schulkin 2007). The trend started replacing 'instinct' with 'behaviour', and the term 'innate behaviour' became favoured. This is reflected in the current dialogue among Jungian authors with regard to 'innatism' (Hogenson 2001, Maloney and Hogenson 2003).

Theo Cope (2006: 17–18) points out that Jung conceived of psychic energy taking the form of instincts (Jung 1928/1948: para. 51–2), although in the Hull translation 'Instinkt' (in German) is translated as 'drive'. In 'Psychological factors determining human behaviour' (Jung 1936/1942), originally written in English, 'energy' is derived from the 'instinct', and 'drive' and 'instinct' appear to be interchangeable, as can be seen in the following, rather complicated, quote: 'The fact that the *energy* can be deployed in various fields indicates the existence of still other *drives* strong enough to change the direction of the sexual *instinct* and to deflect it, at least in part, from its immediate goal' (Jung 1936/1942: para. 239, emphasis added).

In this same work Jung delineates five categories of instincts, each of which can take many different forms of expression:

- hunger (which is more generally considered a part of self-preservation: greed, boundless desire, insatiability, lust for gain, inordinate ambition),
- sexuality,
- drive to activity (urge to travel, love of change, restlessness and play),
- reflection (production of images, speech, abstract thought, dramatic representation, ethical conduct, the production of culture in all forms) and
- creativity (he expresses doubt whether creativity is itself an instinct or if it is closely connected with other instincts).

(Jung 1936/1942: para. 236–46, additions in parenthesis are my own.)

We speak today much less about drives or instincts but rather about behaviour, motivations or needs. For example, Lichtenberg has identified five motivational systems: physiological needs and the related psychological assurance that these will be met, the need for attachment and relationship, the need for exploration and asserting one's self, the need at times to resist and withdraw and the need for sensual/sexual stimulation and enjoyment (Lichtenberg 1992: 1, cited in Jacoby 1999: 38–9).

The use of the term 'value' by Gerald Edelman includes the concept of instinct: 'We define values as phenotypic aspects of an organism that were selected during evolution and constrain somatic selective events, such as the synaptic changes that occur during brain development and experience' (Edelman and Tononi 2000a: 88).

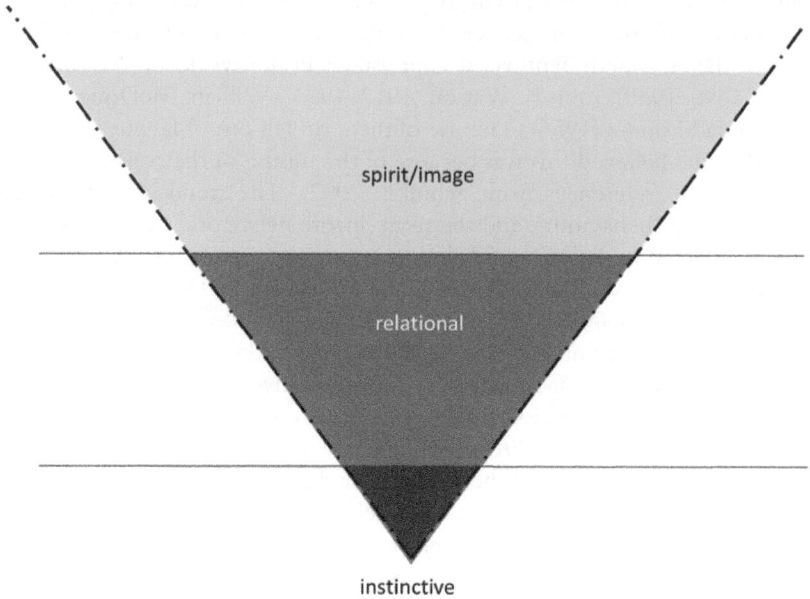

Figure 7.3 The generic archetype, from instinct to image

Jung compared the continuum of the psychoid archetype, from instinct to image, with the electromagnetic spectrum (Jung 1946/1954: para. 417). He compared the instinct with the infrared end of the spectrum below the visible frequency range, with the image extending above the visible frequency range into the ultraviolet. I have modified this one-dimensional representation into two dimensions (Figure 7.3), keeping the instinctive core (dark grey) and the image (light grey) but adding an intermediate relational area in-between to indicate that, as with Jacobi's volcanoes, the image can take on many different forms depending on the cultural environment of the individual.

Instinct as pattern of action

The activation of an instinct often results in unconscious, typical, repetitive and automatic reactions. '*Instincts are typical modes of action, and whenever we meet with uniform and regularly recurring modes of action and reaction we are dealing with instinct*' (Jung 1919: para. 273, italics in the original).

Jung also described archetypes as 'factors and motifs that arrange psychic elements into images'. Factors and motifs are like blueprints and patterns. They form the 'structural dominants of the psyche'. He compared them to a 'crystal lattice' which defines structure and form but not content. The outer shape that the crystal takes depends on a number of environmental factors, such as the shape of the vessel containing the solution, but the inner crystalline structure itself is inherent in the nature of the substance (all quotes from Jung 1942/1948: para. 222, note 2). It is important to note this comparison of the archetype with a pattern as I will come back to it later when considering the relationship of Jung's original theory to complexity and emergence.

> ... the unconscious, as the totality of all archetypes, is the deposit of all human experience right back to its remotest beginnings. Not, indeed, a dead deposit, a sort of abandoned rubbish-heap, but a living system of reactions and aptitudes that determine the individual's life in invisible ways ... it is also the source of the instincts, for the archetypes are simply the forms which the instincts assume
>
> (Jung 1927/1931b: para. 339).

The Kantian basis for Jung's theories has often been discussed and debated, indeed he did so himself, but the archetypes go beyond the Kantian classification of ways of knowing the world, i.e. division into time and space. They become 'impulses' (Jung 1958a: para. 565), 'instincts' (Jung 1919: para. 277), they 'free psychic energy' (Jung 1921/1971 para. 749), they are 'aptitudes' (Jung 1927/1931b: para. 339) and 'behavioural patterns' (Jung 1957/1959: para. 549–50; 1912/1956: para. 224; 1919: para. 270, 274, 398; 1946/1954: para. 398 and others).

The two poles of the archetype

Epigenetics

Modern research in genetics has modified our understanding of what Jung termed 'phylogenetic' and 'instinctual'. Recent epigenetic research has shown that a phenotype can be modified through behaviour (Weaver *et al.* 2004). It has even been proposed that genes and culture *co-evolve*, a term first used to describe the mutual effect of evolution on two species (Richardson and Boyd 2005: 191–236). For example, the use of technology – a development of culture – has led to the evolution of modern humans to be less physically robust than our ancestors. Cultural development modifies behaviour, which in turn alters the survival possibilities of the species, for better or worse. George Hogenson refers to this as the Baldwin effect (Hogenson 2001), after the work by James Mark Baldwin and Conway Lloyd Morgan in 1895, and he shows that Jung was aware of this concept.

This 'co-evolution' of culture and genes was investigated in detail by Eytan Avital and Eva Jablonka (2000). They argue that in environments which change little over the lifespan of the individual, such as the situation with domestic chickens, it is genes which will predominate. Chicks' actions will be determined by genes; they will follow their mothers. The culture, which needs little or no learning, will be passed on principally through a process of genetic assimilation. In such cases, innate, instinctive behaviour predominates. This is not the case with humans. Learning is important in environments which change rapidly in relation to the lifespan of the individual. The more one knows about an unstable environment, the more one is able to adapt. The type of learning involved, whether social (in the context of a group) or asocial (individual), also plays an important role. Social learning predominates in situations where individual learning would be dangerous, as with herbivores which must differentiate between edible and poisonous plants, and in situations where environmental conditions are more stable. This can lead to societies with complex ritual traditions which need to be learned over a relatively long period of time, as is the case with traditional cultures (even that in which Jung grew up). Asocial, personal learning is important in societies which change rapidly during the course of an individual's life. Changing jobs, relocation, uncertain social conditions require the ability to think fast and adapt to changing circumstances.

This suggests to me that the instinctive end of the psychoid is less important for us than it would be for animals living in a more stable environment, such as in the examples Jung gives of the leaf-cutting ant. I believe that the activated instinct evokes an emotional, physical reaction in the body but, for us in the modern, globalised world, even more than in Jung's time, the form of the response to that emotion is to a large extent personally, individually determined. In the society in which Jung lived, in the beginnings of the twentieth century in Switzerland, ritual played a larger role. A concrete example may be a change in the image of the Hero archetype. The traditional hero, after achieving the quest, returns to his or her community (Campbell 1988). A current hero, Jake in the popular film *Avatar,* chooses to stay on a foreign planet rather than bringing their wisdom to his own people. Perhaps this change in *culture* due to our technical knowledge and globalisation is why modern Jungian authors are experiencing a need to modify the theory from how it was originally conceived in the first years of 1900.

One of the most involved examples of co-evolution is the development of speech in prehistoric humans. Within either the discontinuous theory of language development, i.e. that language is the result of a sudden massive genetic mutation, or the continuous theory, i.e. that it evolved slowly over millions of years, it is believed that language evolved from improved motor skills which required the communication of more complicated emotional expression than was possible with the previous limited facial and bodily gestures and vocalisations. Investigating the development of speech in the infant, as well as in prehistory, Greenspan and Shanker, arguing from an evolutionary psychology perspective, conclude that, although genes create a system capable of emotional and perceptual differentiation, it is the dynamic, emotional interaction of infant and caregiver which necessitates the learning of spoken language (Greenspan and Shanker 2004: 187–207).

Modern Jungian authors' variation on the theory of archetypes

Anthony Stevens (1982/2003), one of the few post-Jungian authors to have stressed the instinctive pole of the instinct-image dyad, claims that Jung's theories largely anticipated the theory of epigenetics. Indeed his own work, especially his collaboration with John Price on evolutionary psychiatry, emphasises the instinctive end of that continuum. He is said to hold a 'deep innatist position' (Maloney and Hogenson 2003: 107). Adjusting the previous diagram (Figure 7.3) to represent Stevens' standpoint (Figure 7.4) would greatly increase the infrared end of the psychoid, thereby reducing the relational aspects, but according to him, a large part of the image is also innate, hence below the relational:

For example, a child has an inner image of the archetype of the Good Mother. The pathological mother complex comes from the failure of the actual mother to match that image adequately. Of course no mother can exactly match this image of perfection, but a normal, healthy complex will form if the mother is adequate (Stevens 1982/2003: 74) and an autonomous, pathological one if she is not.

Peter Saunders and Patricia Skar (2001, Skar 2004) identify the archetypes as a class or category of complexes (Saunders and Skar 2001: 312) which 'can be seen as a property of the developmental dynamic that forms the complexes' (Skar 2004: 245), i.e. they are neither pre-existent nor emergent *structures* themselves (ibid.).

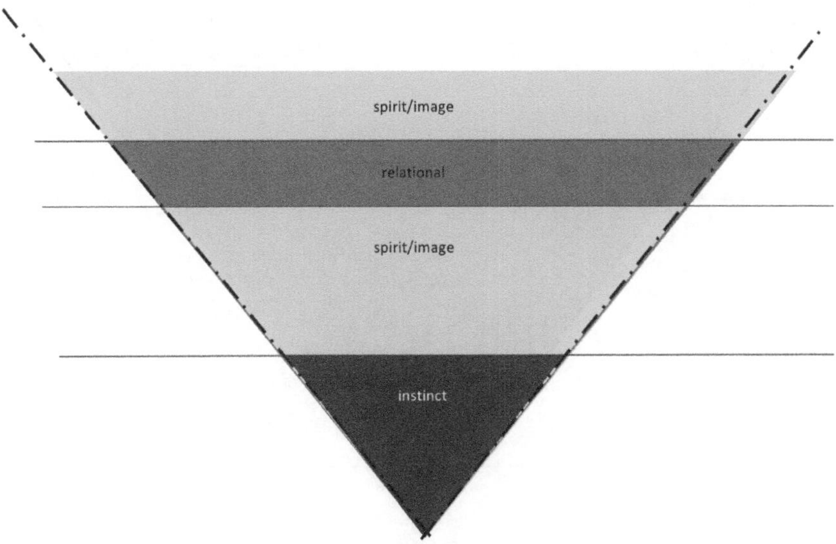

Figure 7.4 Representation of the archetype as viewed by Anthony Stevens

I disagree with their writing when Skar states with reference to this classification: 'It need not have a separate physical existence, either as a heritable structure in the brain or as a gene, *or in any other way*' (Skar 2004: 245; emphasis mine). Although she is referring to the resulting classification schema, she also seems to be negating the instinctive pole of the archetype-as-such. She also says 'When we employ a dynamical systems view of development, we no longer need the "archetype-as-such" to explain the formation of complexes. *In fact, we could do without it altogether and still have the same basic psychological system that Jung proposed*' (Skar 2004: 245, quotes and emphasis in the original). If we do away with the archetype-as-such we do away with the instinctive pole.

The correspondingly modified diagram for the Saunders and Skar model would look like the one shown in Figure 7.5.

The origins of the categories in this model are 'typical situations in life' (Jung 1936/1937: para. 99 quoted in Saunders and Skar 2001: 311). The relational portion is very large. What comes out of the relational dynamic is an archetype as simple classification schema of complexes.

George Hogenson identifies archetypes as 'emergent properties of the developmental system of brain, environment and narrative' (Hogenson 2001: 607; 2009: 185). He further specifies what he means by 'brain' as the 'physiological characteristics of the infant' (Hogenson 2004: 67). The starting point for Hogenson, the instinctive pole of the psychoid, can best be specified, in the quote from Terrance Deacon that he cites, as 'universal biases in the selection processes' (Deacon 1997: 115f quoted in Hogenson 2001: 605). In each of the

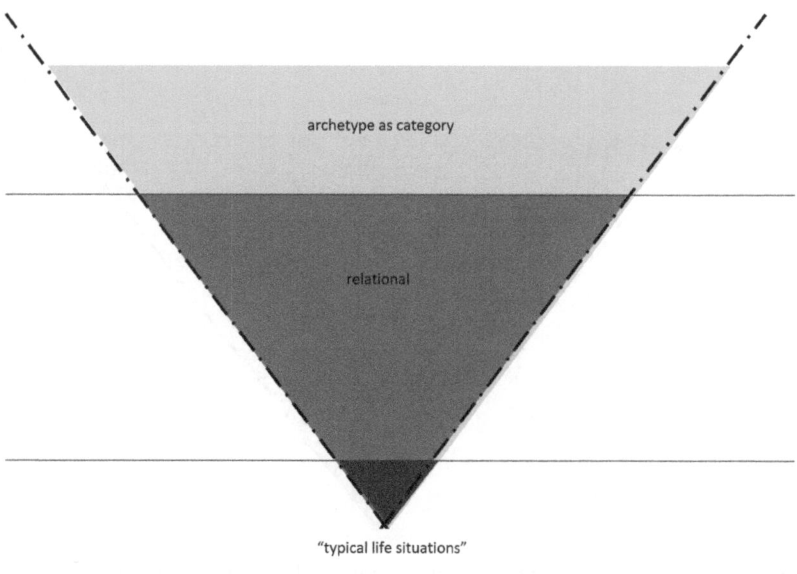

Figure 7.5 Representation of the archetype as viewed by Saunders and Skar

examples Hogenson gives – language, lactose absorption in northern European civilisations (ibid.: 597), and similarities in mythological themes (ibid.: 606–7) – there seems to be some basis for a physical survival advantage, although I would add this might not be the same in each case. He defines archetypes as 'psychological factors' which are 'central to the evolutionary process' (ibid.: 591).

The relationship Hogenson cites as generating the emergent archetypes includes environment and culture (Hogenson 2004, 2005). What emerges is what he terms 'the symbolic' (Hogenson 2005: 277) by which, I suggest, he means something very similar to what I have described as the third level of emergence and meaning, although he puts this in the context of a pattern of action similar to Jung's pattern of behaviour (Jung 1957/1959: para. 549–50; 1912/1956: para. 224; 1919: para. 270, 274, 398; 1946/1954: para. 398).

The diagram modified for the George Hogenson model looks like the one shown in Figure 7.6.

The instinct is not genetic, but could best be described as a bias in evolution, either physical or purely immaterial. The relational process is very important and includes language, narrative and culture. The image pole of the psychoid is an emergent symbolic world 'that the psyche inhabits, realises, or perhaps falls into, rather than as a world that the human mind creates' (Hogenson 2005: 280) thus it pre-exists this process. It is different from consciousness, which is usually depicted as something emergent from the dynamical system of psyche and environment.

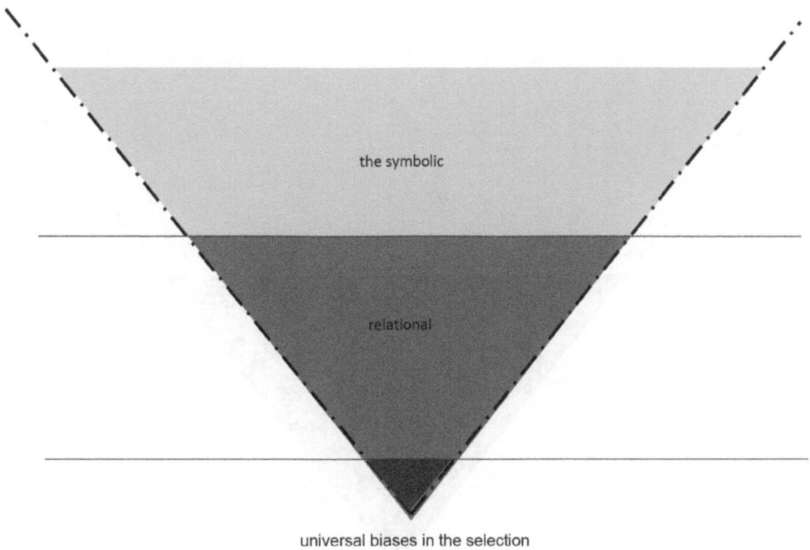

Figure 7.6 Representation of the archetype as viewed by Hogenson

Maxson McDowell (2001), on the other hand, would take the relational component away altogether, replace instinct with the physical laws governing emergence and leave the archetypal image in a relatively pure form (see Figure 7.7). He proposes that dream images are self-organised archetypal images, as in his example of the witch's green eyes becoming the green lawn, consumed by fire.

I expect that he would agree with my hypothesis that the complex is an attractor: 'Within the personality that principle [the archetype-as-such] manifests itself as a psychological vortex (a complex) into which we are drawn' (McDowell 2001: 637, my explanation in square brackets).

Jean Knox quotes Elman in rejecting the earlier idea of the genome as a 'blueprint', stressing rather that the 'algorithm', which is responsible for innate behaviours, is activated by stimuli in the environment (Elman *et al.* 1999: 350 quoted in Knox 2003: 48–9), thus expressing an epigenetic position of interaction between an innate genetic code and inter-subjective culture. She equates the archetype-as-such with the image schema described by cognitive scientist Jean Mandler as the 'earliest and most primitive form of representation' (Knox 2004: 8). These concepts, such as 'PATH', 'UP-DOWN', 'FORCE', 'PART-WHOLE' and 'LINK' (Knox 2003: 56), are suggested by the ability of a baby to recognise a face from a random arrangement of dots and lines (Knox 2003: 50, citing the research of Johnson and Morton 1991). Image schemas are formed in the first days and weeks of a baby's life. This original structure is repeatedly reanalysed and re-encoded into increasingly complex forms. Knox refutes the possibility of any genetically encoded fixed primordial image of the type Jung

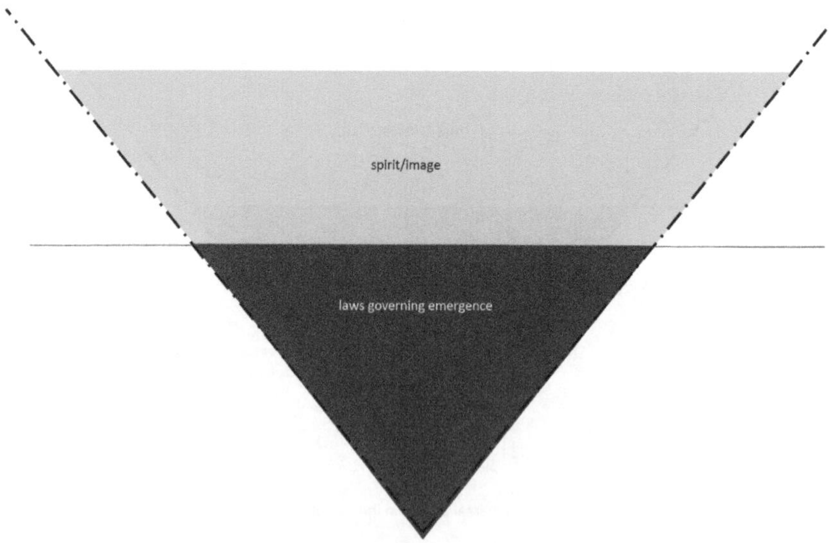

Figure 7.7 Representation of the archetype as viewed by Maxson McDowell

first proposed, concluding that 'Archetypes are not in themselves innate, genetic structures. The evidence from developmental research suggests that archetypes can be equated with image schema … These Gestalts then act as a base for extensive elaboration of these patterns into the symbolic world' (Knox 2003: 66). However, the image schema is not experienced directly, but serves as a pattern or blueprint analogous to the archetype-as-such (Knox 2004: 9).

She views what I have been calling the image pole of the archetype-as-such as 'a process and emergent pattern of relationship that provides meaning for the infant's perception of the physical world and of human relationship' (Knox 2003: 68).

I could go along with Knox in including the image schema as an innate ordering principle and include it with instinct (or emotion) as one pole of the psychoid. The diagram for Knox would then look like Figure 7.8.

The role of the instinct is replaced by the image schema. Where I differ with Knox is in my assertion that the repeated reanalysing and re-encoding of image schemas in ever more concrete forms leads to the formation of the complex or ego-complex, and not the archetype. Knox links the image schema with her internal working model of the archetype. This is stored in implicit memory of interactions principally with parents and key attachment figures (Knox 2004: 10) – the same process of building up the complexes comprising the ego that I describe in Chapter 9.

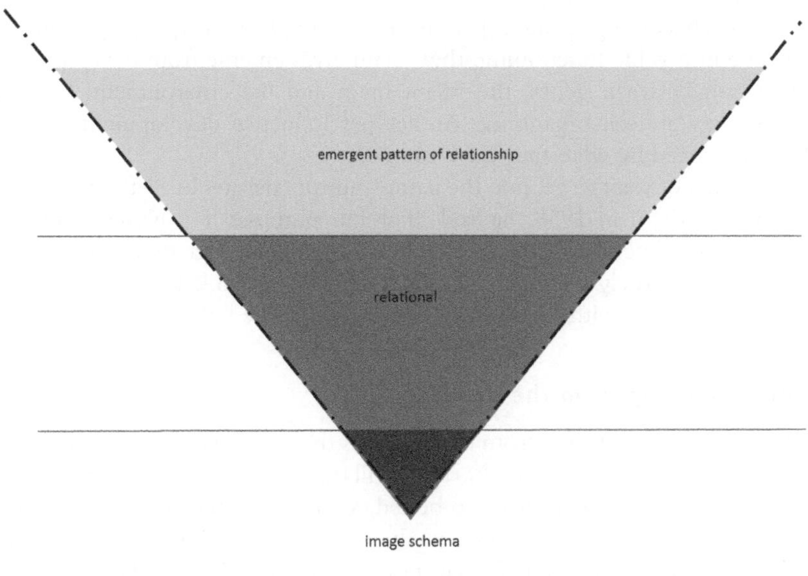

Figure 7.8 Representation of the archetype as viewed by Jean Knox

My conclusions

This discussion of the differing views between modern Jungian authors leads me to conclude that the transition between the two ends of the psychoid, the instinctive and the spiritual/cultural/image, is very ill-defined. There is no clear point, either in the individual or in the collective, at which one stops and the other begins. Different individuals, having different physical and cultural and/ or social backgrounds will experience this division differently. Even over an individual lifetime of learned experiences and adaptation, this dividing line will change. Is that not, in part, what we are hoping for in psychoanalysis? Through the various relationships experienced in the transference, and the bringing of various unconscious contents to consciousness, the individual works through old archetypal images which may have been fixed since childhood. An image of the mother, the anima or the animus, for example, can become more varied, incorporating new insights gained during the analysis.

The cultural relationships one experiences, especially during infancy and early childhood, will also significantly influence one's self-concept, including those characteristics identified above as being central to perceiving oneself as independent agent of one's actions and the degree to which one separates or remains principally a member of a collective. How the continuum from the instinctive pole of the archetype to its expression of the archetypal image, influences then not only the specific form of the archetype but also, as will be shown in the development of the ego-complex, the affective psychic landscape of the individual and the person's self image.

What is becoming apparent here is that, although archetypes play an important role in psychic functioning, they themselves emerge from developmental interaction between genes, the infant brain and the environment. In other words, they are self-organising. Archetypes influence development, and are then influenced by what they have caused.

Jung did not want to get into the nature-nurture debate. In a letter to Michael Fordham, written in 1958, he said: 'For our purposes it is highly indifferent whether archetypes are handed down by tradition and migration or by inheritance. It is an entirely secondary question, since comparable biological facts, i.e. instinctual patterns with animals, are obviously inherited' (Jung 1976: 451).

What is missing from the debate

What I consider is missing from the debate is the simple fact that human babies are very much alike. They are born very ill-adapted to their environment and have a number of basic needs – to be fed, kept warm, held and loved, among others. These needs are inherited in the sense that each child knows, to use colloquial language, *instinctively* that they must be met. Every infant feels good when its tummy is full, when it is warm and has someone to play with – hence the Mother Archetype. A baby cries from fear and insecurity when it is placed on a hard, open surface, but if a caregiver puts their arms on either side of it, about six inches from the body, without even touching it, it will stop. It knew that it was unprotected and was afraid, but with the appearance of limits it feels protected – hence the Father Archetype. Neuroscience may no longer use the term 'instinct', but we know that the amygdala (fear) and the opioids (pleasure) are present from birth and that they are associated with emotions similar to what were before called instincts.

I argue that the fulfilment or not of these basic *needs* is an element in the development of the archetypal image, the experience of strong emotions, and leads eventually to the formation of a complex. These needs arise out of the human nature of the baby and its dependence on the social environment. It has been explained that this dependence is a means by which cultural adaptation can be transmitted in the relationships of the infant with its primary caregivers (Schore 1994). These needs are not transmitted in the genes as such, but arise out of the human nature of the baby.

Specific instincts

Based on a classification of emotion in the work of Louis Stewart (1987) presented in Chapter 5, I proposed the following as the basic instincts along with their association to the emotion. I repeat the table here:

Table 7.1 Instinct, affect and the life situation

Instinct	*Affect*	*Life situation*
Engaging in the world		
To play	Ecstasy (joy)	Encountering the familiar
To learn	Excitement (interest)	Encountering something novel, intriguing
To protect	Caring	Encountering others
To procreate	Desire (sexual attraction)	Founding a family
Existential threats to life (self preservation)		
To flee	Terror (fear)	Confronting the unknown
To submit	Anguish (sadness)	Experiencing loss
To fight	Rage (anger)	Being restricted or controlled
To avoid	Disgust (contempt)	Rejecting someone or something
To freeze	Shame (humiliation)	Being exposed, defenceless
Centring attention		
To startle	Surprise	Sudden confrontation with the unexpected

Through play and curiosity, the infant engages in the world. While encountering something known, he or she plays with it, experiences happiness, and may laugh. Feeling safe, the child may go on to explore new aspects of the object and venture into the unknown, expressing curiosity. Our natural instinct to play and to learn pulls us into the world, not only as infants and children, but throughout life. Infants have means of self-soothing, such as sucking their thumb. Even baby elephants suck their trunk. Through experiencing suffering the infant searches for, and finds, ways of reducing anxiety. How this is done is to a certain extent a learned cultural reaction (Schore 1994), but the impetus for self-protection and self-caring is instinctive. This is what Fordham called the 'defences of the Self' (Fordham 1974), and what Kalsched called the 'self-care system' (Kalsched 1996: 4). I believe that, through projection, this self-care system is extended to concern for those in need – the weak, ill, very young and elderly. I think that empathy is learned, in part, through recognising one's own suffering and then being able to apply this recognition to others one sees in pain or distress.

Fight and flight are the classic reactions to a dangerous situation. Rejection is a natural reaction to someone or something one considers disgusting. In work with trauma victims (Levine 1997), freeze has also been recognised as an instinctive reaction in situations where fight or flight is not possible. In situations lasting for longer time periods, submission is often a reaction which allows survival. Anthony Stevens and John Price (1996) associate this with depression.

Startle is an instinctive reaction which lasts only a fraction of a second. It gets our attention. Afterwards one of the other instincts takes over.

Making an attempt to associate the archetype with instinct I make the following links: protection and caring are associated with the Mother Archetype, procreation and desire with the Anima/Animus, playing with the Trickster and learning, ordering with the Father Archetype. There is too much cultural association with instincts and their related emotions to attempt any further one-to-one correlation, for example fight–rage, could vary from the avenging superhero, the fighter for social justice and equality to villain or terrorist. Indeed the terrorist in one culture could be the hero in a different one.

Neural correlates of instinct and image

Instinct

Recent research in the neural underpinning of innate behavioural patterns has confirmed the importance of the interdependence of genetic programming and environmental stimulus. 'The innate nature of many basic fixed action patterns and fairly invariant species-specific animal behaviours suggests that the underlying neuronal substrates necessary for their execution are genetically determined and developmentally programmed' (Manoli *et al.* 2006: 444, referencing Baker

2001). Based on their research on the Drosophila (fruit fly) and recent studies on vertebrates, Manoli and colleagues believe that the configuration of distinct, genetically determined connections involving neuroendocrine cells in the hypothalamic area 'underlies complex innate behavioural programs' (ibid.).

According to their findings, the hypothalamus plays a central role in determining what we would call instinctive patterns of behaviour (arousal, feeding, sleep, fear, mating and social competition) in vertebrates. Neuroendocrine cells in the hypothalamus, at times in conjunction with the amygdala, release hormones into the blood, thereby causing changes in the entire body. This process is governed to a large extent by the pituitary gland situated close to, and linked closely with, the hypothalamus (Austin 1999: 189). The hypothalamus also has dense interconnections with areas in the cortex and subcortical areas, and can thereby mediate controlled action (Manoli *et al.* 2006: 449). These bodily sensations are then experienced as feelings which, in turn, influence levels of arousal and perception.

These findings explain the inherited nature of archetypes through the genetic influence on the development of these neural systems. They also identify the link between instincts, innate behaviour and emotions. The instinctive reaction or innate behaviour is experienced first in the body through changes in the endocrine system and somatic markers such as heart rate and oxygen levels in the blood. These changes are then re-experienced by the re-entrant feedback loops described by Damasio (1999a) and Edelman and Tononi (2000a) as feelings.

I conclude from this that what has traditionally been called instinct is very closely related to emotion, is linked with the limbic system and is to a certain extent hard-wired, innate. On the other hand, how an individual reacts, and the value placed on the experience, is to a large extent influenced by culture.

Image

The image pole of the archetype as presented by Jung includes a concept of self in relation to the environment, a plan of action and a concept of the goal of the instinctive action.

The neural correlates of the archetypal or symbolic image or experience can be associated with a phenomenon similar to memory and situated in the neocortex. Jung identified 'forgotten memory-images' as part of the subliminal unconscious (Jung 1952: 856). He went on to distinguish between images arising from actual but forgotten sensory perceptions, and images which are innate. The latter either have no relation to once perceived, but now forgotten, sensorial images, or else the relation is subliminal and meaningful, giving the images a special character.

Neuroscience has not investigated this sort of image as *imago*, but the sudden experience of visual insight when control over the instincts is released, as happens in the experience of *kensho* (an experience of enlightenment, sometimes associated with visual hallucinations or visions), originates from the back of the visual cortex and the limbic system (Austin 1999: 460). The feelings associated with the experience of approaching an archetype, classically described as fear, dread, mystery and awefulness (Otto 1917/1923), correlate with activation of the limbic system, in particular the amygdala.

The encounter with an archetypal image can bring a sense of awe. It may be experienced as spiritual alertness or intense significance. These feelings originate from the midline of the limbic thalamus and the mediodorsal, anterior and lateral dorsal thalamic nuclei. Other areas involved are the lateral septum and the cingulate gyrus which curves down to the hippocampus. Meaning is also accentuated by the generation of natural opioids (Austin 1999: 523–4).

Late formulation of entire theory

Jung proposed the archetypes as elemental structural forms of unconscious psychic processes. They are basic to our psychic nature as humans in the same way that internal organs, lungs, liver, etc. are basic to our physical nature. They are in part inherited. They influence our patterns of behaviour and our initial way of interpreting interpersonal relations which will, in turn, influence the form that the archetypes take in any one instance. They are, therefore, self-organising. They are 'in part inherited' because it is only the impulse to act, i.e. the instinct, which is inherited, and not the specific form that action will take. Archetypes are the 'conditions for the forming of representations in general' (Jung 1921/1971: para. 512). Archetypes are indeed connected with the instincts through being an 'image' of the goal of the instinct, i.e. what would happen if the action initiated by the instinct is successful. The 'image' includes the person as actor, the plan of action engaged by the instinct, the environment and the goal of the action.

Archetypes are most readily identifiable through their images as characters and motifs in myth. Here they are depicted with recognisable identities – the hero/heroine, the dying or wounded king etc. – or as life events – the cycle of death and rebirth, the slaying of the dragon, and so forth.

Simply stated, an autonomous complex results from interpersonal relations, and the associations to it are from memories in the personal unconscious. Its constellation is perturbing and takes consciousness away from the ego-complex, but does not risk the fragmentation of the ego. It is, in this sense, neurotic. The constellation, however, of an archetype *per se* is psychotic and threatens to shatter the ego. The psychotic person lives very close to the collective unconscious. The irruption of archetypal images into consciousness is accompanied by very strong, often numinous, emotions.

The relationship between complex and archetype

The following is a somewhat playful review of the relation between the theories of complexes and archetypes within classical Jungian theory, and also ideas from fields well outside psychology: mathematics and information technology. The two theories are actually quite distinct within Jung's writings.

Similarities and differences between complexes and archetypes

One of the major differences between complexes and archetypes is their relation to consciousness. On one hand, complexes are split off from consciousness, giving the impression that they were once, at least in some form, conscious. They split off because of the traumatic nature of the original experience or because they are incompatible with the adaptation of the ego-complex to the outside world (Jung 1936/1942: para. 253). On the other hand, archetypal constellations come from the collective unconscious and cannot be completely integrated into the personality. They may nonetheless manifest as new, creative, artistic and religious phenomena.

However, in other respects the behaviour of both archetypes and complexes may be similar (Jung 1936/1942: para. 254), and archetypes can intervene in our daily lives like complexes (Jung 1961: para. 546).

The difference between the constellation of an autonomous complex and that of an archetype lies in the depth of the unconscious from which the phenomenon arises. The constellation of the complex involves the activation of personal, predominantly implicit, memories. The constellation of the archetype does not involve memory, or if it does (since a complete division between the personal and the collective unconscious cannot exist (Williams 1963)), this involvement is minimal. The sudden intrusion of the archetype into consciousness is perceived as something new, an insight, something unconnected to one's previous experience. The archetype is a part of the collective unconscious while the complex is in the personal unconscious (Jung 1936/1937: para. 88). In analysing a creative work or a dream, if it concerns events in the artist's or the dreamer's past, and/or if the person can relate to the experience, then one is dealing with a complex. If, however, the event takes one unawares, if one is 'transported, or caught up by an overwhelming power' (Jung 1922/1928: para. 128), then one is experiencing the constellation of an archetype. However, Jung is not consistent when speaking of the creative process, referring to a 'new, creative content' (ibid.: para. 19n) as a complex and, at other times, as the manifestation of an archetype (ibid.: para. 125–8).

Archetypes act on the collective level, as can be seen in myth and in philosophical and religious ideas. They manifest collectively as 'social complexes of an archetypal character' (Jung 1961: para. 547).

Complexes, on the other hand, act on the individual level (Jung 1936/1937: para. 88). His comparisons of soul with the personal complex and of spirit with the collective and the archetype make this distinction clear (Jung 1920/1948: para. 588–91). The soul is personal, like a complex; both are encountered many times. The constellation of a complex reminds one of similar previous experiences. The constellation of an archetype brings something unknown; something new has entered one's life. Using Jung's comparison, spirit belongs to another world and only momentarily makes its appearance, like Gabriel at the Annunciation.

Formation of a complex

For Jung the complex which arises from early childhood forms around a discrepancy between the child's instinctive, archetypal expectations and the extent to which the actual caregiver fulfils these expectations: '… the child's instincts are disturbed, and this constellates archetypes which, in their turn, produce fantasies that come between the child and its mother as an alien and often frightening element' (Jung 1938/1954 para. 161). Anthony Stevens, coming from a very biological, instinctive conception of the archetypes, concurs: '… originally the archetype-as-such is unconscious; then, as the child matures in close proximity to its mother, so all those behaviours, feelings, and perceptions determined by the mother archetype are 'released' or activated with the consequent development of the mother complex …' (Stevens 1982/2003: 74).

Basing her conclusions on neuroscientific research, Jean Knox 'refutes any possibility of innate (genetically specified) archetypal imagery' in the interaction between caregiver and infant (Knox 2003: 96). She investigates replacing the traditional instinctive pole of the archetype-as-such with image schemas, a concept developed by cognitive scientists, which are based on perceptual experiences of the infant that develop over time as the infant encounters the world (ibid.: 54–7). The archetypal image pole of the archetype-as-such encompasses 'the innumerable metaphorical extensions which derive from image schemas' (ibid.: 96). This replacement of instinct with image schemas reduces the archetype-as-such to a very elementary, initial tendency that directs learning. Although this process offers a 'scaffolding on which meaning content is organized and constructed' (ibid.: 64), it lacks the fullness and symbolic dimension of the archetype (ibid.: 61). The archetype, building on the perceptions organised by the image schemas, later emerges in the pattern of relationships which are formed between the infant and objects of the external world with which it interacts. The archetype is a process and a pattern of relationship (ibid.: 68).

I accept most of Knox's analysis, but suggest that this tendency of the infant to concentrate on the mother's face, and the basic concepts which she develops from it, have little to do with the archetype as defined by Jung. Modern linguists have also investigated the importance of the body and the infant's early experiences in the construction of a world image (Lakoff and Johnson

1980). This research certainly identifies the importance of early image schemas in organising perception. However, these elementary orienting structures are, in my opinion, insufficient to account for the variety and complexity of archetypes. They lack the energy associated with the archetype, which was instrumental in the development of Jung's theory from primordial image to archetype, and which is an important element in the constellation of a complex. I agree with Knox on the importance of relationship, especially the early experiences of the infant-caregiver pair, but my understanding of Jungian theory suggests that what emerges from this is the complex and not the archetypal image. An orienting mechanism may explain why the infant is fascinated by its mother's face, whereas the complex is more centred around what is communicated in the mother's gaze.

Along with the leaf-cutting ant, which was Jung's example of instinctive, archetypal behaviour, the nest-building practices of birds has long been considered a prime example of instinctive behaviour. Modern research has shown that nest building includes habits, trial-and-error learning, environmental factors and social play-like activities. Along with morphology these are all important factors in how young birds learn to build nests. '… there are no "nest-building" genes; there are nesting practices which, through individual and social learning, have evolved to fit the bird's morphology and ecology …' (Avital and Jablonka 2000: 305) although in some species and under specific conditions certain aspects of nest-building appear to be innate (ibid.: 307). So there is a balance between genes and environment, even in nest-building. Likewise for humans, for whom learning (both social and individual) is much more important, the part played by social learning in the formation of a complex would be much more important than for birds in the building of a nest.

People who refute archetypal theory because it does not explain how the archetypes are inherited are, I believe, concentrating too much on a physical transmission process. One could ask which chromosome or gene transmits the Great Mother, Salomé or the Evil Witch. McDowell (2001) demonstrates that the human genome does not contain enough genes to determine definite neural connections. He argues that what is transmitted is the process by which images will later be formed. On this point he, Jean Knox and I are in agreement.

The function served by the resulting pattern of behaviour should be considered when analysing the development of a complex. The initial instinctive impulse has been modified to fit the environmental constraints of the situation. The complex can, in some cases, be considered as a learned response to a recurring situation. This adaptive response serves a definite purpose and possesses an 'enduring self-regulating property' (Stevens and Price 1996: 20) within the environment in which it evolved. The complex becomes maladaptive when the original experience is later projected onto other situations where it is not applicable and the behaviour is repeated in situations when it is no longer appropriate. Jung illustrated this process in the transformation of the mother complex into an anima projection (Jung 1936/1954: para. 141).

Child development has been studied as a hierarchy of dynamical systems (Lerner 2006: 182–5). At each succeeding phase transition there is feedback from the previous phase, and also changes in the environment, expectations and needs of the individual. Adolescence, involving both major changes in the body and adaptation to new social situations, is a time when complexes are very likely to form. Complexes can also form later in life. They can result from a single traumatic experience, in which the same instinctive mechanism is operative as in the little child fighting for the fulfilment of its basic needs, or from prolonged exposure to a stressful situation.

Self-organisation

The formation of a complex exhibits elements of self-organisation, which is a property of almost all dynamical systems. Self-organisation is characterised by both positive and negative feedback loops. Positive feedback, i.e. reinforcing the formation of the complex, is seen in the repetitive and cumulative nature of the constellation. The pattern of past reactions, which are stored as memories of past experiences of, and emotions associated with, the complex, influences the interpretation of the current situation. This will, in turn, trigger a repetition of the same behavioural reaction. Negative feedback, i.e. hindering the complex, is seen in the reaction of the ego to the pain often caused by the experience of a complex, resulting in a desire to change.

Peter Saunders and Patricia Skar (2001) propose that the complex is a self-organising structure.

> It is generally accepted by neurophysiologists and others interested in the brain and consciousness that self-organisation (in this sense) occurs within the brain and is important in its functioning. On this view, therefore, the core of Jungian thought is consistent with current scientific ideas about how the brain works and is therefore as firmly rooted in biology as it needs to be.
> (ibid.: 311)

Maxson McDowell (2001) agrees that complexes are formed by self-organisation, but differs from Saunders and Skar concerning the role played by archetypes.

Saunders and Skar see the archetype as a class of complexes (op. cit.: 312). This posits the archetype as the outcome, rather than the cause, of the complex, and is therefore contrary to Jung's original theory. As presented above when describing the neural correlates operating during the constellation of the complex, this seeming contradiction is explainable by considering circular causality to be a property of dynamical systems and therefore of the hierarchy of dynamical systems identified by neurobiologists. The complex, stored as memory traces in the neocortex, was, in the most usual case, originally formed by instinctive reactions early in infancy. In my analysis, the instinctive pole of the original archetype-as-such engenders this reaction. As the complex constellates it coalesces around an order parameter, identified as the meaning of the situation at that moment in the person's life, which itself is emergent from the lower-level dynamical systems operating at the beginning of this process. This meaning, or goal, can take the form of what Jung called the archetypal image. This image will then feed back and enslave the system, causing the further constellation of the complex. It is also at this point that new insights arising from new experiences and new relationships (e.g. in therapy) can enter the cycle and change the resulting behaviour.

In contrast to Saunders and Skar, McDowell sees an archetype as a pre-existing ordering principle which underlies the self-organisation rather than being the result of that principle. This seems to me to be more descriptive of the ordering archetype of the Self rather than of archetypes in general. It expresses an ultimate law or order in the brain on the physical level and wholeness on the psychic level. I understand the Self to be the need to find meaning, the final step in becoming conscious. What that meaning is, is determined by the individual archetype, including how the related archetypal image is formed in part by the individual and in part by that person's cultural relationships. Jung quotes Richard Wilhelm's translation of the *Tao Te Ching* to note that Tao does not appear in the world, but is its 'organizer' (Jung 1952: 920).

Through reasoning very close to that of McDowell, George Hogenson (2004: 71) interprets Jung's archetype-as-such to be a 'template' and rejects it because in dynamical systems theory and self-organisation there is no explicit template; the pattern arises from the nature of the system itself and, as it manifests, from interaction with the environment. Thus the pattern is different each time. The archetype is the self-organising nature of the system.

Network of complexes around an archetype

Jung saw complexes as falling into discrete categories (Jacobi 1959: ix, quoted in Saunders and Skar 2001: 306). Saunders and Skar see evidence of this in the various forms that the mother complex can take (2001: 318). Gustav Bovensiepien builds on Jean Knox's analysis of complexes as internal working models where early experiences are continually reworked during a child's development. This re-categorisation builds networks of subjective experience. He sees complexes as sub-networks of the interrelated pattern of neural connections. Staying very close to Jung's early definitions of the complex, Bovensiepien understands the sub-network forming the complex to be defined by the grouping of similar internal working models which are linked by the same 'affective colouring' and 'expectation patterns' (Bovensiepien 2006: 457). He refrains from speaking of specific archetypes, stressing that this model is of a process (as Knox also proposes) and not of a static situation, which he says would be the case if one were speaking of a specific complex.

Bovensiepien also supports McDowell's concept of archetype as organising principle when he states that, 'I assume that the Self (in the Jungian sense) is the dynamical organising principle, according to which of [sic] the complexes come in relation to each other …' (Bovensiepien 2006: 458).

Complexes and the archetypal core

From the general index of the *Collected Works* I checked all paragraphs in which the two words complex and archetype were mentioned, and also where both were in subsequent or preceding paragraphs. There were actually few paragraphs containing both words, and none stating that a complex has an archetypal 'core'.

Surprisingly, there is almost no reference to archetypes in Jung's writings on the theory of complexes. This is because the latter were mostly completed before Jung linked the primordial image to instinct in 1919, giving the beginnings of what we know today as the theory of archetypes. Even in Jung's clear definition of the structure of the complex written in 1928, i.e. after the development of the theory of archetypes, he does not mention the archetype as being part of the nucleus or core of the complex (Jung 1928/1948: para. 18). The 'core', in the sense of the initial cause rather than a structural element, is to be found, according to Jung, in the instinct, and hence only indirectly in the archetype: '… associated with the individually acquired causes of the complex, there was found to be a general human precondition, the inherited and inborn biological structure which is the instinctual basis of every human being' (Jung 1926).

> The use of the term 'archetypal core' probably comes from C. A. Meier: … whenever we succeed in analysing a specific complex right back to its point of origin (which means that the secondary elements that have been assimilated over the years have to be removed like the successive skins of an onion), we finally strike upon the nuclear element; and in most cases this turns out to be a so-called '*archetypal content*'.
>
> (Meier 1984: 177, my emphasis)

Verena Kast maintained the language of the archetypal core of the complex: 'Complexes are energy centres clustered around an emotionally charged core of meaning, …' (Kast 1990/1992: 31) and 'A complex … is defined as contents of the unconscious united by the same emotion and by a mutual core of meaning (archetype)' (ibid.: 32). I understand the 'core of meaning' as the characteristic of the archetype to relate the experience of the complex with that of other people and to put one's life in a mythological context. Hans Dieckmann (1991/1999), particularly in his chapter on 'The Core of the Complex', used this analogy of the archetypal core extensively.

Jung's principal link is between complex and instinct. The instinct provides the energy associated with the complex. In an early work (Jung 1912/1956:

para. 62 and n4) he specifically uses the term 'imago', referring to the archetype as the energetic, collective, living force behind the complex. The imago is activated by an instinctive energy. This energy is characteristic of the person, and the form that the imago takes when it manifests is the complex (Jung 1912/1956: para. 505). 'Again, every instinct has more or less the character of an autonomous complex' (Jung 1922/1928: para. 122).

The activation or constellation of the complex comes about through the emotion generated when an instinctive situation is encountered (Jung 1907/1960: para. 86). The affect is initiated by a relatively small number of sites in the brain stem and the limbic system (Damasio 1999a: 60). Instincts, our essential mechanisms for survival, operate either by directly initiating life-saving actions or by creating emotions which bring the organism to react in a specific manner (Damasio 1994: 114–15). It is the instincts which initiate the emotions. The archetype, as instinct, is the trigger for the activity of the unconscious (Jung 1912/1956: para. 467).

If 'core' refers not to a structural element but rather to an initial cause, then that is to be found in the instinct, hence in the archetype: '... associated with the individually acquired causes of the complex, there was found to be a general human precondition, the inherited and inborn biological structure which is the instinctual basis of every human being' (Jung 1926). The archetypal, instinctual basis of the complex is expressed throughout Jung's work.

> Every emotional state produces an alteration of consciousness ... *abaissement du niveau mental* ... creating a gradient for the unconscious to flow towards the conscious. The conscious then comes under the influence of unconscious instinctual impulses and contents. These are as a rule complexes *whose ultimate basis is the archetype*, the instinctual pattern.
>
> (Jung 1952: para. 856, my emphasis)

Complex as an 'instance' of an archetype

I will now propose a new model for the relation between complex and archetype that uses object-oriented analysis by way of analogy. Object-oriented analysis developed in the mid 1990s in information technology. Information systems model the real world and, in order to do so, need to create parallel structures within the computing system to represent real-world objects. This can be anything from, for example, an employee to a document such as an invoice. There are no fixed rules for how one creates a model. This is the 'art' of design of computer systems. Objects which are too small, for example 'date', will seriously degrade performance while the system is running. Objects which are too large take up unnecessary space and take time to load, also causing poor performance. Object oriented analysis defines, in one of several specific computing languages, a 'class' and identifies, as part of that definition, its relevant attributes. For example, for the class 'Employee' the attributes of 'name', 'address', 'age', 'sex', 'level of education', etc. are defined. Certain actions need to be taken at specific times. For example, when an employee starts or terminates employment, documents may need to be printed, the name or identifying number entered or taken off the payroll, and so forth. Likewise there are 'classes' for the organisational units of the company, for the products it produces, for its customers and suppliers, for any entity in the real world which needs to be represented in the system. A class is an abstraction. It doesn't exist, even virtually in the computer system. It is only a definition.

In object-oriented analysis there is also the concept of an 'object'. An object is intimately related to a class. It is the material realisation, or 'instantiation', of the class. Objects have a virtual existence within the world of the computer, which parallels their real world existence. The class for 'Employee' defines that an employee has a 'name'. The object, a specific instance of that class, has the name 'John Doe' (Booch 1994).

Applying this approach to the concepts of archetype and complex, the archetype corresponds to the class, and the complex to the object. The complex has a real-world existence, a history and real memories associated with it. It instantiates an archetype. For example, the 'Mother Archetype' defines certain types of relationships which can form around the instinct of caring or nurturing (and their negative equivalents). The complex is formed from the interaction and life history of the actual caregiver, the needs and innate disposition of the child, and is bounded by the possibilities which exist within the 'class' (archetype) Mother. The archetype is the '*a priori* principle of organisation' (McDowell 2001: 649), the complex is the actualisation of that principle.

There also exists in object-oriented analysis the concept of a meta-class. Classes associated with a meta-class inherit its attributes and methods. There may be a meta-class 'Person' with the attribute 'name'. If 'Employee' is a class under 'Person' then 'Employee' inherits the attribute 'name' and the instantiated object 'employee' has the name 'John Doe'. An attribute 'department' may exist for the class 'Employee' which is not in the meta-class 'Person' and which will be added to the object when it is created. Applying a parallel logic we could compare the 'Mother Archetype' to a meta-class and the 'Wicked Witch' to a class associated with it.

Archetype as the probability of a complex forming in a state space

Dynamical systems theory deals with possible states of a system. I have argued that a complex, as an attractor, is a state that the psyche is often in.

Archetypes are involved in the formation of the psychic landscape of complexes. What Jung defined as the elements which make up the core of the complex (Jung 1928/1948: para. 18), i.e. the disposition of the infant, its relationship with those around it and the cultural environment, determine whether a particular complex has a higher or lower chance of forming. In mathematics this is called a probability density function. It describes the probability of an event happening, in this case that a complex will form in a state space.

Jung defined the variables of this system when he described the core of a complex, and these can be expressed most generally as the innate disposition of a person and her or his personal experience. These are, of course, impossible to define exactly and to quantify, but we can nonetheless imagine doing so in a graph in three dimensions. In this thought experiment, the x-axis represents the disposition of a person; every possible disposition is represented, from very open and easy-going to very anxious and closed. The influence of instinct, i.e. how it manifests in this particular person, is a part of his or her disposition. The y-axis represents every possible type of experience that this person can have. The z-axis represents the strength of the complex, from zero (no complex) to very positive or very negative. This will then distort the x-y plane formed by all possible disposition-experience combinations into peaks and basins representing positive and negative complexes respectively, resembling a landscape.

The psyche can be imagined as a ball rolling on this surface. As the ball rolls near to a complex, it is attracted to it. The larger the complex the more the psyche-ball is pulled into it. This collection of possible states that the psyche can be in constitutes the state space under the initial conditions of the person's disposition and environment.

I am proposing that the archetype corresponds to the mathematical probability of a complex forming over the course of a person's lifetime at every point on this graph. By considering the type of experience on the y-axis, for example, to range from holding, caring, and supporting to clutching, smothering, and devouring, i.e. the type of aspects usually considered to be related to the Mother Archetype, the complexes represented by the hills and valleys would be mother complexes. By instead mapping experiences involving authority and rules onto the y-axis, the complexes would be father complexes, to use the traditional nomenclature. The Father Archetype corresponds to the probability that a complex will form at each position on this portion of the plane.

Some points represent complexes which are more likely to constellate because either, through evolution, they have proved beneficial to the survival of the species or, during the person's personal history, they have been more often constellated before.

The concept of the archetype as probability is not completely foreign to Jung. Even before his work with Pauli, Jung considered the archetype as the inherited 'possibility of producing the same or similar ideas over and over again' (Jung 1937/1940: para. 165). Considering the Self as the 'container and organizer of all (psychic) possibilities', the moment that an archetype constellates is an indication of the 'possibility of order in wholeness' (Jung 1946: para. 536). 'Possibility' is more vague than 'probability', implying merely potential rather than a quantification of the likelihood of one of several possible outcomes, but it is a closely related concept.

The concept of archetype as probability was strengthened through Jung's work with Pauli. In a letter to Pauli, Jung wrote: 'In physical terms, probability corresponds to the so-called law of nature; psychically, it corresponds to the archetype' (Jung and Pauli 2001: 70, 49J). Both determine a pattern of action. Pauli concurred with this analysis: '... the archetypal element in quantum physics is to be found in the (mathematical) concept of probability – i.e. in the actual correspondence between the expected result ... and the empirically measured frequencies' (ibid.: 64, 47P). Neither is categorically stating that the archetype is probability, but that it corresponds to, or is analogous to, the concept of probability. Behind the probability (in the general case) or the statistical result (in the specific case), there is a cause, some underlying principle or force which is determining this outcome. The archetype-as-such, as instinct, is part of the cause; as image it determines the form. Along with bridging from body to mind, here again is evidence of the transitional, transcendent nature of the archetype, one pole being the underlying cause, and the other the probability, of the manifestation.

My interpretation of an archetype as corresponding to the probability of a complex forming at any particular place in a given state space is compatible with George Hogenson's statement that '... the self [the Jungian Self] is analogous to the differential equation that defines the state space and the phase transitions of an individual's life pattern' (Hogenson 2004: 77, explanation added). A differential equation describes the form of the surface in state space, its peaks and basins. The Self, as both the totality and the ordering principle, is represented in that equation. Correspondingly, each individual point on that surface represents the likelihood of an individual archetype manifesting as a complex.

Summary

The relationship between complex and archetype has been interpreted differently by many post-Jungian authors.

Jung's association was primarily between the complex and instinct, and even then indirectly through the emotion and energy generated by the instinct, and only secondarily between complex and archetype. Although the often quoted assertion that every complex has an archetypal core (of meaning) certainly is in agreement with Jung's theories, it arose from post-Jungian authors and not from Jung himself, at least not from his writings published in the *Collected Works*. The archetype is nonetheless instrumental in the formation of the complex.

Complexes can be correlated with the functioning of the brain as dynamical systems operating on multiple levels of organisation. The archetype can be understood as the principle of self-organisation which determines the form the complex will take, given the disposition of the person and their interactions with their environment. The complex is how the archetype feels in the body. Archetypes can also be viewed mathematically as the probability of a complex forming given the innate character of the individual and his or her environment.

Chapter 8

Constellation of an archetype

This investigation of the constellation of an archetype will be similar to that of the constellation of a complex. I will first define the overriding characteristics of the phenomenon – what it looks and feels like when one experiences it – and thereby identify the attributes of the psychological, emergent macro-state space. Jung's writings on the constellation of archetypes fall into two categories. In the first he explores how this happens in a large number of people, either within a short time span, resulting in a social phenomenon (Jung 1936/1937: para. 98), or over long periods of time (Jung 1953/1956: para. 1529), hence involving a historical or cultural element. This is not how I am using the term. In the second, which corresponds to my usage, the archetype is seen as author in an individual of a creative experience (Jung 1950: para. 1491–2) or religious sentiment of something 'daemonic' or 'divine' (Jung 1942/1948: 223) arising from the 'deeper layers of the unconscious' (Jung 1952: 847) and having a potential transforming effect on the personality (ibid.).

In order to identify the underlying physical correlates, I equate the experience of the constellation of an archetype with what James Austin in his book *Zen and the Brain* (1999) describes as *kensho* and *satori,* both of which may be translated as 'insight wisdom' (ibid.: 303). For each characteristic, I show that both Jung and Austin were referring to the same experience, thereby enabling me to legitimately apply Austin's analysis of the neural correlates of the *kensho/satori* experience to the constellation of an archetype.

With regard to consciousness, the constellation of an archetype is completely different from that of a complex. The constellation of an autonomous complex, or the ebb and flow of the constellation of various complexes within the ego, usually comes from sense perceptions or inter-subjective experience, whereas that of the archetype seems to manifest as an idea, fully formed, from outside.

A synchronistic event could be a form of constellation of an archetype. Some of the events dealt with in this chapter may be considered synchronistic, but I do not explicitly deal with them in that context. Synchronicity is a vast area of study. Synchronistic events involving something occurring simultaneously in the inner and outer world, such as Jung's beetle experience (Jung 1952: para. 843), go beyond the mind/body relation that I am concentrating on.

On a psychological level, the constellation of an archetype could be viewed as a breaking of the symmetry inherent between the various images associated with it – a process reducing the sometimes overly rigid ordering properties of the archetype (Cambray 2010: 63) and leading to life (Krieger 2012). The transcendent function could be seen as such a breaking of symmetry (Meier 2001: 168, cited in Cambray 2009: 59).

Constellation of a complex compared with that of an archetype

The constellation of an autonomous complex is different from the constellation or sudden eruption of an archetype into consciousness. Jung associated the former with 'loss of soul' (Jung 1920/1948: para. 588). There is the possibility that, through dream work, creative self-expression, psychotherapy or psychoanalysis, or simply through life experiences, an autonomous complex can become integrated into the ego-complex. However, Jung associated the constellation of an archetype with 'spirits' and 'daemons', which are completely foreign to the ego and can never be integrated (ibid.: para. 592). He associated such a constellation with 'mental illness, creative inspiration, and religious conversion' (Jung 1916/1953: para. 270). The disposition of the person is an essential factor in this phenomenon. The constellation itself appears to be sudden, but the process leading up to it may have been going on, perhaps subliminally, for some time.

The constellation of an archetype is different from the appearance of an archetypal image in, for example, a dream. A demonic witch in a dream may be said to represent the witch-like characteristics of the negative mother archetype. I understand this to be a complex. The witch in a dream will take on some elements from the dreamer's memories of witches in childhood stories, thus involving an element from the personal unconscious. There are purely archetypal dreams arising from the collective unconscious, but these are rare. Characters in fairy tales are more purely archetypal than those in legend or stories, but they still include cultural influences. For example, the fairy godmother from Cinderella differs from the tame fish in Yeh-hsien, a Cinderella-type tale from about 850 AD in China. So while the archetypal *image* differs, the underlying archetype is universal.

The criterion that I am using to define an archetypal constellation is the absence of memory, both explicit and implicit. Not even the ego is involved as a participant in the phenomenon, but only as an observer. This follows directly from the distinction Jung made between the complex coming from the personal unconscious and the archetype from the collective unconscious. It has been argued earlier that memories of the collective, resulting from influences on the young child through cultural norms, myths and fairy tales, etc., are stored in semantic memory. However, these have all been influenced by the cultural context and are therefore not pure manifestations of the archetype as such.

Characteristics of the experience

One of the best descriptions I have read of the constellation of an archetype is Nietzsche's telling of his experience of writing *Also sprach Zarathustra (Thus Spake Zarathustra)*:

> Has any one at the end of the nineteenth century any distinct notion of what poets of a stronger age understood by the word '*inspiration*'? If not, I will describe it. If one had the smallest vestige of superstition left in one, it would hardly be possible to set aside the idea that one is a mere incarnation, mouthpiece or medium of an almighty power. The idea of revelation, in the sense that something which profoundly convulses and shatters one becomes suddenly visible and audible with indescribable certainty and accuracy, describes the simple fact. One hears – one does not seek; one takes – one does not ask who gives; a thought suddenly flashes up like lightning, it comes with necessity, without faltering – I never had any choice in the matter.
>
> (Quoted in Meier 1984: 18)

From this description we can list a few of the characteristics which appear to be almost universal when people describe this sort of experience: 'revelation', 'profound', 'shatters one suddenly', 'indescribable certainty and accuracy', 'a thought suddenly flashes up like lightning', 'necessity'.

Insight coming from outside

I have stated that the object of consciousness is the relationship between an organism and an object. Here I use the example of the Annunciation as a symbol of the appearance of an archetype in the life of Mary. She is at first occupied with everyday interactions. This relationship could be depicted as shown in Figure 8.1.

She is conscious of herself as subject and of the object. She is also aware that she is conscious. It is her normal state of consciousness. The sudden constellation of an archetype alters this (Figure 8.2).

This is the experience of the sudden eruption of an archetype. Consciousness remains within the person, while the voice or vision is coming from somewhere outside of consciousness.

Jung refers to the story, told in I Samuel 3:1ff, in which Yahweh calls to Samuel, waking him from sleep, as an example of a primordial image or archetype coming into consciousness when the conscious mind is inactive (Jung 1956: para. 260).

The unconscious reaction and the resulting invasion of consciousness are in contrast to the normal conscious situation (Jung 1939b: para. 900). Consciousness splits up perceptions; it differentiates, selects, redefines. The compensatory reaction of the unconscious when this normal fragmentation is stopped is one of totality, wholeness, all-embracing illumination (ibid.).

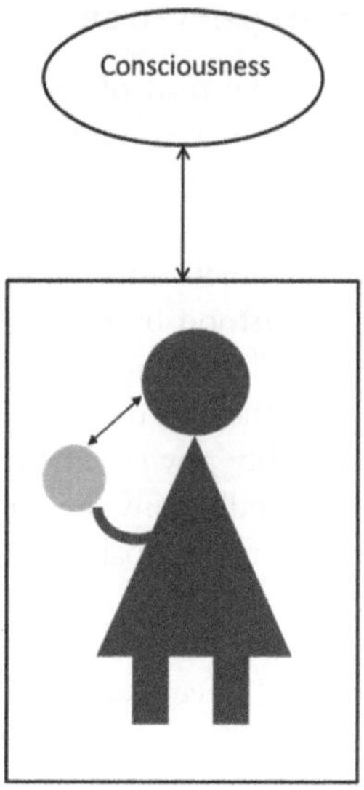

Figure 8.1 Normal consciousness

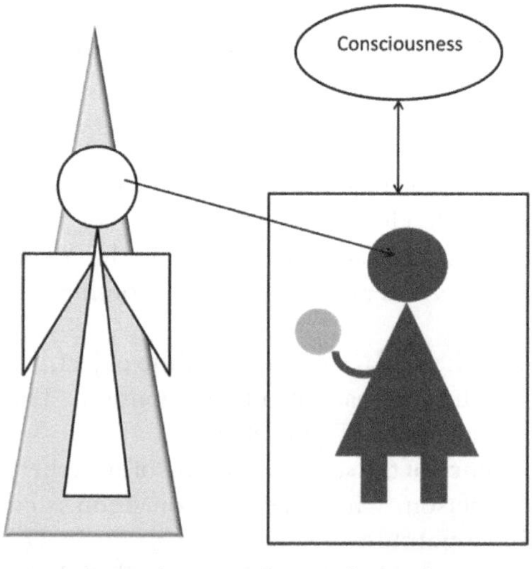

Figure 8.2 Consciousness during the constellation of an archetype

The experience has a feeling of coming in from outside the normal state of consciousness. It indeed brings *in-sight*, but it is a selfless insight since the psychic self or ego is 'lost' (Austin 1999: 569). This is known in Zen as the doctrine of no-mind (Suzuki 1949). Although the experience seems to be coming from outside, the awakening of *prajna* (concentrated insight, direct experiential wisdom capable of bringing about enlightenment) is the realisation of one's true self-nature, which is both conscious and unconscious (ibid. 142–3). In Jungian terms one would speak rather of the ego in service to the Self, rather than ego-less-ness.

Normal thought patterns retrace pathways that have been used before, or are branching off these. The revelation of insight which happens when an archetype constellates traces new pathways through the brain (Austin 1999: 545). The experience is the complete opposite of that feeling when a complex constellates of 'Oh no – I'm trapped doing this again!'

This form of insight was experienced in earlier cultures as the speaking of the gods. 'The primitive does not think; the thoughts come to him' (Jung 1942/1948: para. 240). Julian Jaynes (1976: 255–92) traced what he believed to be the development of consciousness in Greece from 850 to 600 B.C. using the transition in meaning of several words variously translated as mind, spirit or soul. He shows how ideas, which were seen originally as messages from the gods, became 'incarnated', and how humans began to see themselves as capable of self-reflection. Nonetheless, '… we ourselves still feel certain particularly enlightening ideas as "in-fluences", "in-spirations", etc.' (Jung 1942/1948: para. 240).

When the constellating archetype is experienced as coming in from outside, it is perceived as an 'other', a non-ego, a not-I, which is acting on one's conscious mind. The 'other' is subject – that which is acting; one's mind is an indirect object – that which is receiving. 'It is as if the subject-character of the ego has been overrun, or taken over, by another subject, which appears in place of the ego' (Jung 1939b: para. 890). This 'other', which is now subject, is perceived as more powerful, wiser, and greater than the ego.

With the constellation of an archetype, the subject-nature of the ego seems to be taken out of the picture. The ego is overpowered. The ego is so insignificant in relation to the archetype that it is simply of no consequence.

Neural correlates of the sense of self

The experience of the ego-complex, the sense of self, is suspended during the constellation of an archetype; the ego is at most an observer. The experience of self related to the ego-complex results from the activation of autobiographical memories and minor feelings which reoccur frequently, and which we recognise as moods. Many functions associated with the concept of self are situated in the temporal lobe, the limbic system, the central grey, and the medial orbitofrontal areas (Austin 1999: 609–10).

The sudden experience of the constellation of an archetype originates basically from the activation of acetylcholine from neurons with very long axons coordinating areas in the thalamus with areas in the neocortex. Glutamate, which plays a central role in the coordination of internal rhythms, is also involved, but many neurochemicals (dopamine, norepinephrine and serotonin), usually associated with mood and personal memories stored in the association cortices, do not seem to be activated (ibid.: 617–18).

Jung also related the experience to the function of intuition (from the Latin stem *intueri* meaning to look at, hence to look inward) in his theory of psychological types. Thus, for the intuitive 'These images have the value of specific insights, ...' (Jung 1921/1971: para. 611), while for other types such insights come in when the other functions are blocked (ibid.: para. 612).

Fast

The moment of revelation comes unexpectedly. '*Satori* comes upon one unawares, as something utterly unexpected' (Jung 1939b: para. 881). Austin describes *kensho* as the 'lightening strike of profound intellectual illumination' (Austin 1999: 533).

The speed with which a flash of insight is experienced leads Austin to concentrate on the close limbic-cortico links in both hemispheres, which simultaneously activate the fronto-temporal and parieto-occipital regions. This sudden change with retention of coherence suggests a central location in the subcortical regions (Austin 1999: 591).

The same rapid thalamic-cortico link is activated in a startle reaction. This reaction is enhanced by corresponding neurochemical changes (Austin 1999: 592).

Wordless (ineffable) knowing

Prajna is similar to the transcendent function in that it bridges the dualism of our customary way of perceiving (Austin 1999: 547).

The retelling of the story of an event is different from the actual experience. In the flash of knowing which occurs during the constellation of an archetype there is no second, retold version, only the 'real' experience. The insight gained conveys an understanding without being attached to words. One knows in a way similar to knowing through experience, but different from knowing a fact which one can express in language. This is because the centres dedicated to receiving and decoding speech, which lie principally in the left temporal lobe, are being bypassed. The thalamus, which we have seen is a central actor in this drama, has only a few long, fast connections with the temporal lobe (speech), but many long, fast connections to other areas of the neocortex where the experience will later be stored as a memory. Using fMRI imaging with people solving anagrams to study insight, Aziz-Redeh and her colleagues also noted more activation in the right as opposed to the left hemisphere, notably in the right temporal lobe as opposed to the language dominant left temporal lobe (Aziz-Redeh *et al.* 2009: 911). This could also free the temporal lobe (speech) to make its own interpretation of what is going on, albeit somewhat after the fact. This would make it difficult for the temporal lobe to later put into words the understanding that the rest of the neocortex has experienced (Austin 1999: 548).

Certainty

In the moment that the insight strikes one *knows* that it is right. Doubts and old associations are cut through. The knowledge gained has a feeling of being new, fresh. Old doubts and ways of knowing are cut off. 'It is not that something different is seen, but that one sees differently' (Jung 1939b: para. 891). Austin uses the word 'objective' to refer to this quality of the experience. Quite late in his writings Jung began using the expression the 'objective psyche' (Jung 1958a para. 576, Jung 1917/1953 para. 184), by which he meant the collective unconscious rather than the 'subjective psyche', i.e. the personal unconscious (Jung 1917/1953 para. 103n). The use of this term gives a clearer indication that the archetype is coming from a reality not influenced by personal memories; it is coming from somewhere beyond the subjective psyche.

Meaning

The English language fails to differentiate between the type of knowing which comes from learned facts and that which comes directly from encounter and experience. In French, for example, the latter is *connaître* as opposed to *savoir*, and in German it is *kennen* rather than *wissen*. Thus I know as a fact (*je sais, ich weiss*) where my brother lives, but I know from experience (*je connaîs, ich kenne*) the house in which he lives. This latter type of knowledge involves many associations. It is richer, for it is linked to memories, whether pleasant or not.

Experiential knowing is important in psychotherapy:

> This funnelling of the individual conflict into the general moral problem puts psychoanalysis far outside the confines of a merely medical therapy. It gives the patient a working philosophy of life based on empirical insights, which, besides affording him knowledge of his own nature, also make it possible for him to fit himself into this scheme of things.
>
> (Jung 1912/1943 para. 440)

Indeed Jung's psychology is based on his own experience of the psyche.

> Every psychic process has a value quality attached to it, namely its feeling-tone. This indicates the degree to which the subject is *affected* by the process or how much it means to him (in so far as the process reaches consciousness at all). It is through the 'affect' that the subject becomes involved and so comes to feel the whole weight of reality. ... Hence a purely intellectual insight is not enough, because one knows only the words and not the substance of the thing from inside.
>
> (Jung 1959b: para. 61, emphasis in the original)

It is through the direct experience of the constellation of an archetype that one knows, not in the sense of textbook knowledge, but that of a psychological, phenomenological knowing which can reposition the ego in relation to the unconscious. It is the manifold images of the archetype which place the experience in context and carry this sense of meaning. Meaning places fact in context. What is understood is not only one image, but multiple interconnected images. Considering the archetype as a 'pattern of behaviour' (Jung 1946/1954: para. 398), it is not the single instance but the *pattern* which is important. In a painting it is not one object which gives meaning, but the arrangement of objects, the multiple interconnected images.

A feeling of meaning or significance is associated with regions of the brain which interconnect the thalamus within the limbic system, specifically those areas of the thalamus which lie next to, and connect with, the prefrontal cortex (Austin 1999: 524) and other areas of the limbic system, specifically those areas receiving information from the sensory association areas. These are the cingulate gyrus, the entorhinal cortex, which Walter Freeman identifies with the centre of consciousness (Freeman 1999: 136–9), and the hippocampus.

Profound restructuring of the personality

The constellation of an archetype often implies a profound restructuring of the personality. Jung sees this happening in the context of the self-regulating, compensatory nature of the psyche itself. The event takes place because there is a lack in the conscious psyche requiring compensation from the unconscious (Jung 1953: para. 1529). The constellation brings with it 'a superior analysis or insight or knowledge which consciousness has not been able to produce' (Jung 1937/1940: para. 69). It is experienced as if 'two spheres have been brought together which before were kept anxiously apart' (Jung 1916/1953: para. 224).

In Jungian terms, the constellation of an archetype can deeply affect the ego-Self relationship. There is a danger that the ego may be overpowered by the experience, and psychic damage result. If, however, the ego is strong enough the experience can be accepted with no adverse effects. The strengthening of the ego is one of the goals of both Zen meditation and psychoanalysis.

Throughout his book Austin uses the term 'I-Me-Mine' in place of ego to represent the association of 'I' as subject, 'Me' as object, the one to whom things happen, and 'Mine' as those possessions which belong to me, including my thoughts, opinions, and body. The long practice of meditation trains the person to give up temporarily the I-Me-Mine complex. This seems similar to the strengthening of the ego-Self axis spoken of by Erich Neumann (Neumann 1966: 81ff) and Edward Edinger (Edinger 1972) that is also a goal of psychoanalysis. The ego is no longer the centre of the personality, but has experiential knowledge of the Self.

Austin uses the metaphor that after this experience we are left with 'an edifice or brain, built on a more open plan'. Mental boundaries open up, old constructs melt. 'It is a matrix now configured in a way which supports and encourages the natural flow of life's experience. In this uncluttered mental space, no longer do old barriers constrict, block, discriminate' (Austin 1999: 527).

Aziz-Zadeh and her colleagues identified activation in the right prefrontal cortex (PFC) occurring relatively late in the 'Aha!'-experience, starting after about one second. This agrees with other research indicating a relatively slow reaction time of the neocortex as well as linking the right prefrontal cortex with creative insightful solutions (Aziz-Zadeh *et al.* 2009: 913). After the initial insight the prefrontal cortex can step in to sustain attention and tie this experience with memories from prior, relevant happenings, placing it in a temporal and spatial context (Dietrich 2004) and possibly reshaping memories.

One's sense of self, the feeling of who one is, is closely related to affect. Viewed in the context of Antonio Damasio's concept of core and extended consciousness (Damasio 1999a), this restructuring would affect one's sense of core consciousness. Extended consciousness, resting on one's autobiographical memories, is not affected. Core consciousness, however, is related to the basic feedback loop between feeling who we are and a bodily memory of who we were before. It is here that the change has taken place; this basic feeling has been altered, and we no longer feel we are the same as we were a moment ago. Core consciousness, with its relation to the body and to instincts, is related to the archetypal Self.

One consequence of the change of personality which takes place during *kensho* and possibly the constellation of an archetype is that old values disappear. What was judged previously as positive or negative seems to no longer have any importance; both are valued equally. Austin postulates that such a change can come from new forms of amplification and shared configurations between the large pulvinar and the lateral posterior nuclei of the thalamus and posterior regions of the association cortex (Austin 1999: 603).

Meaning not only implies a strong link between perception and recognition, but also involves a flash of understanding that does not come from conscious intellectual processing in the frontal lobes alone, but from activation of the frontal lobes simultaneously with activation of the parieto-occipital cortex that are stimulated jointly by the thalamus (ibid.: 605), and thus activating a global workspace. Austin proposes that it is the levels of ACH (acetylcholine) and opioid in the temporal lobe which impregnate the experience with feelings of significance, numinosity and new meaning (ibid.: 606).

The experience of loss of the psychic self could correspond with the inhibitory effects of GABA and opioids set off in the first flash of insight within the limbic system and the repercussions in the many areas of the brain closely associated with it. It is known from neural imaging that the concept of self is situated in the cortical and subcortical midline structures in the temporal lobe, the limbic system, the central grey, and the medial orbitofrontal cortex (ibid.: 609–10).

Psychic energy

For Jung, archetypal constellation happens because of a flow of energy. In the case of Zen meditation, the energy taken away from the objects of conscious thought is forced into the unconscious and reinforces unconscious contents (archetypes) which then have sufficient energy to break into consciousness (Jung 1939b: para. 898).

Jung identifies the transcendent function as the process by which the shifting of consciousness takes place, resulting in a change in personality (Jung 1939/1954: para. 802). After the fact, one can sometimes see that what appears as a sudden transformation has actually been at work for a long time in the unconscious (Jung 1961: para. 543).

The meditative process of *zazen* together with the use of a *koan*, a puzzle which cannot be solved by logical thinking, forms a period of 'incubation' similar to that taking place in the stalemate that leads to the transcendent function. There is a 'damming up behind the koan' of a reservoir of energy which is released in a burst of insight (Austin 1999: 622).

Breaking into consciousness

The breakthrough into consciousness is often associated with artistic or scientific creativity. It is no coincidence that examples used to describe this occurrence deal with literary inspiration (Niezsche, cited above) and scientific discovery (Robert Mayer's idea of the conservation of energy, cited in Jung 1917/1953: para. 106–7).

Jung spoke of a creative 'instinct' (Jung 1936/1942: para. 245) although he questions the use of this term and speaks of the creative 'impulse' (ibid.). Despite creativity having several characteristics in common with instincts, being dynamic and compulsive, Jung hesitates because it is not apparent in all people.

The eruption into consciousness of an archetype seems to involve the image more than the instinctive pole of the psychoid. This could be understood as symmetry breaking of the instinctive and image poles of the psychoid, or of the opposite attributes (e.g. positive and negative) of the archetype (Meier 2001: 169, Jung's letter to Wolfgang Pauli dated August 1957, quoted in Cambray 2009: 59). The body may experience a startle-like reaction and be suddenly shaken from what appears to be a sleeping state compared to the sudden brilliance of insight which follows, but it is not instinctive in the sense of initiating a fight, flight or freeze response.

Aziz-Zadeh and her colleagues (2009: 913) discovered that one of the distinguishing characteristics of insight was the bilateral insula activation. They explain that the sudden appearance of a solution as a complete gestalt was linked with the *bilateral* activation, as opposed to a predominance in the left insula for a slower, progressive, search solution. Damasio links the insular cortex closely with images of the proto-self (Damasio 2010: 195, 205–6), which may underline the effect this type of experience could have in self-awareness. What breaks into consciousness is a complete image that brings meaning and understanding. Relating this experience to the idea of the global workspace, it is as if a single new idea suddenly takes over the entire brain because it has gained enough psychic energy to assume control and invade the space.

There are no memories associated with this process as there are in the constellation of a complex, which involves memories from the personal unconscious. The archetypal image is free of personal associations.

Putting the pieces together

Insight may be preceded by a long period of seeming inactivity during which the unconscious seems to be working on the problem. This may be days, weeks or even years in the case of a scientific discovery or the work on a koan. The person is working on the problem but with no concrete result. In the study conducted by Lisa Aziz-Zadeh, this is the time between which the subject was presented with an anagram until they eventually found a solution. From the data she presents, one can see mounting activity bilaterally in the insula, the anterior cingulated cortex and, starting a bit later, the right prefrontal cortex. There is also mounting activation in the pons, the bridge between the brain stem and the thalamus. Activity in all of these areas interestingly peaks after approximately 6 seconds. I propose that at about this time a point is reached at which a large enough area to constitute a global workspace is synchronised.

An image was forming in the unconscious, which may be visual, as is often spoken of in mystic experiences, but could involve other senses, like Mozart's description of 'hearing' at one moment an entire symphony. It could also be something abstract like the solution to a mathematical problem. The bilateral activation of the insula is important in the 'gestalt' nature of this solution (Aziz-Zadeh *et al.* 2009: 913). Once this 'image' enters consciousness, the connections from the cortex to the thalamus, which usually serve as feedback regulating perception coming from the senses via the thalamus, initiate activation of the thalamus as if the image were coming from the senses. Through its close connections to the limbic system, the thalamus initiates the release of neurochemicals including opioids possibly responsible for the numinous feelings and the loss of self. Starting at about one second after the feeling of insight, activation in the right prefrontal cortex maintains a high level of attention and endows the event with a feeling of meaning due to connections between the thalamus and this area. Meaning is not sustained by activation of the prefrontal cortex alone but in coordination with the parieto-occipital lobes. Changes to the personality may continue long after the event as the experience is reviewed in memory.

The experience of the loss of self comes from the initial absence of activity in the sensory association cortices where personal memories are stored.

The effects of long-term meditation

A number of experiments have been done using neural imaging during meditation by experienced and novice meditators (Lutz *et al.* 2004, Brefczynski-Lewis *et al.* 2007, Begley 2008: 212–42, Lutz 2012). Assuming that meditation prepares the person to better transform the experience of the constellation of the archetype, as described by Austin (1999), into a positive outcome, there appear to be three lasting effects of meditation on cerebral functioning which reinforce this outcome: the ratio of low gamma to theta frequency in cortical areas, reduction of emotional reactions mediated by the prefrontal cortices and the basal ganglia, and increased reported levels of happiness and well-being.

Base level gamma band activity, particularly in the lower frequencies which were identified as a characteristic of experienced meditators in the Lutz study, 24–42 Hz (Lutz *et al.* 2004), is associated with increased levels of attention, synaptic plasticity and ability to perform complex cognitive functions (Jensen *et al.* 2007), implying a flexible self that is more aware and well-adapted to life.

Experienced meditators also exhibited increased ability to inhibit cognitive and emotional processes such as ruminating over anxious or depressing incidents. This was correlated with decreased activity in the prefrontal cortex associated with a form of metacognition which is constantly monitoring the self in relation to the external world. This implies a lower baseline level of anxiety. Expert meditators also showed a higher level of activity in the left prefrontal cortex which is associated in general with happy feelings (Begley 2008: 238, and Table 6.1 on page 80). The higher proportion of activity in the left, as opposed to the right, prefrontal cortex could also imply a decreased need to control negative emotions, since this activity is often associated with the right brain.

One form of meditation centres on compassion or loving kindness. Emiliana Simon-Thomas and colleagues (2012) conducted an fMRI study while using series of pictures to elicit compassion and pride in subjects. They considered compassion to be a two-step process. The first step was enabling what they called an 'empathy network' including activation in the insula, the medial prefrontal cortex (mPFC), the sensorimotor cortex and several other areas in the lower layers of the cortex. The second step in compassion, after the experience of empathy, was the desire to reach out and care for the victims. During this stage, there was greater medial prefrontal cortex, insula and periaqueductal grey (PAG) response plus increased production of the hormone oxytocin when seeing pain in innocent victims and groups one identified with than in groups one did not. This agrees with studies done by Panksepp (2000 and Table 6.1 on page 80) on parental caring.

The PAG and the insula are included in the cortical midline structures which are highly active in self-referential processing (Northoff 2006). The insular cortex, identified by Northoff and his colleagues as being active in self-referential processing in the emotional, social and agency domains is also included in the generation of the feelings of a core self (Damasio 2010: 205–7).

From this we can conclude that extensive meditation for several hours a day over many years, particularly those meditative exercises that involve loving kindness or compassion, reinforces what in Jungian terms could be called ego strength. Paradoxically, having a strong ego would enable the practitioner to lay it aside in order to experience the constellated archetype, and after the event, to integrate the experience into their own life and to carry the experience into the collective.

Summing up

An experience as profound and encompassing as the constellation of an archetype must be the result of several simultaneous causes. There is no single associated chemical or area of the brain alone, nor does it arise from a sudden massive surge in the *volume* of data being processed. It may be preceded by a long introductory period, sometimes lasting months or years. This could be intense concentration, such as working on a koan, or literary creation, as with Nietzsche's writing of *Also sprach Zarathustra*. It may be triggered by suddenly being in a novel situation, as Austin notes in his own experience of *kensho*, or by the release from concentration, as in sleep. There have been several notable scientific breakthroughs during sleep and dreaming (e.g. Kerkulé's insight into the benzene ring structure). Austin also notes the prevalence of *kensho* type experiences which occur as one is waking in the morning – a trigger that may also have often been overlooked in the attribution of such experiences.

Chapter 9

Development of the ego-complex

The goal of this chapter is to show the effects of considering the complex as an attractor in a dynamic landscape on the Jungian theory of the ego complex as an assembly of complexes. I will point out areas where Jung and modern research overlap as well as areas of difference. I present in detail recent research in neuroscience on the developing brain. It is not my intention to either support or oppose Jung's theories on child development, nor to review the extensive writings of other Jungian authors – this has been done already (Jacoby 1999, Knox 2003) – but to extend Jung's work with research findings which were not available until very recently.

I propose that the ego-complex is a set of shallow attractor states within a basin of attractors through which the psyche travels regularly. The emotions associated with the individual complexes within the ego-complex are experienced as moods and mild feelings. In contrast to this, the emotions associated with autonomous complexes are pronounced affects. The set of complexes comprising the ego-complex is familiar, consisting of stable states experienced repeatedly in everyday life. Long term, persistent neuroses, such as depression or OCD, are deeper states between the ego and the autonomous complex which prevent the normal functioning of the ego, but they may also serve to protect the person from the powerful experience of the autonomous complex. This could be an area of further Jungian research. Like any complex, the set of complexes forming the ego is dependent on both the individual and their environment. They provide a stable base upon which the various persona roles are built.

This model can be seen as a further development of that proposed by Edward Edinger (1985, cited in Cambray 2009: 51), and of the ideas of complexes as hubs in an interactive field (Cambray 2009: 52) and nodes in a network (Bovensiepen 2006).

Although the individual complexes within the ego-complex are dependent on the context, there will often be overriding similarities between them. The emotional contents of these complexes are moods similar to what Antonio Damasio calls 'background feelings'. He differentiates background feelings from moods, stating that moods are made up of both sustained background emotions and normal feelings (Damasio 1999a: 286), whereas background feelings are more transitory and associated closely with core consciousness. Examples of background feelings are enthusiasm, excitement and tranquillity (Damasio 2003: 43). Although the exact context may differ, similar situations may evoke in a person a feeling of mild excitement or anxiety. The emphasis here is on 'mild'. It is not the sudden explosion of feeling associated with an autonomous complex or the constellation of an archetype, but something which may be intriguing or tantalising (Damasio 1999a: 286).

In short, I am making the following associations between types of feelings and types of consciousness:

- Background feeling – core consciousness: This I am calling the emotional landscape, and I will show that it develops in the first months of post-natal life, although there is also evidence that it begins to form prenatally.
- Mood and mild feeling – ego-complex: Moods are associated with the various complexes comprising the ego-complex. They are experienced as mild shifts between frequently experienced, not overwhelming emotions, lasting hours or days.
- Pronounced affect – autonomous complex: The affects associated with the autonomous complex erupt suddenly, are violent and pervasive, but usually dissipate relatively quickly once the stimulus is removed.

Temperament is similar to background feeling in that it is innate or formed during prenatal or very early postnatal experiences. It could be a tendency, for example, to be shy and withdrawn as opposed to outgoing. Temperament is related to what Jung called 'attitude' – extraversion and introversion – which he said is in part innate and which orients an individual's whole psychology 'even in its most fundamental features' (Jung 1921/1971: para. 690). He associates this psychic attitude with 'an essential bias which conditions the whole psychic process' (Jung 1921/1971: para. 941). This is part, but not all, of what I am calling the first layer of the psychic landscape. Lise Eliot links this with the largely genetically determined balance between left and right brain activity, as measured when the person is at rest (Eliot 1999: 296).

'Moods' I associate with the feelings of the ego-complex. They vary slowly. A mood lasts for several hours to several days. 'Emotions' and 'feelings' are as I have defined them in previous chapters: emotions refer to the physiological, neurological state of the brain, while feelings are how emotions are experienced, the felt sense of the emotion. Put perhaps too simply: emotions are generated in the lower limbic structures (the amygdala, the hypothalamus and numerous areas in the upper reaches of the brain stem). Feelings are *experienced* in the limbic cortex, the areas forming the inner partition of the frontal, parietal and temporal lobes, including the orbitofrontal gyrus, the anterior cingulate gyrus and the hippocampus (Eliot 1999: 292). This concurs closely with the importance for consciousness which Walter Freeman places on the multi-sensory convergence that takes place in the entorhinal cortex (Freeman 1999: 137). The lower limbic structures are almost fully developed at birth or very soon after, in contrast to the limbic cortex, which does not begin to develop until about the eighth month.

A basic sense of self

Jung defined the ego as a 'complex factor' (Jung 1959b: para. 1), which I understand to mean a composite entity, composed of a number of elements. He compared infantile consciousness with an 'archipelago' as opposed to the 'firmly-knit ego-complex' (Jung 1946/1954: para. 387) of the adult. He grounded the ego equally in the somatic and the psychic (Jung 1959a: para. 3), and in the 'feeling-tone' of one's own body (Jung 1907/1960: para. 82). A person's somatic perception changes over the course of a day with the moods experienced, giving the ego what I describe as a dynamic character while at the same time supporting a continuous sense of self. This structure, as an assemblage of related but semi-separate objects, I suggest gives the ego strength and flexibility. Jung associated schizophrenia with the splitting of the ego-complex into a plurality of autonomous, dissociated complexes (Jung 1928: para. 498–500).

Arguing from the question of what happens when the sense of self falls away, as during periods of deep absorption in meditation, James Austin postulates that the body sense of self is dependent on a small area in the posterior thalamus where sight, hearing, the vestibular system and other proprioceptive sensations from the head and body converge (Austin 1999: 503). Evidence from imaging studies has shown that, neurologically, the self is an integrated system of cortical and sub-cortical midline structures (Northoff *et al.* 2006). These can be subdivided into a number of different 'selves' based on the functions they perform and their location within the brain, e.g. a visual self, a motor self, an emotional self, etc. The evolutionarily and functionally most elementary of these has been identified as the proto-self, or body-self. This constantly monitors the state of the body, which 'serves as a solid platform for basic *instinctual*-mental existence' (ibid.: 449, emphasis mine). This instinctual element implies that at least an elementary form of it must be in place at birth. In the adult this is located, in part, at the top of the brain-stem and in the limbic system, but also extends to certain midline cortical areas including sensory self-referential processing. I suggest that what we experience as a unified self emerges from the interaction of these different, specific brain areas.

Analysing numerous imaging studies to identify self-referential processing, Northoff and his colleagues have identified a group of cortical midline structures (CMS) which are involved only with regard to self, as opposed to non-self, stimuli (Northoff *et al.* 2006: 449). The tasks studied included verbal, spatial, memory, emotional, facial, social and agency/ownership activities.

Different types of tasks can be identified with different areas within the CMS. I associate these basic pre-self-referential functions with the constant movement within the psychic landscape, thereby laying the basis for the ego-complex. They underlie other processes which may lead to consciousness, but are not themselves conscious. They involve concepts of how one feels, the thoughts one has about oneself, and the control of emotions in social interactions.

An emotional, pre-conscious feeling self develops with the formation of the basic emotional landscape during the initial period of cortical development (about 8 to 15 months) thereby laying the basis for the ego-complex, leading to consciousness, but not itself conscious.

The memories associated with the ego-complex are the autobiographical memories of extended consciousness. They are the stories I tell myself about who I am and contribute to the formation of the autobiographical self. These are stored in a variety of interconnected, mainly cortical, regions in the temporal and frontal lobes that are linked closely with the primary and associative sensory cortices (Damasio 1999a: 223).

The emotions associated with the ego-complex form a backdrop of moods and feelings which we experience continually, but about which we are rarely conscious. These are long term – slow to form or change. They are observable to others in our tone of voice and the prosody of our speech, the quickness and manner of our movements. Damasio associates these with the very basic functioning of internal organs, muscle tension and the nervous system in general (Damasio 1999a: 287). They are what we are feeling when we are not feeling other emotions. I am proposing that these background feelings result from what I am calling the basic landscape, laid down very early in life, during approximately the first 8 months. The image of a landscape to illustrate potential positions within a state space is often used in dynamical systems modelling (e.g. see Haken 1996: 56, Figure 5.4).

I do not consider what are usually called the self-referential emotions (pride, shame, guilt and envy) to be associated with the ego-complex, but rather with autonomous complexes which, when they constellate, take consciousness away from the ego-complex.

Jung linked tightly together the concept of the ego with that of consciousness. He defined the ego as 'a complex of ideas which constitutes the centre of my field of consciousness and appears to possess a high degree of continuity and identity' (Jung 1921/1971: para. 706). Conversely, he defines consciousness as 'the relation of psychic contents to the ego, in as far as this relation is perceived as such by the ego. Relations to the ego that are not perceived as such are unconscious' (ibid.: para. 700). Moreover, 'Consciousness therefore seems to be a necessary precondition for the ego. Yet without the ego, consciousness is unthinkable' (Jung 1926/1960: para. 611). His writing on the relationship between the ego-complex and consciousness is, however, more complicated than these few quotes can convey. I will deal in part with this relationship in the concluding chapter.

If the ego is made up of complexes, what then differentiates a complex that is part of the ego-complex from a so-called autonomous complex that is not associated with the ego? First, the intensity of the emotion: the constellation of an autonomous complex is characterised by a sudden intense emotional experience. Often the emotion is so intense that it hinders an accurate evaluation of the situation and/or makes any reasoned response impossible. This is an instinctive freeze reaction, but maladaptive in the present situation. Emotions associated with the ego-complex are milder, and the changes more gradual. Second, the response during the constellation of an autonomous complex is stereotypic: the same or very similar situations automatically generate the same response. The ego-complex allows for more gradation in interpretations and variations of reaction. Third, the response is often exaggerated in relation to the stimulus. At one time the response might have been appropriate, but with the fixating of the reaction with the stimulus it has become maladaptive. One may also go to some lengths to avoid a situation which might constellate an autonomous complex if one experiences it as particularly harmful, either physically, mentally, or to one's self-image. The consequences of such a complex are judged to be extremely negative.

The ego-complex as a dynamical system

The ego-complex can be looked at as a dynamical system of complexes whose behaviour emerges from the interaction of the various component complexes. It is self-organising in the sense that its responses to internal or external stimulation are determined by interaction within the system. Changes in mood occur as the psyche passes through the different shallow attractor states of the complexes comprising the ego.

Research has not been able to pinpoint one specific area of the brain which generates our sense of self-awareness. On the physical level it is proposed that this is because it is an emergent property of the many areas of the brain functioning synchronously (Austin 1999: 259), although they seem to be closely centred around the temporal lobes, the limbic system, the central grey, and the medial orbitofrontal areas (ibid.: 609–10). On the psychological level the phenomenon of emergence can explain why the ego-complex, while being an assemblage of separate complexes, can still be said to have identifiable characteristics such as self-esteem, self-affirmation, the maintenance of a self-concept and other aspects of the self.

What emerges from this dynamical system is the subjective experience of oneself as a separate, cohesive and distinct individual. This feeling of the self or of oneself, of individual subjectivity as both actor and object, is the centre around which consciousness forms. It is the 'I' around which autobiographic memories can form, memories of myself in relationship with others and with the world and memories about who I am and what it feels like to be me. This feeling memory starts before memories of actual experiences form. It has been argued that this sense of self must be in place before autobiographic memories can begin to form (Howe *et al.* 2009). This feeling sense of self holds all of the complexes of the ego-complex together.

The tendency for humans to develop a sense of self is an inborn part of our nature and predates us phylogenetically. The form that the self takes is shaped by social interaction. We are born about 18 months before the brain is functionally developed in order that it physically completes its development in a social context.

A mathematical model

Andrzej Nowak and his colleagues (2000) conducted a series of experiments using cellular automata, which are mathematical models used to simulate dynamical systems in many physical contexts, to investigate the functioning of the self as a dynamical system. Their research is particularly relevant because many of the concepts they used, both as dependent and independent variables, are analogous to Jungian concepts relating to the complex and the ego-complex. They defined 'press for integration', i.e. the influence of an element's (in our case, a complex's) neighbours, as a variable. If this influence is high, it will tend to keep the complex from breaking off (Nowak *et al.* 2000: 48). This corresponds to what is usually called ego strength. Saying that an ego is strong implies strong bonds between neighbouring complexes within the system. One interesting implication from their research is that people with a weak ego benefit from positive feedback not by learning new things about themselves but by strengthening the bonds with other complexes. This might be achieved, for example, in analysis by the analyst stressing the various accomplishments of the client, in that way making the ego-complex as a whole stronger (ibid.: 50).

Since I will be considering the development of the ego and the influence of inter-subjective interactions on the forming ego later in this chapter, it should be noted here that their research also showed that negative incoming information can cause a negative self-evaluation in the developing ego even where there was a previous natural positive bias. In their simulation, the system realigned with this information, which also had a tendency to scatter the complexes, thereby increasing their dissociation and weakening the ego. However, it had the opposite effect on a developing ego which already had the characteristics of being strong. In this case it tended to cause the complexes to coalesce (ibid.: 50), implying that the same negative experience can have contradictory outcomes depending on the initial ego strength or weakness. This is also something which is of importance in psychotherapy.

On an already formed ego, the effects of *negative* incoming information were relatively slight. 'Taken together, these results suggest that the self-system is quite immune to information that contradicts its current state' (ibid.: 52). On the other hand *positive* feedback 'tends to increase organisation, facilitating the emergence of structure in a system that otherwise would not be able to cohere into subsets of elements' (ibid.: 55), hence the value of empathy and positive feedback in analytic work with some clients.

Development of the ego-complex

Certain areas of Jung's theory of the developing ego-complex correlate with modern research findings. According to Jung, the ego is formed progressively out of the unconscious. It is not a sudden apparition, but develops only over a period of time (Jung 1923/1954, para. 102). This agrees with the current research presented below.

Development of the ego-complex will be considered in three phases:

- The creation of the basic landscape from 0 to 8 months. This consists of development of the implicit, emotional memories in the lower limbic structures and the cerebellum needed for the recognition of patterns of being with others. I associate this basic landscape with what Damasio called background feelings and relate it to core consciousness. It is the foundation on which the ego-complex rests, but is not explicitly part of it.
- The reinforcement of early emotional patterns, thereby forming hills and valleys in the emotional landscape. This occurs from 8 to 15 months. Connections with the limbic cortex, which will enable the infant to begin to control emotional states, develop during this period.
- The consolidation of the top layer of the landscape from 15 to 24 months. This includes the development of language and explicit, autobiographic memory.

What I attempt to show in this next section is that implicit, emotional memory, which is centred in the limbic system, primarily in the amygdala and later also in the hippocampus, develops before the earliest explicit memories, which require coordination between the hippocampus and the neocortex. These implicit emotional memories form the basic layer of the psychic landscape.

It has been proposed that the developmental process is itself a dynamical system during which periods of relative stability are interspersed with periods of rapid growth (Thelen and Smith 1995, Lewis 2000). Thelen and Smith 'characterize development as the continual stabilization and destabilization, over time, of preferred attractor states' (Thelen and Smith 1995: 61). Marc Lewis, professor of neuropsychology, states that 'Self-organization thus provides a single explanation for the multiple facets of development, integrating diverse developmental viewpoints within a larger scientific perspective' (Lewis 2000: 36). It is *not* my intention at this point to prove self-organisation in development in general. I am interested at this point in showing only that activity self-organises and lays down patterns which will be repeated and become entrenched with time. These patterns are stored in implicit emotional memory based in the amygdala before the development of the hippocampus.

The emotional patterns, which will be laid down to form the psychic landscape of the individual, develop from the innate character of the infant and the interactions of the infant-caregiver dyad. I will be comparing neuroscientific research in three areas of brain development:

a) the limbic system (principally the amygdala since most research centres on this) and the sympathetic nervous system, which is in place at birth
b) explicit memory as related to the development of the hippocampus and related organs, and lastly
c) the neocortex and the development of the parasympathetic nervous system.

Difference between implicit and explicit memories

The first layer of the landscape underpinning the ego-complex consists of the very basic emotional patterns laid down during the first hours to first months of postnatal development. These are the first broad, unconscious memories, not of specific events but of emotional states, experienced by the infant. These form the rolling hills of the state space diagram of the psyche. They are not yet attractors or complexes, but tendencies. In other words, I contend that this landscape layer is formed by unconscious emotional memories.

My use of the term 'emotional memory' is based on that of Joseph LeDoux (1995) meaning a conditioned memory created by an unconscious emotional process which has a direct effect on bodily functions such as blood pressure and heart rate, hence *implying* emotions. This implicit emotional memory is linked with the amygdala and the limbic system. In contrast, explicit memories are linked with the hippocampal system in the temporal lobes (ibid.: 201–2).

Explicit memories, which can be associated with either the ego-complex or an autonomous complex, result from the functioning of the hippocampus, which has multiple connections throughout the neocortex (LeDoux 1995: 224). They can connect what is happening currently with memories of past events. The emotional element expressed during the constellation of an autonomous complex comes via paths laid down by the implicit emotional memory which started forming during infancy and is already present in mild form in the ego-complex.

The human brain is capable of forming unconscious memories based on emotional experiences without a functioning hippocampus. This has been demonstrated in patients with extensive damage in both temporal lobes including the hippocampus (Damasio 1999a: 43–7), and is similar to the situation in infants under about 2 years of age whose hippocampus is also not (yet) functioning.

Although memory has been studied in science and philosophy for well over a century, the development of memory in infants and childhood has been relatively ignored until recently. Different types of memory and related functions appear to be the prerogative of different areas in the brain. The study of the development of these differing cognitive functions proves to be a better way of studying memory in babies and small children than the study of memory in adults. However, one must also be wary of a too simplistic structure-to-function mapping since the brain works as an integrated system, a global workplace (Nelson 1995: 723–4).

One must also be careful not to make too simple a differentiation between explicit and implicit memories. It appears clear that explicit memories involve the neocortex and/or precortical areas and therefore cannot be laid down before pathways between them and the hippocampus are formed and functioning (i.e. myelinated) (Eliot 1999: 344, Nelson 1995). The problems arise with the hippocampus and its role in implicit memory. The hippocampus is a complex structure that stands between, and has many connections with, both cortical and sub-cortical structures. Some authors consider it with the limbic system, others as part of the temporal lobe. A number of different types of memory are classified as implicit: procedural memory and skill acquisition associated principally with the striatum, perceptual and conceptual priming through matching with a pre-encoded memory in the neocortex, and conditioning involving mainly the amygdala and in some cases the cerebellum (Lloyd and Newcombe 2009). I am particularly interested in conditioning. It appears that the constellation of an autonomous complex is similar to the conditioned reaction to a stimulus that has been reinforced each time it is activated.

Scientific investigation indicates that the amygdala matures before the hippocampus (LeDoux 1995: 205–6). I argue that implicit emotional memories, linked with the amygdala and the limbic system, form the basic emotional landscape laid down in the infant before the formation of the hippocampus. They will be instrumental in determining moods associated with the ego-complex later in life. These are in place before the formation of autobiographic, explicit memories and are therefore related to what Damasio called core consciousness (Damasio 1999a).

Allan Schore cites research into what I have been calling the emotional landscape, and what he calls the 'affective imprint' which is required both for the creation and the retrieval of subsequent explicit memories (Ciompi 1991: 101, cited in Schore 1994: 180). Going back to studies with new-borns, Schore states that imprinting underlies the formation of the attachment bond and results from early emotional experience (Schore 1994: 180). This early imprinting predestines the infant to certain attachment preferences which underlie future development (ibid.: 111).

The basic landscape

Prenatal memories

Memories are not only stored in the neocortex. Almost every area of the brain stores memories. Memories start forming before birth. Our earliest memories are stored as basic motor patterns in the spinal column and the brain stem long before the hippocampus or the neocortex are functional. Experiments have shown that at 5 to 6 months after gestation a foetus will habituate to a loud noise or a vibration on the mother's abdomen and the baby will 'remember' the sound for up to 24 hours (Eliot 1999: 337). Babies who were read a specific child's book by their mother before birth preferred a tape recording of their mother reading that story over a different one (de Casper and Spence, 1986). All pregnant women know that babies are happiest when mother is resting. This is when they like best to kick and move about. Women who played a specific piece of music before resting found that the babies conditioned to the sound and would start to move *before* the mother rested. The babies retained this conditioning after birth. The same piece of music would calm them more quickly than other music (Eliot 1999: 337).

All of these findings, as well as those given in the next section, are examples of recognition, a simple form of memory in which the neural traces are the same for both storage and retrieval (i.e. one sees something and remembers having seen it before). Recognition involves the hippocampal memory circuit, forming during this time, and is therefore classified as a form of explicit memory, but it is unconscious in the sense that it does not involve memory storage in the neocortex, which only begins to develop after 6 to 8 months after birth. Therefore recognition is termed per-explicit memory (Eliot 1999: 342). 'Normal' memory, recollection from the past, is technically referred to as 'recall'. It is explicit, and only begins at about 8 months when the hippocampal dentate region is fully formed and myelination of pathways within the limbic system is underway (ibid.: 344).

0 to 8 months

Although lacking explicit memories, the basic emotional landscape, starting *in utero*, is laid down as implicit memories in the first 8 months after birth. Already when only 15 *hours* old an infant is able to distinguish its mother's voice (de Casper and Fifer 1980), its mother's smell (MacFarlane 1975) and its mother's face (Field *et al.* 1982, all referenced in Schore 1994), showing that implicit sensory memory is already in place.

During the first day of postnatal life the infant will quiet down more quickly if it hears a recording of its own voice rather than a recording of a different infant (Martin and Clark 1982). This has been used to support the idea that the infant, from birth, has a rudimentary sense of self and can discriminate between itself and its environment (Butterworth 1990). Daniel Stern argues that there is already during the first and second month an *emergent self* present which ties individual experiences together. For this to be so there must be some form of memory present. This emergent self operates as the experiential matrix from which thoughts and feeling will later arise (Stern 1985). This basic emergent, mainly emotional, self is what I am calling the emotional landscape. It is the basis upon which all later emotions will be felt, and acts as a benchmark against which affective evaluations will be appraised.

The brain during this period

It is important in babies this young to differentiate between the lower limbic structures and the limbic cortex. Structures in the lower limbic area are almost, or completely, formed and functioning at birth. These include the amygdala and parts of the basal ganglia (i.e. the striatum which includes the caudate nucleus and the putamen). These are the areas which generate most of the basic emotions and regulate the production of the neurotransmitters GABA and dopamine, among others. The connections between these and the sense organs, particularly the olfactory bulb and the cerebellum, which controls bodily movement at this early age, is almost completely in place and myelinated at birth (Nelson 1995: 731). The striatum is instrumental in the production of dopamine and its close relatives serotonin and noradrenaline, which are all instrumental in moods and emotions. The entorhinal cortex, a doorway between the hippocampus and the cortex for neurotransmitters, has already begun to form synapses by mid-gestation (ibid.: 725). Dopamine releases energy and increases goal-directed behaviour (Austin 1999: 200), so it is reasonable to assume that the infant experiences from birth emotional shifts linked with the production of dopamine. This seems evident when watching the smile on the baby's face as it kicks while lying in the crib.

Another area of the striatum, the caudate nucleus, is the area in which instinctive memories are genetically encoded (Carter 1998: 161) implying that instinct is operating from birth onward.

The upper layers of the limbic system, the limbic cortex, consist of the precortical areas of the frontal, parietal and temporal lobes. They will connect the limbic system with these different areas of the neocortex, which develop much later. The remaining area of the basal ganglion, along with the caudate nucleus, the putamen and the globus palidus, the inner portion of which is instrumental in transmitting inhibitory signals to the thalamus (Internet Encyclopedia of Science), is only myelinated at 8 months, and the outer area not until after the first year (Nelson 1995: 731).

At birth the human hippocampus is just 40% mature, increasing to 50% by 4 to 6 weeks, and is only fully mature by 15 months of age (Kretschmann et at. 1986, cited in Diamond 1990: 401). In contrast to the hippocampus, which is the centre of the explicit memory system, the amygdala, which is the corresponding centre for implicit memory, matures earlier (LeDoux 1995:

205). In addition to the role the amygdala plays in emotions, particularly fear, it is also of decisive importance for socio-emotional behaviours (Adolphs *et al.* 1998; Meunier *et al.* 1999; Bachevalier 2000 and Emery and Amaral 2000, all cited in Bauman *et al.* 2004), particularly in making accurate social judgments (Adolphs *et al.* 1998). There is at present no suitable neuro-imaging technique capable of measuring amygdala activity in the neonate. However, experiments with new-born babies have established that there is an innate orienting mechanism, present at birth (or a few hours afterwards), which is responsible for infants' preference for face-like patterns and direct eye-gazing (Gliga and Csibra 2007: 6). This sensitivity to socially relevant stimuli has been attributed principally to the amygdala and other subcortical structures. The amygdala is sensitive to dark-light patterns, so the poor visual acuity of the new-born would not inhibit this reaction (ibid.: 19–20). George Hogenson proposes that these innate subcortical structures generate the stimulus-response patterns leading to the development of archetypal images (Hogenson 2001: 60, cited in Knox 2003: 51).

Testing for implicit learning has traditionally concentrated on the recognition of statistical regularities, or patterns, often in artificial languages, i.e. on certain sounds in nonsensical words being repeated. These tests have now been replicated with tones (Saffran *et al.* 1999, Saffran *et al.* 2005), visual shapes (Fiser and Aslin 1996, Turk-Browne *et al.* 2005) and tactile stimuli (Conway and Christiansen 2006) (all cited in Perruchet and Pacton 2006: 233). New-borns preferred the sound of words they hadn't heard before, recognising repeated sounds for up to 24 hours (Eliot 1999: 341). Children as young as 5 months have successfully identified patterns (Lloyd and Newcombe 2009: 104). Pattern recognition, a function of the right brain (MacNeilage *et al.* 2009: 64), is the basis for this gentle, repetitive learning which builds up the psychic landscape.

Babies have a universal tendency to stare longer at something they have not seen before. This has been used in numerous experiments to test infants' memory. When presented with two objects, one they have seen before and one they have not, they will show more interest in the novel object. The experimenter can then tell if the baby has forgotten having seen the familiar object. This reaction is reliable in babies of 2 to 3 months, but the tendency has been observed in infants as young as 3 days if the stimulus is repeated in under 2 minutes (Nelson 1995: 726).

The mirror neuron system

In repeated experiments, Meltzoff and Moore (1977, 1983 and 1997) demonstrated that infants from under 1 hour to 21 days old imitate facial expressions (principally tongue protrusion). This was much earlier than had been measured previously. They were not satisfied with explanations of this phenomenon using theories available at the time (1983: 708) and proposed a mechanism involving an initial cross-modal identification (involving more than one form of sense perception) and a period of trial and error until the infant has perfected the movement (1997). There has been some disagreement with other experimental findings, and not all researchers have agreed with their statistics on all facial expressions (tongue protrusion, open mouth and protruding lips). However, some have corroborated their findings for tongue protrusion (Anisfeld 1996). This research needs to be re-evaluated in light of more recent findings concerning mirror neurons.

It is considered that the mirror neuron system (MNS), since it is an assemblage of different neurons and not single neurons, develops over this time (0 to 8 months) and, indeed, throughout childhood and adolescence. At this early stage it is believed to be automatic. The quite long response times of up to several seconds for the first experiences with neonates, and the improvement with repetition implying a learned response, exclude this from being a simple reflexive reaction (Lepage and Théoret 2007). Although there is little controlled experimentation with very young infants, most of the evidence implies that some form of observation/execution of an action is present from birth (ibid: 515). The reason for the improved response time is unclear; it might be the result of learned response to a stimulus, or improved practice in making the movement, or both. Furthermore, tests were not repeated after a specified interval of time to see if the improved response was maintained.

It is noteworthy that the evidence for the MNS in neonates has been principally from facial and mouth movements. The corticobulbar tract, which connects the motor neurons controlling the movement of the face, head and neck with the brain stem, is myelinated and functioning at birth (Bertenthal and Longo 2007: 526–7), whereas the corticospinal tract, which connects the cerebral cortex to spinal motor neurons and controls movement in other areas of the body, myelinates later.

Initial period of cortical development (about 8 to 15 months)

The age of about 8 months comes up repeatedly in literature on infant development. By this time the myelination of the connections between the hippocampus and the limbic cortex is complete, thus forming an important 'watershed' in the development of memory and making possible actual recall as opposed to simple recognition (Eliot 1999: 344). Once memories can be stored for longer and longer periods of time, patterns of memories and emotions can start to form around a rudimentary sense of self, causing deeper valleys in the emotional landscape.

The developed state of the hippocampus and the limbic system at 9 to 12 months after birth makes possible the type of pattern recognition called deferred imitation (Nelson 1995: 727). At 9 months infants can remember and reproduce a series of actions they saw an experimenter perform 24 hours earlier. At 13 months they can remember the actions for up to a week, and at 15 months for a period of 4 months, that is until they are 19 months old (Eliot 1999: 345–6). This is interesting in that, first, it demonstrates that even a simple, non-emotional event can be remembered and reproduced in the same context as it was originally experienced for quite a long period of time and, second, it confirms the age given for the full development of the hippocampus at 15 months (Kretschmann et at. 1986, cited in Diamond 1990: 401) cited on page 146.

At some time between 6 and 12 months the initial form of recognition memory, consisting mainly of communication between the lower limbic system (amygdala and basal ganglia) and the developing hippocampus, is supplanted by a new form enabled by emerging communication with precortical and cortical areas allowing for true recall (Nelson 1995: 728). This new ability is demonstrated in improvement in memory tasks requiring working memory, and is the beginning of explicit memory. Memory up until now has been implicit. Implicit memory continues throughout life, and is readily demonstrated in priming and conditioning. I contend that the shifts between complexes within the ego-complex, which manifest as changes in mood, as well as the constellation of autonomous complexes, are due mainly to shifts between implicit memories. Explicit memory comes in as an additional factor, both during the constellation of a complex and in the life history, starting first as working memory at about 8 months.

This increased communication within the brain not only allows for new and improved memory, but also affects the child's ability to control emotions and is important for differentiating between shifts within the ego complex and the sudden outbreak of an autonomous complex. The child at birth is neurologically not able to control mounting emotions (Schore 1994). This ability will develop rapidly, starting at about 8 to 10 months until about 15 months, in the orbitofrontal cortex which communicates with the limbic system and the frontal cortex (Eliot 1999). This research concurs with findings in attachment theory and supports theories of the influence of early relationship on the formation of both attachments and the ego-complex.

The function of the orbitofrontal cortex to dampen the affect generated by the limbic system is not in place at birth. As has been shown above, the neurons of the neocortex, including the prefrontal cortex, develop during the first two years of life and beyond. Myelination in the prefrontal cortex is very slow, continuing through adolescence and beyond (Jernigan *et al.* 1991; Yakovlev and LeCours 1967, cited in Nelson 1995: 730). This late development increases the extent to which the forming ego-complex is directly influenced by the child's environment.

The infant takes an active part in this interaction with the caregiver. The interactions of the caregiver-infant pair form a pattern which is 'indelibly imprinted' (Schore 1994: 3) into the infant's developing prefrontal cortex. This pattern will shape the infant's future relationships and consequently his or her sense of self and, importantly, self-worth (ibid.). This imprint builds on the basic landscape laid down in the first 8 months and accentuates the hills and valleys of the ego-complex.

Modern research has substantiated the association of early memories and emotions. The interrelationship between the limbic system (feelings) and the prefrontal cortex (cognition), as explained above, shows that cognition can no longer be considered apart from affect. 'Emotions are part of the information represented in memory and consequently affective and cognitive information are interwoven in retrieval' (Sarter and Markowitsch 1985: 368). What is stored in the image-based right hemisphere is an image of the caregiver's facial expression, a memory of what elicited the image, and the body feeling associated with the experience, and thus an expectancy that it will happen again.

This experience-based model, stored in the forming orbitofrontal cortex, contains the basis for expectations that, in times of mounting anxiety, an internalised regulating 'other' can, or cannot, be relied upon to self-regulate the mounting emotion. These expectations form the beginnings of self-identity, of internalised patterns of emotional response; in short, they form a pre-symbolic basis of a sense of self and the experience of that self: self-esteem.

Most babies begin to crawl independently at about 8 to 10 months and take their first wobbly steps by their first birthday. This increased mobility gives them new experiences and puts them into contact with new environments, stimulating growth in perception, coordination, movement and cognition. They can apply what they have learned in new contexts. While very young infants remember only in a context identical with that of the initial event, as babies mature they are increasingly able to apply what they have learned to new situations (Hayne and Simcock 2009: 49–50). Studies comparing memory among children of equal ages showed marked improvement of the children crawling over non-crawlers, and also of those starting to walk over those still crawling. Each increase in mobility increases the application of past experience to new contexts (ibid.).

Interaction between biological, psychological and sociological development has been proposed both by biologists (e.g. Oppenheim 1980) and developmental psychologists (e.g. Kagan 1986 and Alberts 1987). 'The development of social behavior can be understood only in terms of a continuing dialectic between an active and changing organism and an active and changing environment.' (Hinde 1990: 162.) The period at the end of the first year, when the child begins to stand upright, coincides with a maturational advance in the prefrontal cortex allowing for the first exchange of neurotransmitters between the lower limbic system and this area (Nelson 1995; Eliot 1999). At the same time the mother's primary role changes from caregiver to teacher of socially acceptable norms of interpersonal interaction. This transition is crucial for the structural maturation of an adaptive cortical system that can self-regulate emotional states (Schore 1994: 19–20).

There is strong empirical evidence that the maturation within the cortical-limbic structures, and in particular the connections between these areas, is directly influenced by the caregiver-infant relationship (Schore 1994). It is believed that emotional stability is dependent upon mediation between the two subsystems of the autonomic nervous system, i.e. the energy-exciting, subcortical, sympathetic nervous system and the energy inhibiting, cortical parasympathetic nervous system. Jung considered the unconscious sympathetic system to be outside the bounds of the ego (Jung 1926/1960: para. 613). The inhibitory, parasympathetic, cortical structures, which Jung did consider to be part of the conscious ego, develop more slowly and in response to socially acceptable behaviour learned through interaction with the mother and, increasingly, other family members. In this way the developing ego-complex incorporates socially adapted ways of dealing with emotional situations.

The importance of inter-subjective relationship in the development of emotional self-regulation has been discussed in other works (see in particular Schore 1994, and Beebe and Lachmann 2002). The more recent work on the mirror neuron system (MNS) in infants from about 8 to 12 months needs to be included here. It is of particular importance because abnormalities in the MNS have been observed in children with autistic spectrum disorder (Dapretto *et al.* 2005). The MNS has been described as the basis for both imitation learning and our ability to understand and interpret others' actions (Rizzolatti and Craighero 2004, Gallese *et al.* 2004). Early automatic elements of the MNS are in place from birth, as was discussed earlier in this chapter. It appears that neurological changes occurring between 6 and 12 months, and particularly around 8 months, establish the prerequisites for including those components of the MNS necessary for empathic understanding of actions observed in others.

In order for an infant to attribute meaning to an action, either its own or one that it observes, this system must already be functioning if the above theories of MNS are correct. It was observed that infants had the ability to anticipate the goal of an action by 12 months of age, whereas infants under 6 months did not have this ability (Falck-Ytter *et al.* 2006). The measurement of event-related potentials (ERP), which indicate electrical activity in the brain measured during an EEG, in 8-month-old infants confirmed activation in the right hemisphere while watching a person walking. The results correlated with those for adults, indicating that the neurological substrates necessary to distinguish movement develops at about 8 months (Hirai and Hiraki 2005). These studies, together with other EEG, fMRI and near-infrared spectroscopy (NIRS) studies, suggest that a system is in place by 6 to 8 months of age which supports the effective matching of observed to experienced movement (Lepage and Théoret 2007: 519).

If such a system is indeed in place by 8 months, it would play a central role in inter-subjective learning, especially in the experience and control of emotion which lays down the basic emotional landscape of the psyche.

Top layer of the landscape – autobiographical memory

In my analysis concerning dynamical systems modelling I considered autonomous complexes to be independent attractors and the ego-complex to be a central large basin of multiple attractors. Autobiographical memories are linked to that large basin of attractors, whereas autonomous complexes are separate from it.

I agree with theories which state that there is the beginning of a self present practically from birth, but I see this as a feeling-self, an awareness of what it feels like to be me. These are the feelings which make up the basic psychic landscape and are the normal feeling-tone states that the child is used to. They depend on implicit memories that are stored mainly in the lower limbic system, the brain stem and the cerebellum. As the connections with the limbic cortex and the precortical areas mature, explicit memories begin to form. These memories will build on the earlier memories of the feeling-self, and some may be moved to the neocortex where they can eventually become conscious. However, the conscious state of the memory is not of paramount importance, because it is the implicit memories that affect us, as shown through conditioning and priming.

Autobiographical memories are explicit memories of a particular event that occurred at a specific time and place. They are part of a coherent life story. They carry personal significance (Fivush and Nelson 2004: 574); they are stories that have happened to 'me'. Howe and his colleagues argue forcefully that without a sense of self there can be no memories about 'me' and therefore no autobiographical memory (Howe *et al.* 2009: 177). The line representing the relationship between age and memory (the older one is, the more one remembers) has two significant kinks in it. There are almost no memories before the age of 2 and there are very few memories before the age of 7. The earliest memory is usually about the age of 3, with continuous memories related to a life story beginning around 4.5 years (Fivush and Nelson 2004: 574).

Because language also starts at about the same age as autobiographical memory (first reference to past events at 18 months, but only by 20 to 24 months are these continuous and contextual), the question of the relationship between the development of memory and that of language arises. Two alternatives are possible: either language is required for autobiographical memory, or both are dependent on some other process, such as the development of a coherent, stable self. I think it is probably a mixture of both. The concept of self develops in an intersubjective context including language. The infant understands language much earlier than it can speak. Language will in part shape the development of connections between the limbic system and the neocortex. The sense of self develops centred around these forming cortical midline structures (Northoff *et al.* 2006). These structures are in turn required for the coordination of thought and movement necessary for language.

Shift from right to left hemisphere development

By the middle of the second year of life (18 months), development of the orbital prefrontal cortex, with predominance of the right hemisphere and its links with the limbic system, is stable. Two circuits which can moderate affect are in place: the sympathetic, excitatory system with links between the lower limbic system, the cerebellum and the body, which forms early, and the inhibitory, parasympathetic system with links to the limbic precortex, which forms later at 14 to 16 months. The infant's ability to adapt to a changing internal and external environment depends on its capacity to shift between these two mechanisms.

Schore (1994) proposes that there is a major discontinuity in the development of the neocortex at about 15 to 18 months. With the stabilisation of the parasympathetic system, the critical period of inter-subjective social imprinting in the predominantly right hemispheric orbitofrontal cortex begins to wane. The child has incorporated ways of controlling mounting emotions. This is evidenced by the expressions on the child's face of '… "pained", "hurt feelings" in response to shaming prohibitions of the parents …' (ibid.: 226) which demonstrates the existence in the psychic landscape-model of areas centred around distinct emotional states. This same period also corresponds to an increase in the maturation of the dorsolateral prefrontal cortices, principally in the left hemisphere, and is evidenced in the beginnings of language, a negativism on the part of the child (the 'terrible twos'), a lessening of the ties with the mother and an increase in ties with the father (ibid.: 234–7). Austin (1999: 37) proposes that it is precisely this activation of the two lobes that is the basis for the concept of self.

By the end of the first year of life, and thus well before the development of the dorsolateral prefrontal cortex required for speech, the infant has learned an extensive repertoire of signals which it uses to communicate in a social environment. Although it does not possess speech, it has assimilated prosodical rhythms as well as verbal pre-speech patterns (Courage and Howe 2002: 262). The combination of auditory and predominantly visual images is the inspiration of narrative thought, a means by which inter-subjective experiences may begin to be retained as autobiographic memory. Research (Hermans *et al.* 1992; Stern 1989; Bruner 1986, all cited in Schore 1994: 484) suggests that narrative thought is constructed around emotionally charged autobiographic experiences of self-in-interaction-with-other where the other serves to help regulate the emotions experienced. Using the language of object relations, Palombo (1992, cited in Schore ibid.) states that parental self-objects facilitate the stabilisation and regulation of these narratives so that the child is not overwhelmed by their affective content. I understand these to be the foundation of the parental complexes formed, in part, by the infant's early interaction with its parents, and in part from instinctive images the child has of how its needs can be met. These first memories of interactions of self with others, involving differing sensorial images and emotions, are stored in the developing frontotemporal regions as well as the already maturing prefrontal cortex and areas close to the limbic system. It has been shown by brain imaging that these are the principal areas which are activated in self-referential memories (LaBar *et al.* 2006: 59).

The self at 18 months

By the second half of the second year (i.e. after about 18 months) the infant's life has become more complicated. Patterns of arousal and affect, and variations in temperament (the hills and valleys of the psychic landscape) have been laid down. Sensory systems are firmly in place. Motor skills and coordination are quite stable. The child is able to control speech and coordinate vocal sounds with mouth movements. They have usually made the change from crawling to walking, which allows them to explore their universe, giving them much increased stimulation and new experiences. They have established patterns of social interaction with parents, other family members and friends and, importantly, with other children.

Schore proposes that this change at around 18 months corresponds with the onset of the maturation of the dorsolateral prefrontal association cortex, and that this underlies the lateralisation of right and left hemispheres (Schore 1994: 234–9). This could lead to the assumption that maturation is responsible for the sudden spurt in language ability at this same time, although a close reading of Schore shows that he does not explicitly state this. Other researchers are more reluctant to attribute this change to any single cause, including brain development, e.g.: '... although there is extensive neurological development throughout the first 2 postnatal years, there does not appear to be consistent evidence of a particular advance that coincides with the apparent shift in cognitive performance at 18 months' (Courage and Howe 2002: 267).

At 18 months of age there is a major change of affect in the child. On the psychological level Margaret Mahler noted that the exploratory period comes to an end and is replaced by the fearful mood of what she termed the 'rapprochement phase' (Mahler *et al.* 1975). Biologically, it has been noted that there is a discontinuity in mental abilities and a reorganisation of cognitive functions at this time (Lewis, Jaskir and Enright 1986, cited in Schore 1994). Sociologically, by this time the child has been in contact with other children, and the beginnings of socialisation and peer interaction have increased the infant's palette of possible affective states (Schore 1994: 491).

It has been emphasised by several schools of psychology (e.g. Self psychology, Object relations) as well as modern researchers (Sugerman and Jaffe 1990, cited in Schore 1994) that the changes which take place at about 18 months involve a transformation of the concept of the self. The structures and modes of processing of information and affects which are put into place at this time are long-term. They will form the basis for subsequent interpersonal interactions (Schore 1994: 491).

It is at this time that the autonomous self emerges. The self now takes over functions which were previously performed by the external 'other'. This is done by the internalisation and integration of self-objects (Kohut 1971).

It is also at this time that the child is first able to recognise a picture of his or her own face. This is a function of the now-developing frontal lobes. It indicates that the child is aware of itself as an object for other people. It can also put itself in the place of those other people and see itself as an object (Broucek 1982: 371).

All of the elements which Damasio defined as necessary for the establishment of extended consciousness are now present. The brain is monitoring changes in the outer world through sense perceptions. It is monitoring the body for changes and it now has the beginnings of memory images, in the form of either emotional patterns or true memories. There are not a lot of memories, and the cognitive facilities are not yet present, but this is the beginning of extended consciousness.

The effect of language

It is not clear what effect language has on memory. Children begin recalling recent current events almost as soon as they begin speaking (Eliot 1999: 347). They can, on occasion, also recall events which occurred before they learned to speak. Verbal recall is conscious, so when a child speaks of a preverbal event, he or she is bringing into consciousness something that was experienced before there were words to put it in context. This shows that language is not required for memory storage, and that non-linguistic memories can be retrieved.

Other researchers (Hayne and Simcock 2009: 52–3), while not denying that this can occur, conclude that it is very rare and incomplete when it does happen. Infants' memories are highly contextual, as was shown above. Out-of-context recognition increased with age, but even at 6 months significant improvement in memory was demonstrated if tests were conducted in conditions similar to the initial exposure (Eliot 1999: 339). The argument is that language is important in forming an inner context in which memories are stored and retrieved.

Language is not only a means to express personal memories, it also provides a structure within which personal experiences can be organised (Fivush and Nelson: 2004: 574). It is not clear to what extent preverbal memories include both an emotional tone from the psychic landscape and content of events and things which happened, since the infant has no words with which to refer to these. When children who are just learning to speak give an account of an incident which occurred 6 to 12 months earlier, they use only words which were part of their vocabulary when that event occurred (Simcock and Hayne 2002, cited in Fivush and Nelson: 2004: 574). This implies that they can only express in words what was remembered in words. I believe these memories build on the first emotional layer of the psyche, forming the hills and valleys which will constitute both the ego-complex and the autonomous complexes.

Both parents play a role in the development of language, and hence of the autobiographical self, that is similar to the one played by the primary care-giver in learning to control emotions. By encouraging expression and elaboration in the recounting of events by the child, the parent is aiding it to build organisational representations of their experiences (Fivush and Nelson 2004: 574).

Pillemer and the fire

One of the few well-documented cases of childhood memories and language is that conducted by David Pillemer (Pillemer *et al.* 1994: 95–106) following a fire in a child care centre. He interviewed two groups of children, one group aged 3.5 years and the other 4.5 years, at 2 weeks, and again at 7 years, after the event. At 2 weeks all of the 3.5 year olds remembered the event, but almost none told a coherent story about it – none stated where they were at the time the fire broke out (in the building) or what was the cause of the fire (burning popcorn). Almost all of 4.5 year olds included these details in a coherent telling of their experiences. Pillemer argues that at 4.5 years the children had begun developing what he termed the 'socially accessible verbal system', whereas the 3.5 year olds had not. After 7 years, Pillemer was able to locate most of the children again. The children who were over 4 years old at the time of the fire remembered it fairly well, and over a third were able to give an 'intact narrative account' of what happened. In contrast, almost none of those who were 3 years old at the time remembered the event or were able, in response to questioning, to give an accurate response (Pillemer *et al.* 1994, retold in Neisser 2004). David Pillemer and Sheldon White (1989) identified two basic types of memory which form the dual memory system. There is, first, a non-verbal image-based system and, second, what they called a 'socially accessible system'. This division corresponds basically to that between declarative and non-declarative memory, with the additional specification that the nonverbal, image-based system is present from birth and addressed by situational, affective cues. These memories are expressed through behaviour and emotion, as opposed to the verbal, narrative-based, socially accessible system which develops during pre-school and early school childhood. In the terms of this system the older children had, at the time of the fire, the beginning of declarative memory and were able to encode the memory in a narrative form, whereas the younger children were operating in a nonverbal, image-based system and were less able to structure their memories. The older children were able to situate the event in their life at the time it happened (they began their stories with where they were at the time the fire broke out), and had a fuller understanding of what was happening (the cause of the fire). They had the beginnings of an ego-complex and were therefore able to link this event to it. This memory could be associated into the basin of attractors which was the forming ego. The children at 3.5 years were not able to do this and the attractor formed by the images of the fire and the emotions experienced remained cut off from other events. This memory would remain disassociated from the forming ego. As a single event, and because it was handled by the adults present without inflicting undue fear, the memories would fade and the event would never become long-term memory in the association cortices. This was shown by the fact they did not remember it. If the event had been repeated, or other events occurred which touched on the same or very similar emotions, or the event was traumatic enough, I propose that additional memories would build around this event but remain dissociated from the ego-complex basin of attractors, thus forming into an autonomous complex. The younger child would be more at risk because, not having language, the memory is stored in implicit memory, more related to emotion and body reactions. The child also lacks the ability to express what it feels and so cannot share its experience and fears with the other children and adults.

Language and the development of the self

Language seems to play an important role in the concretisation of a sense of self by integrating memories with felt experience. In the retelling of an experience, as in the above example, the child is forced to place themselves in a time sequence, in a specific place in relation to the other children, and to confront the fear they experienced. This retelling then connects several dissimilar regions and functions of the brain, creating for the child the beginnings of the global workspace, which is identified with consciousness. The retelling also identifies oneself as an actor in the drama. It reinforces a time sequencing of the events; 'I was in my room when the fire alarm went off, then I ran into the hall and saw other children, then the teacher told us to go outside, then I was on the lawn'. It links external events with interior feelings. It identifies a 'me', a 'self' within a social context. The retelling forces the child to concentrate on the event for a certain period of time, strengthening attention span and concentration. All of these activities build on one another in intricate feedback loops leading to the emergence of a sense of self as a distinct and unique entity.

Jung placed the development of the ego at between two and four (Jung 1930/1933: para. 754–5), which has been contested as being much too late (Schore 1999), but this depends on exactly what one considers the ego to be. If one defines it to be a basic, bodily sense of being an individual, I agree that Jung's estimate of 2 to 4 years is very late. However, considered in the above context, and in relation to long-term memory, Jung's proposal seems justified.

Language and separation

Language does not simply extend what was before: along with the forming of the concept of self, it adds a new dimension. As the child matures, it learns in discussion with its parents that its version of an event may differ from that experienced by others. Memories are subjective representations of events, both in relation to what actually happened and, especially, in relation to the emotions experienced. The child thereby learns that it is separate from all others, and that experiences can never be completely shared with another.

In the retelling of an event some things are inevitably left out. Not all of the rich detail of the original felt experience can be shared. A choice must be made. Certain things are told, while others not (Stern 1985). What is lost Lacan called the 'real' (Lacan 1973/1977: 53–60). This real is not reality. It is very hard even to know the real because we do not have words to describe it. In describing the part that we know, we shatter the wholeness of the experience. Even the part that we think we can communicate is subject to misunderstanding and misinterpretation.

What is lost results also from the process of categorisation described by Deacon as the third level of communication. Of the three referencing mechanisms present in language (iconic, indexical and symbolic), Deacon argues that only the third, the formation of categories, is symbolic (Deacon 1997: 69–92). His concept of symbolic overlaps with that of Jung (Jung 1921/1971: para. 814). Deacon proposes that, once a person or animal is able to identify the characteristics of an object and to match those characteristics with those of a second object, i.e. to form categories, this is evidence of symbolic thought. By putting things into categories, the details of each object are lost. To the extent that these details could be expressed, Jung would call it a sign, but if the details of the association are lost, one is no longer able to consciously express the meaning and emotional associations, this could be called a symbol also in Jungian terms.

It may be that, because of the differing specialisation of the left and right brain hemispheres, early emotion-carrying visual images are inaccessible to the language-dominated left hemisphere that matures later. This disconnection may remain throughout life (Schore 1994: 447). But it may also be the opposite. The visual right brain forms the images that the left brain puts into words. Thoughts often begin as an image, which is subsequently expressed.

Attributes of a complex applied to the ego-complex

Because the ego is an assembly of complexes, its state will vary over time depending on which of the complexes is constellated. Below are listed the characteristics defined above of the autonomous complex, modified where necessary to apply to the ego-complex.

The first level of the dynamical hierarchy (milliseconds):

- **Perception**: Perception changes constantly, initiating transitions from complex to complex within the ego-complex. Some people may have a predisposition to one form of perception over another.

- **Instinct**: The major instinct associated with the ego-complex is the life instinct, which can take on many subtle forms. In everyday life, instincts are less involved than during the constellation of the autonomous complex.
- **Emotions**: The emotional mix also changes constantly. Emotions associated with the ego-complex are experienced as moods and tend to be more of a mixture than any single one of the individually defined emotions.

The second level of the hierarchy (200 to 500 milliseconds):

- **Energy generated**: One's level and direction of energy is constantly shifting.
- **Level of awareness/attention**: Shifts in the level of awareness and the object of attention are experienced constantly. Perceptual images are constantly being evaluated as potentially interesting or dangerous. The evaluation is done with respect to the emotions evoked and memories from past experiences.
- **Personal memories**: Memories associated with the ego-complex constitute one's autobiographic memory. These are mainly things which can be consciously remembered, but the ego-complex begins to form around implicit memories, and these unremembered memories persistently influence the continual movement taking place within the ego-complex.

The third level of the hierarchy (seconds to tens of seconds):

- **Symbolic image**: The image of oneself in relation to others and the environment is constantly changing. This image is the beginning of thought. An idea starts first as an image before it is translated into language. This idea, as image, can have many meanings; before it is fixed in language it is unclear. The process of putting an idea into words fixes one meaning and excludes the others to the unconscious. This fixing of one meaning is similar to the fixing of attention – only a small portion of the idea can be retained.
- **Interpretation/Meaning**: The meaning of one's life or of one's current activities. The fixing of the idea/image, which is constantly changing with perception, and the incorporation of memories keeps the stream-of-consciousness-type script constantly running.

Since this is a continuous process, the running dialogue of interpretation lags behind the present and is constantly being interrupted with new perceptual input and the ebb and flow of emotions.

Chapter 10

The psychic landscape

The persona

My use of the term 'persona' is different from what is usually meant. It does not contradict Jung's original definition, but extends it.

Jung defines the persona as 'a functional complex that comes into existence for reasons of adaptation or personal convenience …' (Jung 1921/1971: para. 801). I do not believe that he used the term 'complex' unless he intended it to be in the context of what he was calling at this time 'complex psychology'.

The persona interfaces between the ego and the collective. It is the face I wear to the world, but since neither the ego nor the situations one faces in the world are constant, I argue that the persona too is not always constant. I propose that, like the ego-complex, the persona-complex is a set of complexes. Persona-complexes in this set can be more or less flexible. Some may be more similar to the ego-complexes, others may be closer to the unconscious and approach the autonomous complexes in feeling-tone. However, the latter differ from autonomous complexes in that persona-complexes never completely break their relation with the ego-complex. They also vary in intensity when they constellate and how they are experienced; some are very mild, while others approach the dramatic quality of autonomous complexes.

Although interfacing between the ego and the collective is necessary, one must be careful not to identify with the persona (Jung 1916/1953: para. 305), which should remain a socio-cultural interface between the ego-complex and the collective. The persona can present a stereotypic image, limiting one to age, gender and socially determined roles.

Murray Stein, one of the few modern Jungian authors who deals with the persona at some length, stresses the role of the persona as protection: 'It operates like the skin on the body, providing a protective barrier between the ego and the outside' (Stein 1998: 128). He presents it as the opposite of the shadow (ibid.: 106) and as complementary to the anima/animus (ibid.: 111). Stein points out that Jung was aware of the effect of the milieu on attitude, meaning a stance or comportment of the individual, i.e. behaving in a certain way, and thus adopting a certain persona to align with the environment (ibid.:

112–13). He cites Jung as identifying two sources of the persona: 'expectations and demands of society' and 'the social aims and aspirations of the individual' (Jung 1921/1971: para. 798 quoted in Stein 1998: 115).

By having a persona role to fall back on at times when the ego is threatened, I experience the persona as also protecting me from the constellation of the autonomous complex, hence not only protecting from the outside, but also from the inside. The ability of the persona to do this has not been addressed by any Jungian authors that I have found. The persona in this situation comes close to what Hester McFarland Solomon describes as the 'as-if' personality (Solomon 2004), although the 'as-if' personality is more pervasive and central to the personality as a whole.

The persona has been built up as a standard way of reacting to situations which cause anxiety and/or in which one feels threatened. If one had not developed these ways of reacting, the defenceless ego would be left to deal with the full emotional impact of the constellated autonomous complex.

The persona develops significantly in adolescence as one experiences the need to define oneself. It increases feelings of self-esteem, differentiates one from one's parents and expresses expectations of one's future social role. It maintains coherence in situations when the ego is threatened with dissociation.

I contend that persona complexes form as point attractors within the basin of attractors constituting the ego-complex and that they function as defences because they avoid a direct confrontation with the full power of the archetypal energies of the autonomous complex. The reaction of someone playing a persona role to a perceived threat may not be ideal, it may not even be how they would wish to react, but it is better than what they imagine could happen if the absolute worst-case scenario were to be played out.

If the roles which form the persona are complexes, then they too have the characteristics of a complex defined above: they are states in a psychic landscape (attractors), often experienced in relation to something perceived, identified by a specific emotional content and autobiographic memories, and implicitly and/or explicitly related to similar incidents in the past personal history of the subject.

Jung evokes the role the persona plays in mediating the relationship between the outer object and an inner attitude (Jung 1921/1971: para. 801). This suggests to me the possibility of positioning the roles comprising the persona on Cartesian axes, with one axis representing the person's inner attitude or self-image and the other their evaluation of the outer object (see below).

The persona is an adaptation from a collective image of how a person should react. 'Fundamentally the persona is nothing real: it is a compromise between individual and society as to what a man *should* appear to be' (Jung 1916/1953: para. 246, italics added). To the extent that 'the persona was [is] only a mask of the collective psyche' (ibid.), it is a mask of the collective *conscious* psyche as opposed to the collective *unconscious* psyche. I am referring to the collective conscious psyche as expressed, for example, in myths and legends of how a person in a given situation *should* react (Campbell 1988). This collective image is, at the same time, modified by the individual self (Jung 1916/1953: para. 246). Here again we could apply Cartesian coordinates, this time to individual vs. the collective.

When hearing a myth or fairy tale, a simplified world, populated with stereotyped characters - the omnipotent hero, the all-loving mother, etc. - is created in the mind of the listener, in which these become role models that one subsequently tries to live up to. Jung gives an example of this in the case of the 'the supremely wise, very grown-up, all-understanding mother-daughter-beloved' (ibid.: para. 248).

Modern researchers Marc Lewis and Natalka Junyk have also identified the existence of stable roles within the psychic landscape as

> reciprocal interactions among cognitive interpretations and emotional states fuel the emergence and stabilization of idiosyncratic patterns, which constrain further development and perpetuate their own logic. ... We argue that self-organizing defences play a special role in personality development, not because they are particularly "adaptive" solutions but because they transform indeterminacy into crystallized outcomes that constrain all subsequent development.
>
> (Lewis and Junyk 2002: 43)

I believe that persona complexes form in a state space particular to each individual and defined by their self concept in the context of their social situation. The state space is different for each emotional state.

The state space model

I will now adapt the state space model presented by Marc Lewis and Lori Douglas (1998: 176). I see the autonomous complex as what they label the 'original painful attractor', but reject their idea of a 'repeller' as the opposite of an attractor, because I have not found it anywhere else in dynamical systems theory. The persona can, in some situations, play the role of what they label a 'defensive attractor', being a complex associated with the ego-complex and for the most part conscious. I also investigate contrasting someone's self-evaluation with his or her evaluation of the other by using these as the x and y axes respectively in the following diagrams. I have added the concept of the ego-complex and the varying background emotions. Lewis and Douglas presented this model only in the context of anxiety. I suggest that its use is much broader and that it is a valuable tool in mapping a person's psyche in a wide variety of situations. It gives a more complete image of the psyche than that usually used in relation to the Word Association Experiment (Kast 1980: 27, Vezzoli *et al.* 2007: 99). In analysis, or more particularly during a training analysis, it could be developed together with a client or student, allowing a means to visualise their reactions.

Example 1: Psychic landscape in a threatening situation

Figure 10.1 depicts a state space model of the psyche of someone (let us call him John) at one particular instant. It represents a situation in which he feels his ability is threatened, perhaps by a test or a confrontation with a superior at work. It corresponds closely with that originally proposed by Lewis and Douglas (1998). The state of the psyche can be anywhere within the dotted envelope, and it is very unlikely that conditions exist outside this area, although theoretically not impossible. The vertical axis measures John's estimation of his ability to deal with the event currently occurring in the real world. This varies from completely incapable, inept, unable to express himself or to reveal his capabilities, to brilliant, very confident of his ability, with intermediary levels of just average and capable, but not overly so.

The horizontal axis measures John's judgement of the extent to which the other people involved in the event are open and accepting. This ranges from seeing them as receptive, actively encouraging and visibly on his side, to open, but not as positive as in the first case, to rather rejecting, needing to be won over, to closed and actively discouraging at the extreme negative end.

The light grey area represents the basin of attractions for John's ego-complex. The background emotion being experienced in each configuration is indicated. For example, if he sees himself as quite capable of handling the situation, but experiences those around him as being closed and not receptive to his intervention, he may be hurt, having feelings that the rejection is unwarranted

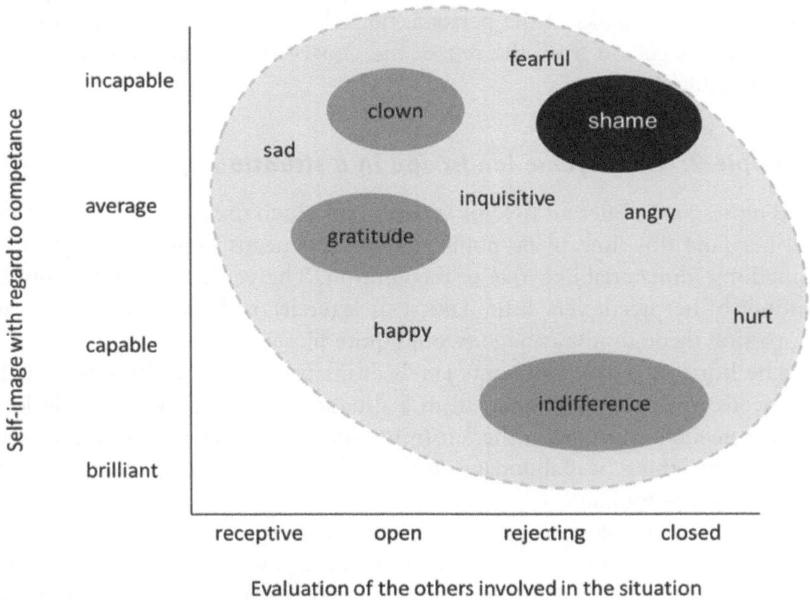

Figure 10.1 The psychic landscape in a threatening situation

and unfair. If he sees himself as incompetent and unable to handle this situation, and also judges the people around him to be rejecting, he might be fearful as he does not know what the outcome will be. This is just a picture of one person; someone else might experience different emotions.

The darker grey ovals represent personas, typical ways of handling this situation that John has learned in the past. These may have been due to constellations often experienced, as a result of which his reactions have become stereotypical. These may be areas that he finds particularly difficult to deal with, and has thus developed a persona, a role to play in such situations. If he feels unable to handle the situation, but judges the people around him to be relatively open, he may play the clown, laughing and joking to cover his nervousness, trying in this way to win the others over. If he knows himself to be competent in this situation, but experiences the others as rejecting and not accepting of the aid or advice he is offering, then he may feign indifference to mask his somewhat hurt feelings. If he judges himself to be only average and the others as being quite open to being receptive he may be overly polite, expressing much gratitude.

The black oval represents an autonomous complex around shame that John might fall into if he feels himself to be incapable in this situation and that the others are critical and rejecting. His ineptitude is being exposed. This area is actually outside of, and cut off from, the ego-complex, as if it were a deep well, a third dimension in the two-dimensional representation. While outside of this area of the autonomous complex the 'ball' of the psyche can roll relatively freely from area to area within the ego-complex and even quite readily put on and take off the masks of the persona, but when it falls into the autonomous complex it is cut off from the rest of the ego-complex and can only get out with difficulty.

Example 2: The psychic landscape in a situation of need

This represents a different psychic situation in which the same person (but let's call her Jane this time to be politically correct) needs something physical or something immaterial like love or recognition. The vertical axis represents the amount of her need: very little (take it or leave it), to large (desperately want it), passing through just average (would quite like it).

The horizontal axis represents Jane's estimation of the availability of what she needs in her environment; from a situation where there is very little of what is needed available on the left (minimum), it is very rare, to there being much of this thing, it is abundant on the right, with an adequate amount represented in the middle.

If Jane's need is quite large, but the availability of what she needs is merely adequate or less, she may be depressed to sad, depending on the ratio of need to availability. If, however, her need is less and availability is higher, then she may be happy, and even playful with those around her.

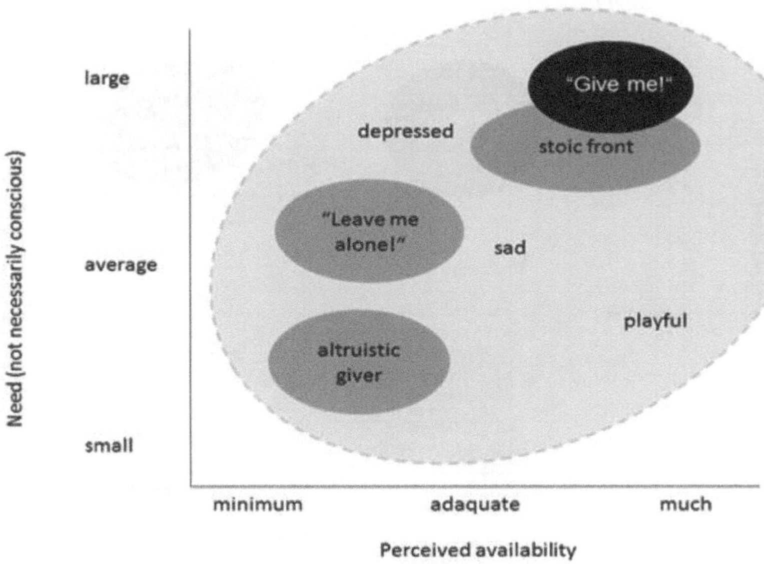

Figure 10.2 The psychic landscape in a situation of need

If her need is small, for example she has more than enough of something which is not abundant in her environment and which others need, then Jane may enjoy being altruistic and give it away for free. This role of benevolent giver may be one that is quite beneficial for her self-esteem. A different person may well react differently. If, however, her need is a bit greater for something which is still no more abundant in her environment, she may cut off relations with others and put up a front that warns them 'Leave me alone!' to hide her need. In a different situation, if her need is great and there is quite a bit of what she needs available, she may put up a false stoic front for some time, claiming 'I really didn't want that anyway'. This may be a last valiant effort on the part of the psyche to avoid the full weight of the autonomous complex – 'Give me what I need. You have enough and my need is great. Just give it to me' – expressed with all of the pain and anger of the rejection that accompanies it.

Example 3: The psychic landscape of a narcissistic person

A last example depicts the relationship between what one of these individuals (John again) is trying to accomplish and what he feels he is actually accomplishing. This may involve, for example, working with other people or getting a job done using physical tools and objects.

John may have invested very little effort in this project, somewhat more effort, a lot or very much effort as depicted on the vertical axis. He may perceive the success he has achieved as being none at all (failure), a little, an

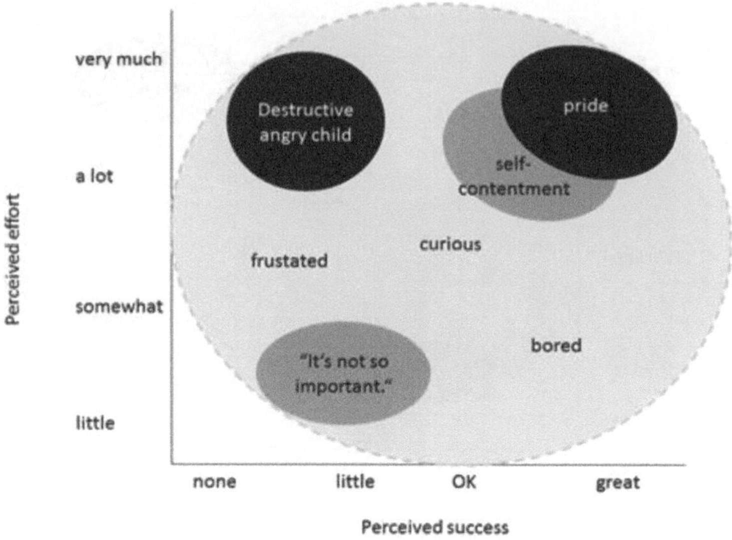

Figure 10.3 The psychic landscape of a narcissistic person

average amount (OK) or that he has had great success and achieved all he hoped for, and maybe more. These are depicted on the horizontal axis.

If he was very successful, but had invested little effort and cared little about the outcome, John may be bored. However, if he invested quite a bit of effort and really tried, but had little success he may be frustrated. If he invested about the same amount of effort and achieved moderate success he may be intrigued, curious as to what exactly is happening and what could be changed to improve the situation. These are all normal emotions of the ego-complex.

If, however, John has invested a lot of effort and feels he has accomplished the job, he may wear a mask of contentment, but close to that may be a narcissistic complex of pride, not only in his own result, but feelings of superiority over others who couldn't match his success. On the other hand, if he has failed to accomplish the task despite trying hard, the autonomous complex of the destructive, angry child, a form of narcissistic rage, may constellate. If he hasn't tried very hard, or feels that the job was unimportant, he may dismiss his failure as of little importance, wearing a mask of disinterest.

It can be seen from these models that the autonomous complexes and, to a lesser extent, the various persona-complexes are situated towards the edges of the model, where the circumstances are at their most extreme. The persona-complexes may also appear in situations in which there is increased emotion, to show socially acceptable ways of handling it.

Integration of the complex

The constellation of an autonomous complex, and the break with the ego-complex which this entails, is often experienced as disagreeable, painful and frightening. An early goal in Jungian psychoanalysis is often to make the client aware of what is happening during the constellation of a complex. A subsequent goal is to find out how to ameliorate the dissociation felt at this time. This dissociation comes from the complex's autonomous nature (Jung 1921/1928: para. 266), so the goal is an integration process to link the autonomous complex with the other complexes of the ego. On a psychological level, integration means acknowledging the feeling, and accepting it as part of oneself. On a neurological level this means tying the memories associated with the autonomous complex to the other autobiographical memories and thereby weakening the strong associations with the limbic system.

While the constellation of the autonomous complex can be seen as a phase transition on both the physical and psychological levels, the integration of the complex can also be seen as a series of milder transitions, each involving a modification of the entire state space leading to a larger, more flexible ego-complex.

Jung suggests that one of the principal ways of doing this is by working with projections, both as they occur naturally and, importantly, as they manifest within the analytical relationship as transference. 'Practical analysis has shown that unconscious contents are invariably projected at first upon concrete persons and situations. Many projections can ultimately be integrated back into the individual once he has recognized their subjective origin ...' (Jung 1946: para. 357).

Often an analysis is seen as a long process of slowly feeling better, punctuated by a few experiences of major change. These together form the interplay of minor and major phase transitions in the psychological space and related changes in the physical space. Through projection onto the analyst of emotions linked with long-term, perhaps unconscious, memory these memories, and more importantly the emotion linked with them, may become conscious. Each of these recovered emotions, either from memories, dreams or projections, is a small phase transition on the physical level which may coalesce subsequently in a major phase transition on the psychological level. The complex does not disappear; it is changed, particularly with regard to the emotion, to fit into the ego, thereby broadening the ego-complex.

Jung warns that the images, especially of parental complexes, which arise in this process, are charged with the energy they had in childhood. Their integration will bring an influx of energy into the unconscious which will manifest in dreams and fantasies (Jung 1935c: para. 218). The image as it manifests during the constellation of the complex is highly charged with instinctual emotions. They are iconic in that there is a direct relationship between the image and the instinctive situation (Deacon 1997). All of the energy and emotion associated with that situation may be re-experienced. This image needs to be separated from these emotions to incorporate the latter into the psychic landscape by creating more connections between the memories of the ego-complex and the limbic system. The image can then be put into words and incorporated into the ego-complex. This involves a link between the image-based right hemisphere and the language-based left hemisphere. There will be a transformation of the entire personality as the network of neural connections expands. 'Once these unconscious components are made conscious, it results not only in their assimilation to the already existing ego-personality, but in a transformation of the latter' (Jung 1946/1954: para. 430).

Extinction

To the extent that the constellation of an autonomous complex is a conditioned response, integration of the complex corresponds with the extinction of this response. Studies done with rats on de-conditioning their reaction to a tone followed by a mild electric shock correspond with findings with people suffering severe phobic reactions, i.e. although the fear reaction can be controlled for many years, the experience of a sudden re-exposure can bring it back in full force. This leads Joseph LeDoux to conclude that 'Like extinction, therapy does not erase the memory that ties fear reactions to trigger stimuli. Both processes simply prevent the stimuli from unleashing the fear reaction' (LeDoux 1996: 145–6). Therefore what is important is changing the *perception* of the emotion, the body state, and the expected outcome, thereby changing the psychic landscape. Most forms of extinction of conditioned responses rely on strengthening input to the amygdala from the medial prefrontal cortex, thereby dampening the conditioned response (ibid.: 170). I suggest that, by concentrating on bringing unconscious events into consciousness, psychotherapy may have this same neurological effect.

Although the constellation of a complex involves unconscious, implicit memories, there are also explicit memories of the person's reactions during previous experience with the complex. Integrating the complex depends not so much on actually remembering the original event, thus turning implicit into explicit memory, as on the recognition of the existence of the complex and its importance and meaning in the life of the individual. I have identified meaning/interpretation as the order parameter which enslaves the other components of the complex to constellate. It is the understanding, acceptance and integration of this meaning which will lead to the weaving of the autonomous complex into the web of the ego-complex on the psychic landscape. From the point of view of DST, with the removal of the order parameter of meaning the enslavement process does not take place, the person is then freer to deal with the emotional situation.

Integration as an emergent property

If the psyche is considered to be a hierarchy of dynamical systems then the integration of an autonomous complex is a process of self-organisation. 'Integration [of individual elements into a self-concept] is not achieved through the control of a higher order structure, but rather is an emergent property deriving from the local interactions among the elements themselves' (Nowak *et al.* 2000: 41). I propose that this same process of self-organisation is at work when autonomous complexes are woven more closely into the ego-complex.

Nowak's simulations showed that not all elements of a system need to become integrated, nor one global system formed. Only certain elements may become integrated into independent clusters (in this context principally the ego-complex and the autonomous complexes). Global integration (i.e. connecting all of the autonomous complexes to the ego-complex, thereby forming one universal cluster) is rarely achieved, and not necessarily desirable. What may appear to be conflicting characteristics, (e.g. friendliness and aggression) are advantageous in different situations (Nowak *et al.* 2000: 41). This loose construction corresponds with the ego-complex as archipelago (Jung 1946/1954: para. 387). When clusters (complexes) are integrated, it is through interaction of the elements with neighbouring elements in a different cluster, perhaps first by forming a new persona or integration into an existing persona.

One of the interesting findings of Nowak and his colleagues was that people with low 'press for integration' (a weak ego) benefit from social interactions which give them coherent, self-relevant feedback, irrespective of whether it is positive or negative, but not from conflicting or ambivalent feedback. This aids their self-integration, strengthening the ego by forming a more consistent self-concept (Nowak *et al.* 2000: 50).

Chapter 11

Three bridges and consciousness

In this work I have shown that, although the *reason* behind the constellation of an autonomous complex may be unconscious due in part to its 'strangeness' (Jung 1928/1948: para. 19 and note 19), the *process* of this constellation generates consciousness. This applies to the ego-complex as well as to autonomous complexes and, albeit in a different way, to the archetypes. I have concentrated on the role of emotion and the body in this process. Basing my research on Jung's original work with regard to the complex, I have identified the phenomenological correlates of the constellation of an autonomous complex. This has not, to my knowledge, been attempted before. I have dealt in detail with the development of the brain in the infant in order to stress the importance of unconscious emotional patterns and implicit memories in the psychic landscape of the adult.

My goal was not to justify Jung or Jungian theory. Rather, my starting point was to investigate the emergence of consciousness. I have compared three topics in Jungian theory – the constellation of an autonomous complex, the idea of the psychoid, and the ego as an assembly of complexes – with current neuroscientific research and explored their implications for consciousness. By applying DST and modelling of the neural correlates of psychological states I have demonstrated that the complex is an attractor state in the psychic landscape.

Each of the three experiences investigated is unique. Ego-consciousness is the everyday experience of consciousness, with changes in mood, basic emotional patterns and scope, from diffuse awareness to focussed concentration. The constellation of an autonomous complex upsets this usual consciousness with sudden eruptions of acute emotional, potentially traumatic, experiences. The constellation of an archetype brings complete, symbolic knowledge in the form of sudden insight, and in doing this throws light on the formation of ideas.

Through my investigations I have identified three concepts or processes which I consider of primary importance to the emergence of consciousness: the emergence of symbolic meaning, the concept of self and the formation of a global workspace resulting from the coordination/synchronisation over many psychological and physical levels.

By applying the theories of DST to research findings in neuroscience, I have identified a large degree of overlap between these findings and Jung's concept of the feeling-toned complex. I believe that starting from the experience of the feeling-toned complex to explain how consciousness emerges from brain and body has shed some light on the process.

Using this approach, I have also investigated the ego as an assembly of interrelated complexes. I have posited the persona as an assembly of functional complexes in the psychic landscape and illustrated the defensive role it can play with relation to the ego-complex and the autonomous complexes.

I have developed a tool which can help the therapist to visualise the psychic landscape of the client, thereby aiding the therapeutic process.

The process of symbolisation and meaning

The emergence of the symbol and its link to meaning within the life of the individual is the top level in the hierarchy of dynamical systems during the constellation of the autonomous complex. This final step is crucial for the establishment of consciousness. It is the order parameter which synchronises the lower levels of the hierarchy and guarantees emergence. Our tendency to do this is, I believe, an expression of the Self as the central process in the emergence of consciousness. The form the symbolic image takes is determined by the individual archetypes and their expression within a cultural environment. The Self can then, in this sense, be seen as the totality of the expression of these archetypes in an individual's life.

Reviewing the three hierarchical levels of emergence, we can say that the first level brings together perception, instinct and emotion, the second level involves possible changes in awareness, the level of energy experienced and memories recalled, and the third level results in the formation of a symbolic image and meaning related to the individual.

The memories activated in the second level are, according to the classification of Terrence Deacon, an indexical relationship (Deacon 1997: 77). The same stimulus could evoke a number of memories, creating not only a record of past events, but a prediction of what will happen in the near future. From these indexical relationships there emerges, through a process of self-organisation, a symbolic representation which conveys meaning.[1] The evaluation-interpretation-meaning then locks the system in the attractor state of the constellated complex, thus eliminating all other possible outcomes of the situation. This evaluation-interpretation-meaning may be expressed in words, but even if it is not, it coordinates the emotions and possible outcomes around a central self figure. It aligns the body and mind, preparing for possible physical action. It integrates the present, the past and the anticipated future. There are no longer a number of possible outcomes that can be logically decided between, but only one outcome; the others are eliminated.

On the physical micro-level the initial perception initiates instinctive responses very deep in the brain, at the top of the brain stem and the limbic system. From here the reaction goes simultaneously in two directions, into the body to prepare for an immediate reaction, and into the cortex stimulating implicit memory. A multi-modal image then forms. The anterior cingulate cortex mediates the memories, image and emotions, projecting possible outcomes. Finally, the frontal cortex interprets what is happening in terms of the meaning for the individual as consciousness develops in this global workspace.

This formulation of the meaning and the elimination of other envisioned results is what is happening during the constellation of an archetype (tenths of a second), the constellation of a complex (seconds to tens of seconds), and continually during the subtle changes within the ego-complex (minutes to hours). Moreover, it happens (or should happen) over the course of a lifetime, as Jung acknowledged when he spoke of the loss of meaning as the neurosis of modern society.

The formation of a symbol, or categorical relationship, as described by Deacon (1997), allows humans to manipulate larger and larger groups of information in decision-making to evaluate complicated situations and plan ahead. Categories can be considered in place of individual details. The reverse process is happening when meaning is extracted from a symbolic image, as when we use metaphor in speech. Abstract speech is almost entirely metaphoric (Lakoff and Johnson 1980: 272) and is pervasive in everyday thought and action (ibid.: 3). Lakoff and Johnson argue that this is because our thought processes are largely metaphoric. In metaphor, the characteristics of the categorical association are reviewed and similarities are identified. Thus, by using language, we are constantly evaluating metaphor, applying multi-modal images involving both hemispheres of the brain.

During the constellation of many autonomous complexes, meaning, directly related to what is being perceived as threatening to one's physical or psychological well-being, emerges. In trying to integrate such a complex into the ego after the immediate situation has passed, one realises that its meaning is more generally related to one's past and future. During the constellation of an archetype, the meaning seems to be in the object or thought itself, thereby manifesting almost as illumination.

During ordinary ego-consciousness the process is more complex. In the hierarchical model proposed above, it is the extraction of meaning from the symbol which enslaves the psyche. We know that it takes about half a second to become conscious in an experimental situation (Dehaene and Naccache 2001). Roughly half of this time is taken to form the first and second levels of the hierarchy. During this time, global, synchronous patterns are forming (Freeman 1999: 185). It is the global nature of this pattern which consequently directs attention to the initial stimulus (ibid.: 185–6), thus exhibiting the circular causality of self-organisation. During the constellation of an autonomous complex, because of the high emotional content and possibility of danger, other normal processing is stopped as attention focusses on the immediate situation. In the normal flow of ego-consciousness, which often lacks highly emotional content, attention may wander from one external object to another, interrupted by memories recalled in relation to what is perceived, or by previous thoughts. This process is continually generating consciousness. Daniel Amit (1989: 42) associated meaning with the convergence of a dynamical system on an attractor state. This is exactly what meaning is doing in the three cases I have considered: the constellation of the complex and the archetype, and the random flow of consciousness in the ego-complex.

The emergence of symbolic representation takes place in the prefrontal cortex, but is highly dependent on sensory-based images retained in the various sensorial association cortices. Symbols 'are relationships between tokens [memories], not tokens [memories] themselves' (Deacon 1997: 266. Explanation added). This emergence involves 'widely distributed neural systems' (ibid.) and, including the emotion involved, it could be called a 'global workspace' (Baars 2005). The process of putting things into words may be blocked momentarily by the flood of emotion during the constellation of a complex, as measured in the Word Association Experiment. This bypassing of words may favour the formation of an image, which is phylogenetically more primitive. More than language, Jung stressed the generation of an archetypal image by the psyche as part of the process of bringing unconscious thoughts and emotions into consciousness.

Thought

An idea is an image, abstracted or categorised from the original situation and (usually) put into words which fixes its meaning. Vittorio Gallese and George Lakoff (2005) have demonstrated that just imagining an action produced a neural pattern identical to actually seeing or carrying out the action. I am proposing that, in bringing something into consciousness, a similar but reverse action is taking place. A vague, multi-modal sensorial image is formed and is then brought into consciousness either as an image or as words. Certainly this is the case with the constellation of the archetype, as described by Mozart: 'I can see the whole of it at a single glance in my mind, as if it were a beautiful painting ... I do not hear it in my imagination at all as a succession ... but all at once, as it were' (Wolfgang Amadeus Mozart, quoted in William James (1890/1950), quoted in Hunt 1995: 139).

The passage from image to word is a passage from the right hemisphere, with its many connections to the limbic system, to the left neocortex. It involves a global workspace in the brain. The word, however, lacks some of the multiplicity and emotional content of the image. Explaining in words is a process of differentiation, which Jung considered to be one of the primary functions of the ego, that brings unconscious objects into consciousness.

When applied to oneself it is a process of slowly becoming aware of who one is, of developing self-awareness and self-realisation - in short, of becoming conscious.

We manipulate categories in thought. We can both put things into categories and use an image to represent a category and manipulate it. Emotions are carried over, transferred and placed in new, abstract settings.

Concepts of self

Being conscious is being aware that we are aware. We categorise the bundle of feelings and experiences about ourselves into a concept of 'self'. We are attentive not only to things outside ourselves, but to inner objects: thoughts, memories and feelings.

What is usually called simply 'the self' is composed of a number of cortical midline structures active when the subject is involved in self-referential thought processes (Northoff *et al.* 2006: 449). The highest level of self, identified as the autobiographical self (Damasio 1999a), is the only self which is available to consciousness. It is involved in higher-order processing, is verbal, involved in judgements, imagination, and explicit memory encoding and retrieval. It is principally associated with the neocortex, including the lateral prefrontal cortex (analysis and decision-making). Applying the concepts of symbolisation presented above, I propose that this self has itself become symbolised; it can therefore become an object of consciousness, thus leading to the second level awareness, self-consciousness or self-awareness.

The following simplified table relates consciousness and unconscious processing. For each level I have proposed the type of consciousness (extended or core), the corresponding concepts in analytical psychology with respect to the psychoid and the types of thinking or feeling experienced at each level.

Table 11.1 Levels of consciousness

Level of conscious/unconscious	*Type of consciousness*	*Psychoid pole*	*Body/mind coordination*
Conscious – higher order processing	Extended consciousness	Archetypal image	Directed thinking (verbal) Non-directed thinking (image based)
Unconscious – pre-self-referential and emotional processing	Core consciousness		Body sensations and feelings
Deep unconscious – body functions and instinctive processing	Proto self	Instinct	Regulation of body functions

- Higher-order processing, called extended consciousness (or simply consciousness), involves both directed, verbal thought, and non-directed, image-based thought. I contend that this starts somewhat just above the core self of core consciousness and includes the autobiographical self of extended consciousness. Consciousness includes both stream of consciousness type thinking, a diffuse type of consciousness when, for example, walking in the woods, and willed, concentrated, conscious reflection. Jung made the same distinction in terms of directed (verbal) and non-directed (image-based) thinking (Jung 1912/1956: para. 14–17). The constellation of a complex, or of an archetype, involves the sudden eruption of the archetypal image, and the accompanying meaning, into consciousness, thereby disrupting normal extended consciousness.
- Unconscious, called also pre-self-referential processing because it does not involve the concept of a developed self, is related to core consciousness and the experience of body sensations and feelings. I equate this, together with the deep unconscious, with the Jungian Self.
- Deep unconscious, emotional and instinctive processing is linked to the very basic mechanisms regulating body functions. It is related to the instinctive pole of the psychoid. I equate this with the archetypes of the collective unconscious.

Unconscious processes

It is not only consciousness that is important. Alongside the global workspace of consciousness, unconscious processes are constantly active. The proto-self continues to monitor what is taking place in the body, and perception is always watching for cues that something needs attention. Memories are constantly being activated in the unconscious. The first two levels of the hierarchal dynamical systems described above are going on in the background. It is the third level, the process of symbolisation and the accompanying meaning within the life situation, which is required for full extended consciousness.

I attribute the gentle changes within the ego-complex to this constant monitoring of the body and the environment. Because we are dealing with an open system, objects may be perceived, or bodily sensations felt, which change one's stream of consciousness without one actually becoming aware of them. Once extended consciousness develops, either within an individual or a species, it functions all of the time except during periods of deep sleep (and even then hearing and touch continue). So the conscious self is occupied with an endless, unimportant personal narrative until either the will or something perceived disturbs the stream of thought. Jung explained this as the unconscious complexes lacking the psychic energy necessary to become fully conscious (Jung 1946/1954: para. 363). He identified emotion as supplying the missing psychic energy (Jung 1938/1954: para. 179). During the constant flux of complexes they go through the first two hierarchal levels of constellation, but never reach level three. However, their influence continues in the background, affecting perception, levels of awareness, memories and feelings experienced.

Coordination/synchronisation over multiple layers

Any one of the constellation of a complex, of an archetype, or an act of will can align unconscious and conscious processing and lead to consciousness. The process is started by awareness, either deliberately or as an instinctive reaction. It continues when perception triggers an instinct and related emotion, there is a corresponding change in the levels of awareness and energy in the body, and principally implicit memories are activated. From this a symbolic image emerges, putting the situation in context of the individual life. Through circular causality this meaning enslaves the system of mind and body. It culminates when the three levels of processing, corresponding to the various layers of the self (e.g. the visual self, emotional self, motor self) are synchronised into a global workspace.

The proto/emotional self, together with the means of its control and expression learned during the first 15 months and now incorporated in the basic psychic landscape, gives the feeling of emotional consistency, i.e. relatively fixed instinctual patterns of emotions which are evoked in interpersonal relationships.

These established patterns of self-referential processing, along with the autobiographical narrative, provide the experience of coherence and continuity, i.e. the feeling of being the same over time.

Note

1 'The critical point is that when such a systematic set of tokens becomes available, it allows a shift in mnemonic strategy that results in a radical transformation in the mode of representation' (Deacon 1997: 89).

References

Note: *CW* = *The Collected Works of C.G. Jung*

When two dates are given, the first is the date of the original publication, independent of the language of publication. The second is the date of the first publication of the *CW* in which the article appears. Original titles are given when known.

Achard, Sophie, Raymond Salvador, Brandon Whitcher, John Suckling, and Ed Bullmore (2006). 'A resilient, low-frequency, small-world human brain functional network with highly connected association cortical hubs'. *Journal of Neuroscience*. 26(1): 63–72; doi: 10.1523/JNEUROSCI.3874-05.2006.

Adolphs, R, D. Tranel, A.R. Damasio (1998). 'The human amygdala in social judgment'. *Nature* 393: 470–74.

Alberts, J.R. (1987). 'Early learning and ontogenetic adaptation'. In: *Perinatal development: A psychobiological perspective* (N.A. Krasnegor, E.M. Blass, M.A. Hofer and W.P. Smotherman, editors) pp. 11–37. Orlando, FL: Academic Press.

Allain, H., M. Bourin, J.M. Reymann, D. Bentue-Ferrer, A. Patat, S. Schuck and A. Lieury (1999). 'Emotion, anxiolysis and memory'. *Human Psychopharmacology: Clinical and Experimental*. 14: 80–6.

Allefeld Carsten, P. beim Graben, Jiri Wackermann and H. Atmanspacher (2008). 'Identifying emergent states from EEG dynamics'. *FENS Forum Abstracts*. 4: 056.2.

Allefeld, Carsten, H. Atmanspacher and Jiri Wackermann (2009). 'Mental states as macrostates emerging from EEG dynamics'. *Chaos*. 19(1).

Amit, Daniel J. (1989). *Modeling brain function: The world of attractor neural networks*. Cambridge: Cambridge University Press.

Andersen C.M. (2000). 'From molecules to mind: how vertically convergent fractal time fluctuations unify cognition and emotion'. *Consciousness and Emotion*. 1: 193–226. doi: 10.1075/ce.1.2.02and.

Anderson, Stephen J. and Martin A. Conway (1997). 'Representations of autobiographical memories'. In: *Cognitive models of memory* (Martin A. Conway, editor) pp. 217–46. Hove: Psychology Press.

Anisfeld, Moshe (1996). 'Only tongue protrusion modeling is matched by neonates'. *Developmental Review*. 16: 149–61.

Atmanspacher, Harald and Peter beim Graben (2007). 'Contextual emergence of mental states from neurodynamics'. *Chaos and Complexity Letters*. 2(2/3): 151–68.

Austin, James H. (1999). *Zen and the brain*. Cambridge, MA, London: MIT Press.

Avital, Eytan and Eva Jablonka (2000). *Animal traditions: Behavioural inheritance in evolution.* Cambridge, MA: Cambridge University Press.

Aziz-Zadeh, Lisa, Jonas T. Kaplan, and Marco Iacoboni (2009). '"Aha!": The Neural Correlates of Verbal Insight Solutions'. *Human Brain Mapping.* 30: 908–916.

Baars, Bernard J. (1988). *A cognitive theory of consciousness.* Cambridge, MA: Cambridge University Press.

——(1997a). *In the theater of consciousness: The workspace of the mind.* Berkeley, California: The Wright Institute.

——(1997b) 'Contrastive phenomenology: A thoroughly empirical approach to consciousness'. In: *The nature of consciousness: Philosophical debates* (Ned Block, Owen Flanagan and Güven Güzeldere, editors) pp. 187–201. Cambridge, MA: MIT Press.

——(2005). *Global workspace theory of consciousness: toward a cognitive neuroscience of human experience.* San Diego, CA: The Neurosciences Institute.

Bachevalier, J. (2000). 'The amygdala, social cognition, and autism'. In: *The amygdala: a functional analysis* (J.P. Aggleton, editor) pp. 509–43. New York: Oxford UP.

Baddeley, Alan D., Michael W. Eysenck, Michael Anderson (2009). *Memory.* East Sussex: Psychology Press Ltd.

Baker, B.S. (2001). 'Are complex behaviors specified by dedicated regulatory genes?' *Reasoning from Drosophila Cell.* 105: 13–24.

Bauman, M.D., P. Lavenex, W. A. Mason, J.P. Capitanio and D.G. Amaral (2004). 'The development of mother–infant interactions after neonatal amygdala lesions in rhesus monkeys'. *The Journal of Neuroscience.* 24(3): 711–21.

Beauregard Mario, Johanne Lévesque and Pierre Bourgoulin (2001). 'Neural correlates of conscious self-regulation of emotion'. *The Journal of Neuroscience.* 21: 1–6.

Beebe, Beatrice and Frank M. Lachmann (2002). *Infant research and adult treatment: co-constructing interactions.* Hillsdale, N.J.: The Analytic Press.

Beggs J.M. and D. Plenz (2003). 'Neuronal avalanches in neocortical circuits'. *Journal of Neuroscience.* 23: 11167–77.

——(2004). 'Neuronal avalanches are diverse and precise activity patterns that are stable for many hours in cortical slice cultures'. *Journal of Neuroscience.* 24: 5216–29. doi: 10.1523/JNEUROSCI.0540–04.2004.

Begley, Sharon (2008). *Train your mind, change your brain: how a new science reveals our extraordinary potential to transform ourselves.* New York: Ballantine Books. First published 2007 by Mind and Life Institute.

Benton, D., P.Y. Parker and R.T. Donohoe (1996). 'The supply of glucose to the brain and cognitive functioning'. *Journal of Biosocial Science.* 28: 463–79.

Bernard, Luther Lee (1924). 'The classification of instincts.' Chapter 8 in *Instinct: A study in social psychology.* pp. 148–71. New York: Henry Holt and Co.

Bertenthal, Bennett I. and Matthew R. Longo (2007). 'Is there evidence of a mirror system from birth?' *Developmental Science.* 10(5): 526–9.

Blaney, P.H. (1986). 'Affect and memory: A review'. *Psychological Bulletin.* 99(2): 229–46.

Blasi, Augusto and Robert J. Oresick (1987). 'Self-inconsistency and the development of the self'. In: *The book of the self* (Young-Eisendrath, editor). New York: New York University Press.

Bleuler, Eugene (1911/1950). *Dementia Praecox oder Gruppe der Schizophrenien/Dementia Praecox or the Group of Schizophrenias.* New York: International Universities Press.

Boes, Aaron D., Daniel Tranel, Steven W. Anderson and Peg Nopoulos (2008). 'Right anterior cingulate cortex volume is a neuroanatomical correlate of aggression and defiance in boys'. *Behavioral Neuroscience.* 122(3): 677–84.

Booch, Grady (1994). *Object-oriented analysis and design: With applications.* Redwood City, California: The Benjamin/Cummings Publishing Company, Inc.

Bovensiepen, Gustav (2006). 'Attachment-dissociation network: some thought about a modern complex theory'. *Journal of Analytical Psychology.* 51(3): 451–66.

Bowlby, John (1973). *Attachment and loss. Vol. 2: Separation.* London: The Hogarth Press.

Brefczynski-Lewis, J.A., A. Lutz, H.S. Schaefer, D.B. Levinson and R.J. Davidson (2007). 'Neural correlates of attentional expertise in long-term meditation practitioners'. *Proceeds of the National Academy of Science* 104(27): 11483–88.

Bridgeman, Bruce (1996). 'What we really know about consciousness: Review of "A cognitive theory of consciousness"'. *Psyche.* 2(30).

Brooke, Roger (1991a). *Jung and phenomenology.* London and New York: Routledge.

——(1991b). 'Psychic complexity and human existence: A phenomenological approach'. *Journal of Analytical Psychology.* 36: 500–18.

Broucek F.J. (1982). 'Shame and its relationship to early narcissistic developments'. *International Journal of Psycho-Analysis.* 63: 369–78.

Browne, Chris, Richard Evans, Nick Sales and Igor Aleksander (1997). 'Consciousness and neural cognizers: A review of some recent approaches'. *Neural Networks.* 10(7): 1307–16.

Bruce, Darryl (2001). 'Fifty years since Lashley's In Search of the Engram'. *Journal of the History of the Neurosciences.* 10(3): 308–18

Bruner, J. (1986). *Child's talk.* New York: W.W. Norton.

Buckner, Randy L. (2010). 'Human functional connectivity: New tools, unresolved questions'. *Proceedings of the National Academy of Sciences.* 15 June 2010, 107(24): 10769–70.

Butterworth, G. (1990). 'Self-perception in infancy'. In: *The self in transition: From infancy to childhood* (D. Cicchetti and M. Beeghly, editors) pp. 119–38. University of Chicago Press, Chicago.

Cambray, Joseph (2006). 'Towards the feeling of emergence'. *Journal of Analytical Psychology.* 51(1): 1–20.

——(2009). *Synchronicity: Nature and psyche in an interconnected universe.* Carolyn and Ernest Fay Series in Analytical Psychology. College Station: Texas A & M University Press.

——(2010). 'Emergence and the self'. In: *Jungian psychoanalysis* (Murray Stein, editor) pp. 53–66. Chicago: Open Court Publishing Company.

Campbell, Joseph (1988). *The power of myth,* Tape 2 'The message of the myth'. Mystic Fire Audio.

Carter, Rita (1998). *Mapping the mind.* Berkeley: University of California Press.

Caserta F., H.E. Stanley, W.D. Eldred, G. Daccord, R.E. Hausman and J. Nittmann (1990). 'Physical mechanisms underlying neurite outgrowth: a quantitative analysis of neuronal shape'. *Physical Review Letters.* 64: 95–8. doi: 10.1103/PhysRevLett.64.95.

Campbell, Joseph (1988). The power of myth, Tape 2 'The message of the myth'. Mystic Fire Audio.

Chalmers, David (1995). 'Facing up to the problem of consciousness'. *Journal of Consciousness Studies.* 2 (3): 200–19.

Christianson, Sven-Ake (1992). 'Emotional stress and eyewitness memory: A critical review'. *Psychological Bulletin.* 112(2): 284–309.

Ciompi, L. (1991). 'Affects as central organizing and integrating factors: A new psychological/biological model of the psyche'. *British Journal of Psychiatry.* 159: 97–105.

Cohen, N.J. and L. Squire (1980). 'Preserved learning and retention of pattern-analyzing skill in amnesia: Dissociation of knowing how and knowing that'. *Science* 210: 207–9.

Conway, C.M. and M.H. Christiansen (2006). 'Statistical learning within and between modalities: Pitting abstract against stimulus-specific representations'. *Psychological Science* 17(10): 905–12.

Coopersmith, R. and M. Leon (1986). 'Enhanced neural responses by adult rats to odors experienced early in life'. *Brain Research* 37: 400–3.

Cope, Theo A. (2006). *Fear of Jung: The complex doctrine and emotional science.* London: Karnac.

Costa, M.E., M. Sigman and F. Bonomo. (2009). 'Scale-invariant transition probabilities in free word association trajectories'. *Frontiers in Integrative Neuroscience*: 3(19). Published online 2009 September 11. Prepublished online 2009 June 12. doi: 10.3389/neuro.07.019.2009

Courage Mary L. and Mark L. Howe (2002). 'From infant to child: The dynamics of cognitive change in the second year of life'. *Psychological Bulletin* 128(2): 250–77.

Damasio, Antonio (1994). *Descartes' error: Emotion, reason, and the human brain.* New York: Penguin Putnam.

——(1999a). *The feeling of what happens: Body, emotion and the making of consciousness.* London: Vintage.

——(1999b). 'Commentary'. *Neuro-psychoanalysis* 1: 38–9.

——(2000). 'A neurobiology for consciousness'. In: *Neural correlates of consciousness: Empirical and conceptual questions.* (Thomas Metzinger, editor) pp. 111–20. Cambridge, MA: MIT Press.

——(2003). *Looking for Spinoza: Joy, sorrow, and the feeling brain.* Orlando: Harcourt, Inc.

——(2010). *Self comes to mind.* New York: Pantheon Books.

Damasio, A.R. and D. Tranel (1988). 'Domain-specific amnesia for social knowledge'. *Neuroscience Abstracts* 14: 1289.

Dapretto, Mirella, Mari S. Davies, Jennifer H. Pfeifer, Ashley A. Scott, Marian Sigman, Susan Y. Bookheimer and Marco Iacoboni (2005). 'Understanding emotions in others: Mirror neuron dysfunction in children with autism spectrum disorders'. *Nature Neuroscience.* doi: 10.1038/nn1611.

Darwin, Charles (1872). *The expression of the emotions in man and animals.* London: John Murray.

Deacon, Terrence W. (1997). *The symbolic species: The co-evolution of language and brain.* New York and London: W.W. Norton and Company.

de Briun, J.P.C. (1990). 'Social behaviour and the prefrontal cortex'. *Progress in Brain Research* 85: 485–500.

de Casper, A. and W. Fifer (1980). 'Of human bonding: newborns prefer their mothers' voices'. *Science.* 208: 1174.

de Casper, A. and M. Spence (1986). 'Prenatal maternal speech influences newborn's perception of speech sounds'. *Infant Behaviour and Development.* 9: 133–50.

Dehaene, Stanislas and Naccache Lionel (2001). 'Towards a cognitive neuroscience of consciousness: basic evidence and a workspace framework'. *Cognition.* 79: 1–37.

Dehaene, Stanislas and Jean Pierre Changeux (2004). 'Neural mechanisms for access to consciousness'. In: *The cognitive neurosciences III* (Michael Gazzaniga, editor-in-chief) pp. 1145–58. Cambridge, MA: MIT Press.

del Castillo J. and B. Katz (1954). 'Quantal components of the end plate potential'. *Journal of Physiology.* 124: 560–573.

Del Cul, Antoine, Sylvain Baillet and Stanislas Dehaene (2007). 'Brain dynamics underlying the nonlinear threshold for access to consciousness'. *Plos Biology* 5(10). Open access. www.plosbiology.org.

Dennett, Daniel (1984). 'Cognitive wheels: The frame problem of A.I.' In: *Mind, machines and evolution* (C. Hookway, editor). Cambridge: Cambridge University Press.

——(1991). *Consciousness explained.* Boston: Little Brown and Company.

Dennett, Daniel and M. Kinsbourn (1992). 'Time and the observer: The where and when of consciousness in the brain'. *Behavioral and Brain Sciences.* 15: 183–247.

Diamond, Adele (1990). 'Rate of maturation of the hippocampus and the developmental progression of children's performance on the delayed non-matching to sample and visual paired comparison tasks'. *Annals of the New York Academy of Sciences.* 608: 394–433.

Dieckmann, Hans (1991/1999). *Complexes: Diagnosis and therapy in analytical psychology.* Originally published in 1991 as *Komplexe: Diagnostik und Therapie in der analytischen Psychologie* (1991). Wilmette, Illinois: Chiron Publications.

Dietrich, Arne (2004). 'The cognitive neuroscience of creativity'. *Psychonomic Bulletin & Review.* 11(6): 1011–26.

DSM-IV-TR (2000). *Diagnostic and statistical manual of mental disorders,* Fourth edition, Text Revision. Washington D.C.: The American Psychiatric Association.

Dubuc Bruno (2002). *The brain from top to bottom.* (McGill University website developed, researched and written by Bruno Dubuc). http://www.thebrain.mcgill.ca/flash/index_d.html.

Easterbrook, J.A. (1959). 'The effect of emotion on cue utilization and the organization of behaviour'. *Psychological Review.* 66(3): 183–201.

Edelman, Gerald M. (2004). *Wider than the sky: A revolutionary view of consciousness.* London: Penguin Books.

Edelman, Gerald M. and Giulio Tononi (2000a). *A universe of consciousness: how matter becomes imagination.* New York: Basic Books.

——(2000b). 'Reentry and the dynamic core: Neural correlates of conscious experience'. In: *Neural correlates of consciousness: Empirical and conceptual questions* (Thomas Metzinger, editor) pp. 139–51. Cambridge, MA: MIT Press.

Edinger, Edward (1972). *Ego and archetype.* Boston and London: Shambhala.

——(1984). *The creation of consciousness: Jung's myth for modern man.* Toronto: Inner City Books.

——(1985). *Anatomy of the psyche.* La Salle, IL: Open Court.

Ekstrom, Soren (2004). 'The mind beyond our immediate awareness: Freudian, Jungian, and cognitive models of the unconscious'. *Journal of Analytical Psychology.* 49(5): 657–82.

Eliasmith, Chris (2007). 'Attractor networks'. *Scholarpedia.* 2(10): 1380.

Eliot, Lise (1999). *What's going on in there? How the brain and mind develop in the first five years of life.* New York, Toronto, London, Sydney, Auckland: Bantam Books.

Elman, Jeffrey L., E.A. Bates, M.H. Johnson, A. Karmiloff-Smith, D. Parisi and K. Plunkett (1999). *Rethinking innateness: A connectionist perspective on development.* Cambridge, MA and London: MIT Press.

Emery N.J. and D.G. Amaral (2000). 'The role of the primate amygdala in social cognition'. In: *Cognitive neuroscience of emotion. Series in affective science* (R.D. Lane and L. Nadel, editors). pp 156–91. New York: Oxford UP.

Encyclopædia Britannica (2006). 'Instinct' Encyclopædia Britannica. Ultimate Reference Suite DVD.

Erdmann Erika and David Stover (1991). *Beyond a world divided: Human values in the brain-mind science of Roger Sperry.* San Jose: Authors Choice Press.

Falck-Ytter Terje, Gustaf Gredeback and Claes von Hofsten (2006). 'Infants predict other people's action goals'. *Nature Neuroscience.* 9(7): 878–9.

Fell, Juergen (2004). 'Identifying neural correlates of consciousness: The state space approach'. *Consciousness and Cognition*. 13: 709–29.

Field, T., R. Woodson, R. Greenberg and D. Cohen (1982). 'Discrimination and imitation of facial expressions by neonates'. *Science*. 218: 179–81.

Fiser, J. and R.N. Aslin (1996). 'Statistical learning by 8-month-old infants'. *Science* 274: 1926–8.

Fivush, Robyn and Katherine Nelson (2004). 'Culture and language in the emergence of autobiographical memory'. *Psychological Science*. American Psychological Society. 15(9): 573–7.

Fodor, Jerry Alan (1983). *The modularity of mind*. Cambridge, MA: MIT Press.

Fordham, Michael (1974). 'Defences of the self'. *Journal of Analytical Psychology*. 19(2): 192–99.

Freeman, Walter J. (1991). 'The physiology of perception'. *Scientific American*. 264(2): 78–85.

——(1997). 'Nonlinear neurodynamics of intentionality'. *Journal of Mind and Behavior* 18(2–3): 291–304.

——(1999). *How brains make up their minds*. London: Weidenfeld and Nicolson.

Freeman, Walter J. (2000a). 'Brain dynamics: Brain chaos and intentionality'. In: *Integrative neuroscience: Bridging together biological, psychological and clinical models of the human brain* (Evian Gordon, editor) pp. 163–71. Sydney: Harwood Academic Publishers.

——(2000b). 'Emotion is essential to all intentional behaviours'. In: *Emotion, development, and self-organization: Dynamic systems approaches to emotional development* (Marc D. Lewis and Isabela Granic, editors) pp. 209–35. Cambridge: Cambridge University Press.

Freeman, Walter J. and Giuseppe Vitiello (2005). 'Nonlinear brain dynamics as macroscopic manifestation of underlying many-body field dynamics'. *Physics of Live Reviews*. 3(2): 93–118.

Frey-Rohn, Liliane (1974). *From Freud to Jung: A comparative study of the psychology of the unconscious*. (Fred E. Engreen and Evelyn K. Engreen, translators). New York: G.P. Putnam's Sons.

Friston, Karl, J. Kilner and L. Harrison (2006). 'A free energy principle for the brain'. *Journal of Physiology* 100: 70–87.

Gallese, Vittorio, Christian Keysers and Giacomo Rizzolatti (2004). 'A unifying view of the basis of social cognition'. *Trends in Cognitive Sciences*. 8(9): 396–403.

Gallese Vittorio and George Lakoff (2005). 'The brain's concept: The role of the sensory-motor system in conceptual knowledge'. *Cognitive Neuropsychology*. 22(3/4): 455–479.

Gilden D.L. (1997). 'Fluctuations in the time required for elementary decisions'. *Psychological Science*. 8: 296–301. doi: 10.1111/j.1467–9280.1997.tb00441.x.

——(2001). 'Cognitive emissions of 1/f noise'. *Psychological Review*. 108: 33–56. doi: 10.1037/0033–295X.108.1.33.

Gliga, Teodora and Gergely Csibra (2007). 'Seeing the face through the eyes: A delevopmental perspective on face expertise'. Central European University, Budapest, http://web.ceu.hu/phil/csibra/papers/gliga_csibra2007.pdf.

Grandjean, Didier, David Sander and Klaus R. Scherer (2008). 'Conscious emotional experience emerges as a function of multilevel, appraisal-driven response synchronization'. *Consciousness and Cognition*. 17: 484–95.

Greenspan, Stanley I. And Stuart G. Shanker (2004). *The first idea: How symbols, language, and intelligence evolved from our primate ancestors to modern humans*. U.S.A.: Da Capo Press.

Haken, Herman (1983). *Synergetics: An introduction: Nonequilibrium phase transitions and self-organization in physics, chemistry, and biology*. New York: Springer-Verlag.

——(1988/2000). *Information and self-organization*. Berlin, Heidelberg, New York: Springer.

——(1996). *Principles of brain functioning: A synergetic approach to brain activity, behavior and cognition*. Berlin, Heidelberg, New York: Springer-Verlag.

Haken, H., J.A.S. Kelso and H. Bunz (1985). 'A theoretical model of phase transitions in human hand movements'. *Biological Cybernetics*. 51, 347–56.

Hayne, Harlene and Gabrielle Simcock (2009). 'Memory development in toddlers'. In: *The development of memory in infancy and childhood* (Mary L. Courage and Nelson Cowan, editors) pp. 43–68. Hove and New York: Psychology Press.

Hebb, D.O. (1949). *The organization of behavior*. New York: Wiley & Sons.

Hermans, H.J., H.J.G. Kempen and R.J.P. van Loon. (1992). 'The dialogical self: Beyond individualism and rationalism'. *American Psychologist*. 47: 23–33.

Hilgetag C.C. and M. Kaiser (2004). 'Clustered organization of cortical connectivity'. *Neuroinformatics*. 2: 353–60. doi: 10.1385/NI:2:3:353.

Hillman, James (1962). *Emotion: A comprehensive phenomenology of theories and their meanings for therapy*. London: Routledge.

Hinde, R. (1990). 'Causes of social development from the perspective of an integrated developmental science'. In: *Causes of development* (G. Butterworth and P. Bryant, editors) pp. 161–85. Hillsdale NJ: Lawrence Erlbaum Associates.

Hirai, Masahiro and Kazuo Hiraki (2005). 'An event-related potentials study of biological motion perception in human infants'. *Cognitive Brain Research*. 22: 301–4.

Hobson, J.A., E.F. Pace-Schott and R. Stickgold (2000). 'Dreaming and the brain: Toward a cognitive neuroscience of conscious states'. *Behavioral and Brain Sciences*. 23: 793–842.

Hogenson, George B. (2001). 'The Baldwin effect: A neglected influence on C.G. Jung's evolutionary thinking'. *Journal of Analytical Psychology*. 46(4): 591–611.

——(2004). 'What are symbols symbols of? Situated action, mythological bootstrapping and the emergence of the self'. *Journal of Analytical Psychology*. 49(1): 67–81.

——(2005). 'The Self, the symbolic and synchronicity: virtual realities and the emergence of the psyche'. *Journal of Analytical Psychology*. 50(3): 271–84.

Howe Mark L., Mary L. Courage and Maki Rooksby (2009). 'The genesis and development of autobiographical memory'. In: *The development of memory in infancy and childhood* (Mary L. Courage and Nelson Cowan, editors) pp. 177–96. Hove and New York: Psychology Press.

Hunt, Harry T. (1995). *On the nature of consciousness: Cognitive, phenomenological and transpersonal perspectives*. New Haven and London: Yale University Press.

Internet Encyclopedia of Science. http://www.daviddarling.info/encyclopedia/G/globus_pallidus.html

Izard, Carroll E., Brian P. Ackerman, Kristen M. Schoff and Sarah E. Fine (2000). 'Self-organization of discrete emotions, emotion patterns, and emotion-cognition relations'. In: *Emotion, development, and self-organization: Dynamic systems approaches to emotional development* (Marc D. Lewis and Isabela Granic, editors) pp. 15–36. Cambridge: Cambridge University Press.

Jacobi, Jolande (1959). *Complex/archetype/symbol in the psychology of C.G. Jung*. (Ralph Mannheim, translator). New York: Putnam and Sons.

——(1962). *The psychology of C.G. Jung*. New Haven and London: Yale University Press.

Jacoby, Mario (1999). *Jungian psychotherapy and contemporary infant research: Basic patterns of emotional exchange*. London and New York: Routledge.

Jaffé, Aniela (1970/1984). *The myth of meaning in the work of C.G. Jung*. (Translated from the German.) Zurich: Daimon Verlag.

James, William (1887). What is instinct? *Schribners Magazine*. I: 355–65.

——(1890/1950). *The principles of psychology, volume one.* First published by Henry Holt & Co., current edition New York: Dover Publications, Inc.

Jaynes, Julian (1976). *The origin of consciousness in the breakdown of the bicameral mind.* Boston: Houghton Mifflin Company.

Jensen O., J. Kaiser and JP. Lachaux (2007). 'Human gamma-frequency oscillations associated with attention and memory'. *Trends in Neuroscience.* 30(7): 317–24.

Jernigan, T.L., D.A. Trauner, J.R. Hesselink and P.A. Tallal (1991). 'Maturation of human cerebrum observed in vivo during adolescence'. *Brain.* 114: 2037–49.

Johnson, M.H. and J. Morton (1991). *Biology and cognitive development: The case of face recognition.* Oxford: Blackwell.

Johnston, Elizabeth (1997). *Investigating minds.* Online lecture notes chapter 8 Infantile Amnesia. Department of Psychology. Sarah Lawrence College. http://pages.slc.edu/~ebj/IM_97/Lecture6/L6.html, accessed 30 October 2011.

Jones, Dan (2007). 'The depth of disgust'. *Nature.* 447: 768–71.

Jung, C.G. (1907). 'On the psychophysical relations of the association experiment'. *Experimental Research* (Sir Herbert Read, Michael Fordham, Gerhard Adler, editors; William McGuire. Leopold Stein in collaboration with Diana Rivère, translator. (1973)) *CW* 2: 483–91. London: Routledge.

——(1907–8). 'Further investigations on the galvanic phenomenon and respiration in normal and insane individuals'. *Experimental Research* (Sir Herbert Read, Michael Fordham, Gerhard Adler, editors; William McGuire. Leopold Stein in collaboration with Diana Rivère, translator. (1973)) *CW* 2: 483–91. London: Routledge.

——(1907/1960). 'The psychology of dementia praecox'. *The psychogenesis of mental disease* (R.F.C. Hull, translator. (1960)), *CW* 3: 1–151. The Bollingen Foundation. New York: Pantheon Books, Inc.

——(1909/1949). 'The significance of the father in the destiny of the individual'. *Freud and psychoanalysis* (Sir Herbert Read, Michael Fordham and Gerjard Adler, editors. R.F.C. Hull, translator (1961)), *CW* 4: 301–23. the Bollingen Foundation. New York: Pantheon Books.

——(1912/1943). 'New paths in psychology'. *Two essays on analytical psychology* (Sir Herbert Read, Michael Fordham and Gerhard Adler, editors. R.F.C. Hull, translator. (1953/1966)), *CW* 7: 245–68. London: Routledge.

——(1912/1956). *Symbols of transformation: An analysis of the prelude to a case of schizophrenia* (R.C.F. Hull, translator. (1956)). *CW* 5. London: Routledge and Kegan Paul

——(1913/1955). 'The theory of psychoanalysis' (originally published in German with the title 'Versuch einer Darstellung der psychanalytischen Theorie'). *Freud and psychoanalysis* (Sir Herbert Read, Michael Fordham and Gerjard Adler, editors. R.F.C. Hull, translator. (1961)), *CW* 4: 83–226. The Bollingen Foundation. New York: Pantheon Books.

——(1916/1953). 'The relations between the ego and the unconscious'. *Two essays on analytical psychology* (Sir Herbert Read, Michael Fordham and Gerhard Adler, editors. R.F.C. Hull, translator. (1953/1966)), *CW* 7: 123–241. London: Routledge.

——(1917/1953) 'On the psychology of the unconscious'. *Two essays on analytical psychology* (Sir Herbert Read, Michael Fordham and Gerhard Adler, editors. R.F.C. Hull, translator. (1953/1966)), *CW* 7: 1–119. London: Routledge.

——(1919). 'Instinct and the unconscious'. *The structure and dynamics of the psyche,* (Sir Herbert Read, Michael Fordham, Gerhard Adler and William McGuire, editors. R.F.C. Hull, translator. (1960/1969)), *CW* 8: 129–38. The Bollingen Foundation. Princeton N.J.: Princeton University Press.

——(1920/1948). 'The psychological foundations of belief in spirits'. *The structure and dynamics of the psyche* (Sir Herbert Read, Michael Fordham, Gerhard Adler and William McGuire, editors. R.F.C. Hull, translator. (1960/1969)) *CW* 8: 301–18. The Bollingen Foundation. Princeton N.J.: Princeton University Press.

——(1921/1928). 'The therapeutic value of abreaction'. *The practice of psychotherapy* (Sir Herbert Read, Michael Fordham, Gerhard Adler and William McGuire, editors. R.F.C. Hull, translator. (1954/1966)) *CW* 16: 125–38. The Bollingen Foundation. Princeton N.J.: Princeton University Press.

——(1921/1971). *Psychological types* (Sir Herbert Read, Michael Fordham, Gerhard Adler and William McGuire, editors. R.F.C. Hull, a revisions of the translation by H.G. Baynes) *CW* 6. London: Routledge.

——(1922/1928). 'On the relation of analytical psychology to poetry'. *The spirit in man, art, and literature* (Sir Herbert Read, Michael Fordham, Gerhard Adler and William McGuire, editors. R.F.C. Hull, translator. (1966)) *CW* 15: 65–83. The Bollingen Foundation. Princeton N.J.: Princeton University Press.

——(1923/1954). 'Child development and education'. *The development of personality* (Sir Herbert Read, Michael Fordham, Gerhard Adler and William McGuire, editors. R.F.C. Hull, translator. (1954)) *CW* 17: 47–62. London: Routledge.

——(1926). 'Foreword to third edition: The significance of the father in the destiny of the individual'. *Freud and psychoanalysis* (Sir Herbert Read, Michael Fordham and Gerjard Adler, editors. R.F.C. Hull, translator. (1961)), *CW* 4: 302. The Bollingen Foundation. New York: Pantheon Books.

——(1926/1960). 'Spirit and life'. *The structure and dynamics of the psyche* (Sir Herbert Read, Michael Fordham, Gerhard Adler and William McGuire, editors. R.F.C. Hull, translator. (1960/1969)) *CW* 8: 319–37. The Bollingen Foundation. Princeton N.J.: Princeton University Press.

——(1927/1931a). 'Mind and earth'. *Civilization in transition* (Sir Herbert Read, Michael Fordham, Gerhard Adler and William McGuire, editors. R.F.C. Hull, translator. (1964/1970)) *CW* 10: 29–49. The Bollingen Foundation. Princeton N.J.: Princeton University Press

——(1927/1931b). 'The structure of the psyche'. *The structure and dynamics of the psyche* (Sir Herbert Read, Michael Fordham, Gerhard Adler and William McGuire, editors. R.F.C. Hull, translator. (1960/1969)) *CW* 8: 139–58. The Bollingen Foundation. Princeton N.J.: Princeton University Press.

——(1928). 'Mental disease and the psyche'. *The psychogenesis of mental disease* (Sir Herbert Read, Michael Fordham, Gerhard Adler and William McGuire, editors. R.F.C. Hull, translator. (1960)), *CW* 3: 226–31. The Bollingen Foundation. New York: Pantheon Books, Inc.

——(1928/1948). 'On psychic energy'. *The structure and dynamics of the psyche* (Sir Herbert Read, Michael Fordham, Gerhard Adler and William McGuire, editors. R.F.C. Hull, translator. (1960/1969)) *CW* 8: 3–66. The Bollingen Foundation. Princeton N.J.: Princeton University Press

——(1930/1933). 'The stages of life'. *The structure and dynamics of the psyche* (Sir Herbert Read, Michael Fordham, Gerhard Adler and William McGuire, editors. R.F.C. Hull, translator. (1960/1969)) *CW* 8: 387–403. The Bollingen Foundation. Princeton N.J.: Princeton University Press.

——(1930/1950). 'Psychology and literature'. *The spirit in man, art, and literature* (Sir Herbert Read, Michael Fordham, Gerhard Adler and William McGuire, editors. R.F.C.

Hull, translator. (1966)) *CW* 15: 84–105. The Bollingen Foundation. Princeton N.J.: Princeton University Press.

——(1934/1948). 'A review of the complex theory'. *The structure and dynamics of the psyche* (Sir Herbert Read, Michael Fordham, Gerhard Adler and William McGuire, editors. R.F.C. Hull, translator. (1960/1969)) *CW* 8: 92–105. The Bollingen Foundation. Princeton N.J.: Princeton University Press.

——(1935/1953). 'Psychological commentary on "The Tibetan book of the dead"'. *Psychology and religion: West and east* (Sir Herbert Read, Michael Fordham, Gerhard Adler and William McGuire, editors. R.F.C. Hull, translator. (1958/1969)) *CW* 11: 509–26. The Bollingen Foundation. Princeton N.J.: Princeton University Press.

——(1935a). 'The Tavistock lectures'. *The symbolic life* (Sir Herbert Read, Michael Fordham, Gerhard Adler and William McGuire, editors. R.F.C. Hull, translator. (1950/1976)) *CW* 18: 5–182. The Bollingen Foundation. Princeton N.J.: Princeton University Press.

——(1935b). 'Über Grundlagen der Analytischen Psychologie'. *Das Symbolische Leben Erste Halbband: Verschiedene Schriften.* Olten u. Freiburg im Breisgau: Walter-Verlag.

——(1935c). 'General problems of psychotherapy'. *The practice of psychotherapy* (Sir Herbert Read, Michael Fordham, Gerhard Adler and William McGuire, editors. R.F.C. Hull, translator. (1954/1966)) *CW* 16: 3–125. The Bollingen Foundation. Princeton N.J.: Princeton University Press.

——(1936/1937). 'The concept of the collective unconscious'.*The archetypes and the collective unconscious* (Sir Herbert Read, Michael Fordham, Gerhard Adler and William McGuire, editors. R.F.C. Hull, translator. (1959/1969)) *CW* 9i: 42–53. The Bollingen Foundation. Princeton N.J.: Princeton University Press.

——(1936/1942). 'Psychological factors determining human behaviour'. *The structure and dynamics of the psyche* (Sir Herbert Read, Michael Fordham, Gerhard Adler and William McGuire, editors. R.F.C. Hull, translator. (1960/1969)) *CW* 8: 114–25. The Bollingen Foundation. Princeton N.J.: Princeton University Press.

——(1936/1954). 'Concerning the archetypes, with special reference to the anima concept'. *The archetypes and the collective unconscious* (Sir Herbert Read, Michael Fordham, Gerhard Adler and William McGuire, editors. R.F.C. Hull, translator. (1959/1969)) *CW* 9i: 54–72. The Bollingen Foundation. Princeton N.J.: Princeton University Press.

——(1937/1940). 'Psychology and religion'. *Psychology and religion: West and east* (Sir Herbert Read, Michael Fordham, Gerhard Adler and William McGuire, editors. R.F.C. Hull, translator. (1958/1969)) *CW* 11: 3–106. The Bollingen Foundation. Princeton N.J.: Princeton University Press.

——(1938/1954). 'Psychological aspects of the mother archetype'. *The archetypes and the collective unconscious* (Read, Sir Herbert, Michael Fordham, Gerhard Adler and William McGuire, editors. R.F.C. Hull, translator. (1959/1969)) *CW* 9i: 75–112. The Bollingen Foundation. Princeton N.J.: Princeton University Press.

——(1939a). 'On the psychogenesis of schizophrenia'. *The psychogenesis of mental disease* (Sir Herbert Read, Michael Fordham, Gerhard Adler and William McGuire, editors. R.F.C. Hull, translator. (1960)) *CW* 3: 233–49. The Bollingen Foundation. New York: Pantheon Books, Inc.

——(1939b). 'Foreword to Suzuki's 'Introduction to Zen Buddhism''. *Psychology and religion: West and east* (Sir Herbert Read, Michael Fordham, Gerhard Adler and William McGuire, editors. R.F.C. Hull, translator. (1958/1969)) *CW* 11: 538–57. The Bollingen Foundation. Princeton N.J.: Princeton University Press.

——(1939/1954). 'Psychological commentaries on 'The Tibetan book of the great liberation''. *Psychology and religion: West and east* (Sir Herbert Read, Michael Fordham, Gerhard Adler and William McGuire, editors. R.F.C. Hull, translator. (1958/1969)) *CW* 11: 316–23. The Bollingen Foundation. Princeton N.J.: Princeton University Press.

——(1940/1951). 'The psychology of the child archetype'. *The archetypes and the collective unconscious* (Sir Herbert Read, Michael Fordham, Gerhard Adler and William McGuire, editors. R.F.C. Hull, translator. (1959/1969)) *CW* 9i: 151–81. The Bollingen Foundation. Princeton N.J.: Princeton University Press.

——(1940/1954). 'Transformation symbolism in the mass'. *Psychology and religion: West and East* (Sir Herbert Read, Michael Fordham, Gerhard Adler and William McGuire, editors. R.F.C. Hull, translator. (1958/1969)) *CW* 11: 201–98. The Bollingen Foundation. Princeton N.J.: Princeton University Press.

——(1942/1948). 'A psychological approach to the dogma of the trinity'. *Psychology and religion: West and East* (Sir Herbert Read, Michael Fordham, Gerhard Adler and William McGuire, editors. R.F.C. Hull, translator. (1958/1969)) *CW* 11: 107–200. The Bollingen Foundation. Princeton N.J.: Princeton University Press.

——(1942/1953). 'The spirit Mercurius'. *Alchemical studies* (Sir Herbert Read, Michael Fordham, Gerhard Adler and William McGuire, editors. R.F.C. Hull, translator. (1967)) *CW* 13: 251–349. The Bollingen Foundation. Princeton N.J.: Princeton University Press.

——(1945/1954). 'The philosophical tree'. *Alchemical studies* (Sir Herbert Read, Michael Fordham, Gerhard Adler and William McGuire, editors. R.F.C. Hull, translator. (1967)) *CW* 13: 251–349. The Bollingen Foundation. Princeton N.J.: Princeton University Press.

——(1946). 'The psychology of the transference'. *The practice of psychotherapy* (Sir Herbert Read, Michael Fordham, Gerhard Adler and William McGuire, editors. R.F.C. Hull, translator. (1954/1966)) *CW* 16: 163–323. The Bollingen Foundation. Princeton N.J.: Princeton University Press.

——(1946/1954). 'On the nature of the psyche'. *Structure and dynamics of the psyche* (Sir Herbert Read, Michael Fordham, Gerhard Adler and William McGuire, editors. R.F.C. Hull, translator. (1960/1969)) *CW* 8: 159–234. The Bollingen Foundation. Princeton N.J.: Princeton University Press.

——(1950). Foreword to Allenby: 'A psychological study of the origins of monotheism'. *The symbolic life* (Sir Herbert Read, Michael Fordham, Gerhard Adler and William McGuire, editors. R.F.C. Hull, translator. (1950/1976)) *CW* 18: 656–9. The Bollingen Foundation. Princeton N.J.: Princeton University Press

——(1952). 'Synchronicity: An acausal connecting principle'. *Structure and dynamics of the psyche* (Sir Herbert Read, Michael Fordham, Gerhard Adler and William McGuire, editors. R.F.C. Hull, translator. (1960/1969)) *CW* 8: 417–531. The Bollingen Foundation. Princeton N.J.: Princeton University Press.

——(1953). *Psychology and alchemy* (Sir Herbert Read, Michael Fordham, Gerhard Adler and William McGuire, editors. R.F.C. Hull, translator.) *CW* 12. The Bollingen Foundation. Princeton N.J.: Princeton University Press.

——(1953/1956). 'Letter to Père Bruno'. *The symbolic life* (Sir Herbert Read, Michael Fordham, Gerhard Adler and William McGuire, editors. R.F.C. Hull, translator. (1950/1976)) *CW* 18: 673–8. The Bollingen Foundation. Princeton N.J.: Princeton University Press.

——(1955–6). *Mysterium coniunctionis* (Sir Herbert Read, Michael Fordham, Gerhard Adler and William McGuire, editors. R.F.C. Hull, translator.) *CW* 14. The Bollingen Foundation. Princeton N.J.: Princeton University Press.

——(1957/1959). 'Recent thoughts on schizophrenia'. *The psychogenesis of mental disease* (Sir Herbert Read, Michael Fordham, Gerhard Adler and William McGuire, editors. R.F.C. Hull, translator. (1960)), *CW* 3: 250–5. The Bollingen Foundation. New York: Pantheon Books, Inc.

——(1958a). 'Schizophrenia'. *The psychogenesis of mental disease* (Sir Herbert Read, Michael Fordham, Gerhard Adler and William McGuire, editors. R.F.C. Hull, translator. (1960)), *CW* 3: 256–71. The Bollingen Foundation. New York: Pantheon Books, Inc.

——(1958b). 'Flying saucers'. *Civilization in transition* (Sir Herbert Read, Michael Fordham, Gerhard Adler and William McGuire, editors. R.F.C. Hull, translator. (1964/1970)) *CW* 10: 307–433. The Bollingen Foundation. Princeton N.J.: Princeton University Press.

——(1958c). 'A psychological view of conscience'. *Civilization in transition* (Sir Herbert Read, Michael Fordham, Gerhard Adler and William McGuire, editors. R.F.C. Hull, translator. (1964/1970)) *CW* 10: 437–55. The Bollingen Foundation. Princeton N.J.: Princeton University Press.

——(1959a). Foreword to *Complex/archetype/symbol in the psychology of C.G. Jung*. (Jacobi 1959) New York: Putnam and Sons.

——(1959b). *Aion* (Sir Herbert Read, Michael Fordham, Gerhard Adler and William McGuire, editors. R.F.C. Hull, translator.) *CW* 9ii. The Bollingen Foundation. Princeton N.J.: Princeton University Press

——(1961). 'Symbols and the interpretation of dreams'. *The symbolic life* (Sir Herbert Read, Michael Fordham, Gerhard Adler and William McGuire, editors. R.F.C. Hull, translator. (1950/1976)) *CW* 18: 185–264. The Bollingen Foundation. Princeton N.J.: Princeton University Press.

——(1961/1963). *Memories, dreams, reflections*. (Aniela Jaffé, recorder/editor) London: HarperCollins.

——(1971). *Psychologische Typen*, 9.ten Auflage. Olten u. Freiburg im Breisgau: Walter-Verlag.

——(1976). *C.G. Jung Letters Volume 2: 1951–1961*. (Gerhard Adler, editor, in collaboration with Aniela Jaffé. R. F. C. Hull, translator.) London: Routledge & Kegan Paul Ltd.

——(1988). *Nietzsche's Zarathustra: Notes on the seminar given in 1934–1939*. (James L. Jarrett, editor). London: Routledge.

Jung, C.G. and Wolfgang Pauli (2001). *Atom and archetype: The Pauli/Jung letters 1932–1958*. (C. A. Meier, editor) Princeton N. J.: Princeton University Press.

Jung, C.G. and Franz Riklin (1904/1919). 'The associations of normal subjects'. *Experimental Researches*. (Sir Herbert Read, Michael Fordham, Gerhard Adler, editors William McGuire. Leopold Stein in collaboration with Diana Rivère, translator. (1973)) *CW* 2: 3–196. Princeton N.J.: Princeton University Press.

Kagan, J. (1986). 'Presuppositions in developmental inquiry'. In: *Value presuppositions in theories of human development* (L. Cirillo and S. Wapner, editors) pp. 63–78. Hillsdale, NJ: Lawrence Erlbaum Associates.

Kaiser M., M. Görner and C.C. Hilgetag (2007). 'Criticality and spreading dynamics in hierarchical cluster networks without inhibition'. *New Journal of Physics*. 9: 110–23. doi: 10.1088/1367-2630/9/5/110.

Kalsched, Donald E. (1996). *The inner world of trauma: archetypal defenses of the personal spirit*. London: Routledge.

Kast, Verena (1980). *Excerpts in English from 'Das Assozuiationsexperiment in der therapeutischen Praxis'* (by Irene Gad, privately printed). Fellbach-Oeffingen: Bonz Verlag.

——(1990/1992). *The dynamics of symbols: Fundamentals of Jungian psychotherapy*. Originally published as *Die dynamic der symbole* (Susan A. Schwarz, translator). New York: Fromm International Publishing Corp.

——(1997). *Father-daughter, mother-son: Freeing ourselves from the complexes that bind us*. Rockport, MA: Element.

Kauffman, Stuart A. (1993). *The origins of order: Self organization and selection in evolution*. New York and Oxford: Oxford University Press.

Kelso, Scott (1995). *Dynamic patterns: The self-organization of brain and behavior*. Cambridge, MA: MIT Press.

Kiebel, Stefan J., Jean Daunizeau and Karl J. Friston (2008). 'A hierarchy of time-scales and the brain'. *PloS Computational Biology*. 4(11). doi: 10.1371/journal.pcbi.1000209.

Kim, Sang Hee and Stephen Hamann (2007). 'Neural correlates of positive and negative emotion regulation'. *Journal of Cognitive Neuroscience*. 19(5): 776–98.

Kitzbichler, Manfred G., Richard N.A. Henson, Marie L. Smith, Pradeep J. Nathan and Edward T. Bullmore (2011). 'Cognitive Effort Drives Workspace Configuration of Human Brain Functional Networks'. *Journal of Neuroscience*. 31(22): 8259–70.

Knox, Jean (2003). *Archetype, attachment, analysis: Jungian psychology and the emergent mind*. London and New York: Routledge.

——(2004). 'From archetypes to reflective function'. *Journal of Analytical Psychology*. 49(1): 1–19.

——(2011). *Self-agency in psychotherapy: Attachment, autonomy, and intimacy*. New York and London: W.W. Norton and Company.

Kobak, R.R. and A. Sceery (1988). 'Attachment in late adolescence: Working models, affect regulation, and representations of self and others'. *Child Development*. 59: 135–46.

Kohut, H. (1971). *The analysis of the self*. New York: International Universities Press.

Kolb, B. and I.Q. Whishaw (1990). *Fundamentals of human neuropsychology* (3rd edn). New York: W.H. Freeman.

Koyré, Alexandre (1957/2008). *From the closed world to the infinite universe*. Radford, Virginia: Wilder Publications.

Kramer, Mark A., Uri T. Eden, Kyle Q. Lepage, Eric D. Kolaczyk, Matt T. Bianchi and Syndey S. Cash (2011). 'Emergence of Persistent Networks in Long-Term Intracranial EEG Recordings'. *Journal of Neuroscience*. 31(44): 15757–67.

Krämer, Ulrike M., Sarah Büttner, Gerhard Roth, and Thomas F. Münte (2008). 'Trait Aggressiveness Modulates Neurophysiological Correlates of Laboratory-induced Reactive Aggression in Humans'. *Journal of Cognitive Neuroscience*. 20 (8): 1464–77.

Kretschmann, H.-J., G. Kammradt, I. Krauthhausen, B. Sauer and F. Wingert (1986). 'Growth of the hippocampal formation in man'. *Bibliotheca Anatomica*. 28: 27–52.

Krieger, Nancy (2012). 'Symmetry breaking and breaking into consciousness: Mirrors, metaphor, and meaning'. In: *The playful psyche: Entering chaos, coincidence, creation* (Stacy Wirth, Isabelle Meier, and John Hill, editors. Nancy Cater, consulting editor). New Orleans: Spring Journal Books.

LaBar, Kevin and Roberto Cabeza (2006). 'Cognitive neuroscience of emotional memory'. *Nature Reviews: Neuroscience*. 7: 54–64.

Lacan, Jacques (1973/1977). *The four fundamental concepts of psycho-analysis*. First published as *Le Séminaire de Jacques Lacan, Livre XI*, 'Les quatre concepts fondamentaux de la psychanalyse' (Alan Sheridan, translator). Vintage: London.

Lakoff, George and Mark Johnson (1980). *Metaphors we live by*. Chicago and London: The University of Chicago Press.

Lamme, Victor (2006). 'Towards a true neural stance on consciousness'. *Trends in Cognitive Sciences.* 10(11): 494–501.

Lane, Richard D., Eric M. Reiman, Beatrice Axelrod, Lang-Sheng Yun, Andrew Holmes, and Gary E. Schwartz (1998). 'Neural correlates of levels of emotional awareness: Evidence of an interaction between emotion and attention in the anterior cingulate cortex'. *Journal of Cognitive Neuroscience.* 10(4): 525–35.

Lashley, Karl Spencer (1950). 'In search of the engram'. In: *Society of Experimental Biology Symposium No. 4: Psysiological Mechanisms in Animal Behaviour.* Cambridge: Cambridge University Press.

Lazarus Richard S. (1991). *Emotion and adaptation.* New York: Oxford University Press.

LeDoux, Joseph (1995). 'Emotion: Clues from the brain'. *Annual Review of Psychology.* 46: 209–35.

——(1996). *The emotional brain.* New York: Simon & Schuster.

——(2002). *Synaptic self.* New York: Penguin Books.

Lehmann, D. (1989). *Microstates of the brain in EEG and ERP mapping studies.* Berlin and Heidelberg: Springer-Verlag.

Leichtman, M., Q. Wang and D. B. Pillemer (2003). *Autobiographical memory and the construction of a narrative self: Developmental and cultural perspectives* (R. Fivush and C.A. Haden, editors) pp. 73–98. Mahwash N.J.: Erlbaum.

Lenaerts, Tom, Dominique Chu and Richard Watson (2005). 'Dynamical hierarchies'. *Artificial Life.* 11: 403–5.

Lepage, Jean-François and Hugo Théoret (2007). 'The mirror neuron system: grasping others' actions from birth?' *Developmental Science.* 10(5): 513–23.

Lerner, Richard M. (2006). *Handbook of Child Psychology* Volume 1. (William Damon and Richard M. Lerner, editor). Hoboken, N.J.: John Wiley and Sons.

Le Van Quyen, M. (2003). 'Disentangling the dynamic core: a research program for a neurodynamics at the large-scale'. *Biological Research.* 36(1): 67–88. doi: 10.4067/S0716-97602003000100006

Levine, Peter (1997). *Waking the tiger: Healing trauma.* Berkeley California: North Atlantic Books.

Lewis, Marc D. (2000). 'The promise of dynamic systems approaches for an integrated account of human development'. *Child Development.* 71: 36–43.

——(2005). 'Bridging emotion theory and neurobiology through dynamic systems modeling'. *Behavioral and Brain Sciences.* 28: 169–245.

Lewis, Marc D. and Lori Douglas (1998). 'A dynamic systems approach to cognition-emotion interactions in development'. In: *What develops in emotional development?* (Michael F. Mascolo and Sharon Griffin, editors) pp. 159–88. New York: Plenum Press.

Lewis, Marc D. and Natalka Junyk (2002). 'The self-organization of psychological defences'. In: *The psychological meaning of chaos: Translating theory into practice* (Frank Masterpasqua and Phyllis A. Perna, editors) pp. 41–73. Washington D.C.: American Psychological Association.

Lewis, M., J. Jaskir and M. Enright (1986). 'Development of mental abilities in infancy'. *Intelligence.* 10: 331–54.

Lévy-Bruhl, Lucien (1910). *Les fonctions mentales dans les sociétés inférieures.* Paris: Les Presses universitaires de France. First edition.

Lichtenberg, J.D. (1992). 'Hass im Verständnis der Selbstpsychologie: Ein motivationssystemischer Ansatz'. *Sexualität und Aggression aus der Sicht der Selbstpsychologie* (C Schöttler, editor) pp. 48–76. Frankfurt/Main: Suhrkamp.

Liu, Xu, Steve Ramirez, Petti T. Pang, Corey B. Puryear, Arvind Govindarajan, Karl Deisseroth, and Susumu Tonegawa (2012). 'Optogenetic stimulation of a hippocampal engram activates fear memory recall'. *Nature*. 484: 381–5 (19 April 2012) doi: 10.1038/nature11028.

Lloyd Narianne E. and Nora S. Newcombe (2009). 'Implicit memory in childhood: Reassessing developmental invariance'. In: *The development of memory in infancy and childhood* (Mary L. Courage and Nelson Cowan, editors) pp. 93–114. Hove and New York: Psychology Press.

Lorenz, Konrad (1956). 'The objective theory of instinct'. In: *L'instinct dans la comportement des animaux et de l'homme* (P.P. Grasse, editor). Paris: Masson et Cie.

Lutz, Antoine, Lawrence L. Greischar, Nancy B. Rawlings, Mathieu Ricard and Richard J. Davidson (2004). 'Long-term meditators self-induce high-amplitude gamma synchrony during mental practice'. *Proceedings of the National Academy of Science*. 101(46): 16369–73.

Lutz, Antoine (2012). 'Le cerveau méditative'. *Cerveau & Psycho*. 52: 27–33.

MacFarlane, A. (1975). 'Olfaction in the development of social preferences in the human neonate'. In: *Parent-infant interaction* (H. Hofer, editor). Amsterdam: Elsevier.

MacLean, Paul (1969). 'A triune concept of the brain and behaniour'. In: *A triune concept of the brain and behaniour* (T.J. Boag and D. Campbell, editors) Lectures given in 1969. First published in 1973.

MacNeilage, P.F., L.J. Rogers, and G. Vallortigara (2009). 'Origins of the left and right brain'. *Scientific American*. 301: 60–7.

Mahler, Margaret, F. Pine and A. Bergman (1975). *The psychological birth of the human infant*. New York: Basic Books.

Main, Mary, N. Kaplan and J. Cassidy (1985). 'Security in infancy, childhood and adulthood: A move to the level of representation'. *Monographs of the Society for Research in Child Development*. 50: 66–104.

Maloney, Alan and George B. Hogenson (2003). 'Responses (to Archetype theory, evolutionary psychology and the Baldwin effect). *Journal of Analytical Psychology*. 48(1): 101–16.

Mangan, Bruce (1995). 'The Dead Hand: Commentary on Baar's on contrastive analysis'. *Psyche*. 1(14).

Manoli, Deven and S., Geoffrey W. Meissner and Bruce S. Baker (2006). 'Blueprints for behavior: Genetic specification of neural circuitry for innate behaviors'. *Trends in Neuroscience*. 29(8).

Marreiros, Andre C., Enno Stephan Klaas and Karl J. Friston (2010). 'Dynamic causal modeling'. *Scholarpedia*. 5(7): 9568

Martin, G. and R. Clark (1982). 'Distress crying in neonates: species and peer specificity'. *Developmental Psychology*. 18: 3–9.

McClelland, James L. and David E. Rumelhart (1985). 'Distributed memory and the representation of general and specific information'. *Journal of Experimental Psychology: General*. 114(2): 159–88.

McDougal, David, Dave Van Lieshout and John Harting (2013). 'Medical Neuroscience Unit 2 Brain Stem Superior Colliculus'. University of Wisconsin. http://www.neuroanatomy.wisc.edu/virtualbrain/BrainStem/23Colliculus.html Accessed 2 April 2013.

McDougall, W. (1910). 'Instinct and intelligence'. *British Journal of Psychology*. 3(3): 250–66. doi: 10.1111/j.2044-8295.1910.tb00204.x.

McDowell, Maxson J. (2001). 'Principle of organization: a dynamic-systems view of the archetype-as-such'. *Journal of Analytical Psychology*. 46(5): 637–54.

Meier C. A. (1984). *The unconscious in its empirical manifestations*. Volume one of *The psychology of C.G: Jung*. Boston: Sigo Press.

——(2001). *Atom and archetype: The Pauli/Jung letters 1932–1958*. C. A. Meier, editor. Princeton: Princeton University Press.

Meltzoff A. and M. Moore (1977). 'Imitation of facial and manual gestures in human neonates'. *Science*. 198: 75–8.

——(1983). 'Newborn infants imitate adult facial gestures'. *Child Development*. 54: 702–9.

——(1997). 'Explaining facial imitation: A theoretical model'. *Early Development and Parenting*. 6: 179–92.

Meunier M, J. Bachevalier, E.A. Murray, L. Malkova and M. Mishkin (1999). 'Effects of aspiration versus neurotoxic lesions of the amygdala on emotional responses in monkeys'. *European Journal of Neuroscience*. 11: 4403–4418.

Moskowitz, Andrew (2005). 'Pierre Janet's influence on Bleuler's concept of Schizophrenia'. A presentation at the First Symposium of the Pierre Janet Gesellschaft in Freiburg, Germany. 3–4 June, 2005.

Munakata Yuko (2004). 'Computational cognitive neuroscience of early memory development'. *Development Review*. 24(1): 133–53.

Nakanishi K. and F. Kukita (1998). 'Functional synapses in synchronized bursting of neocortical neurons in culture'. *Brain Research*. 795: 137–46. doi: 10.1016/S0006-8993(98)00283-2.

Neisser, Eric (2004). 'Memory development: New questions and old'. *Developmental Review*. 24(1): 154–8.

Nelson, Charles (1995). 'The ontogeny of human memory: A cognitive neuroscience perspective'. *Developmental Psychology*. 31(5): 723–38.

Neumann, Erich (1954). *The origins and history of consciousness*. Bollingen Series XLII. New York: Princeton University Press.

——(1966). *Narcissism, Normal Self-formation and the Primary Relation to the Mother*. New York: Analytical Psychology Club.

Northoff Georg, Heinzel Alexander, Moritz de Greck, Felix Bermpohl, Henrik Dobrowolny and Jaak Panksepp (2006). 'Self-referential processing in our brain – A meta-analysis of imaging studies on the self'. *Neuroimage*. 31: 440–57.

Nowak Andrzej, Robin R. Vallacher, Abraham Tesser and Wojciech Borkowski (2000). 'Society of self: The emergence of collective properties of self-structure'. *Psychological Review*. 107(1): 39–61.

Oppenheim, R.W. (1980). 'Metamorphosis and adaptation in the behavior of developing organisms'. *Developmental Psychobiology*. 13: 353–6.

Ornstein, Robert (1992). *The evolution of consciousness: of Darwin, Freud, and cranial fire: The origins of the way we think*. New York: Simon & Schuster.

Ortony, Andrew and Terence J. Turner (1990). 'What's basic about basic emotions?' *Psychological Review*. 97(3): 315–31.

Otto, Rudolf (1917/1923). *The idea of the holy*. London Oxford New York: Oxford University Press.

Palombo, J. (1992). 'Neurocognitive deficits, developmental distortions, and incoherent narratives. *Psychoanalytic Inquiry*. 13: 85–102.

Panksepp, Jaak, Brian Knutson and Douglas L. Pruitt (1998). 'Toward a neuroscience of emotion'. In: *What develops in emotional development?* (Michael F. Mascolo and Sharon Griffin, editors) pp. 53–83. New York: Plenum Press.

Panksepp, Jaak (2000). 'The neuroscience of emotion: An evolutionary-neurodevelopmental view'. *Emotion, development, and self-organization: Dynamic systems approaches to emotional development* (Marc D. Lewis and Isabela Granic, editors) pp. *236–64.* Cambridge: Cambridge University Press.

——(2005). 'On the embodied nature of core emotional affects'. *Journal of Consciousness Studies.* 12(8–10): 158–84.

Papez, J. W. (1937). 'A proposed mechanism of emotion'. *Archives of Neurological Psychiatry.* 38: 725–43.

Paz-Alonso, Pedro M., Rakel P. Larson, Paola Castelli, Deborah Alley and Gail S. Goodman (2009). 'Memory development: Emotion, stress, and trauma'. In: *The development of memory in infancy and childhood* (Mary L. Courage and Nelson Cowan, editors) pp. 197–239. Hove and New York: Psychology Press.

Penrose, Oliver (1986). 'Phase transitions on fractal lattices with long-range interactions'. *Journal of Statistical Physics.* 45(1,2): 69–88.

Perez-Mercader, Juan (2004). 'Coarse-graining, scaling and hierarchies'. In: *Nonextensive entropy-interdisciplinary applications* (M. Gell-Mann and C. Tsallis, editors) pp. 357–76. Oxford: Oxford University Press.

Perruchet, Pierre and Sebastien Pacton (2006). 'Implicit learning and statistical learning : one phenomenon, two approaches'. *Trends in Cognitive Sciences.* 10(5): 233–8.

Perry, J. W. (1970). 'Emotions and object relations'. *Journal of Analytical Psychology.* 15(1): 1–12.

Peterson, Frederick and C.G. Jung (1907). 'Psychophysical invertigations with the galvanometer and pneumograph in normal and insane individuals'. *Experimental Research, CW* 2. pp. 492–553 (Sir Herbert Read, Michael Fordham, Gerhard Adler, editors; William McGuire) London: Routledge.

Phan, K.L., T. Wager, S.F. Taylor and I. Liberzon (2002). 'Functional neuroanatomy of emotion: a meta-analysis of emotion activation studies in PET and fMRI'. *NeuroImage.* 16: 331–48.

Pillemer, David B. and S.H. White (1989). 'Childhood events recalled by children and adults'. *Advances in Child Development and Behavior.* 21: 297–340.

Pillemer, David B., M.L. Picariello and J.C. Pruett (1994). 'Very long-term memories of a salient preschool event'. *Applied Cognitive Psychology.* 8: (95–106).

Pinker, Steve (1997). *How the mind works.* London: Penguin Books.

Plutchik, R. (1994). *The psychology and biology of emotion.* New York: HarperCollins College Publishers.

Prifitera, Aurelio (1981). 'Jungian personality correlates of cerebral hemispheric preference'. *Journal of Analytical Psychology.* 26(2): 151–62.

Read, Sir Herbert, Michael Fordham, Gerhard Adler and William McGuire (editors) (1973). 'Editorial Note'. *Experimental Research, CW* 2. London: Routledge.

Redfearn, J.W.T. (1994). 'Introducing subpersonality theory: A clarification of the theory of object relations and of complexes, with special reference to the I/not-I gateway'. *Journal of Analytical Psychology.* 39(3): 283–309.

Reviere, Susan L. (1996). *Memory of childhood trauma: a clinician's guide to the literature.* New York, London: The Guilford Press.

Revonsuo, Antti (2000). 'Prospects for a scientific research program on consciousness'. In: *Neural correlates of consciousness: Empirical and conceptual questions* (Thomas Metzinger, editor) pp. 57–75. Cambridge, MA: MIT Press.

Richardson, Peter J. and Robert Boyd (2005). *Not by genes alone.* Chicago: University of Chicago Press.

Rilling, J., J. Winslow and C. Kilts (2004). 'The neural correlates of mate competition in dominant male rhesus macaques'. *Biological Psychiatry*. 56(5): 364–75.

Rizzolatti, Giacomo and Laila Craighero (2004). 'The mirror-neuron system'. *Annual Review of Neuroscience*. 27: 169–92. doi: 10.1146/annurev.neuro.27.070203.144230.

Robinson H. P. C., M. Kawahara, Y. Jimbo, K. Torimitsu, Y. Kuroda and A. Kawana (1993). 'Periodic synchronized bursting and intracellular calcium transients elicited by low magnesium in cultured cortical neurons'. *Journal of Neurophysiology*. 70: 1606–1616.

Rossi, Ernest (1977). 'The cerebral hemispheres in analytical psychology'. *Journal of Analytical Psychology*. 22(1): 32–51.

Saffran, J.R., E.K. Johnson, R. N. Aslin and E.L. Newport (1999). 'Statistical learning of tone sequences by human infants and adults'. *Cognition*. 70: 27–52.

Saffran, J.R., Karelyn Reeck, Aimee Niebuhr and Diana Wilson (2005). 'Changing the tune: Absolute and relative pitch processing by adults and infants'. *Developmental Science*. 8: 1–7.

Sandner, D. and J. Beebe (1982). 'Psychopathology and analysis'. In: *Jungian analysis* (Murray Stein, editor) pp. 294–334. La Salle: Open Court.

Sarter M. and H.J. Markowitsch (1985). 'The involvement of the amygdala in learning and memory: a critical review with emphasis on anatomical relations'. *Behavioral Neuroscience*. 99: 342–80 .

Saunders, Peter and Patricia Skar (2001). 'Archetypes, complexes and self-organization'. *Journal of Analytical Psychology*. 46(2): 305–23.

Schaefer, Alexandre, Fabienne Collette, Bierre Philippot, Martial Van der Linden, Steven Laureys, Guy Delfiore, Christian Degueldre, Pierre Maquet, Angre Luxen and Eric Salmon (2003). 'Neural correlates of 'hot' and 'cold' emotional processing: A multilevel approach to the functional anatomy of emotion'. *Neuroimage*. 18: 938–49.

Schore, Allan N. (1994). *Affect regulation and the origin of the self: the neurobiology of emotional development*. Hillsdale, New Jersey and Hove, UK: Lawrence Erlbaum Associates, Publishers.

——(1999). 'Commentary'. *Neuro-psychoanalysis*. 1:49–54.

Schrank, Roger C. (1982). *Dynamic memory: A theory of reminding and learning in computers and people*. Cambridge, London and New York: Cambridge University Press.

Schrank, Roger C. (1999). *Dynamic memory revisited*. Cambridge, London and New York: Cambridge University Press.

Schulkin, Jay (2007). 'Curt Richter: Psychobiology and the concept of instinct'. *History of Psychology*. 10(4): 325–43.

Sevelinges, Yannick, Stephanie Moriceau, Parker Holman, Cathrine Miner, Kyle Muzny, Remi Gervais, Anne-Marie Mouly and Regina M. Sullivan (2007). 'Enduring effects of infant memories: Infant odor-shock conditioning attenuates amygdala activity and adult read conditioning'. *Biological Psychiatry*. Society of Biological Psychiatry. 62: 1070–9.

Shalit, Erel (2002). *The complex: Path of Transformation from Archetypt to Ego*. Toronto: Inner City Books.

Shin, Y.-W., J.-S. Lee, O.-S. Han and B.-Y. Rih (2005). 'The influence of complexes on implicit learning'. *Journal of Analytical Psychology*. 50 (2): 175–90.

Sidoli, Mara (1993). 'When the meaning gets lost in the body: Psychosomatic disturbances as a failure of the transcendent function'. *Journal of Analytical Psychology*. 38(2): 175–90.

——(2000). *When the body speaks: The archetypes of the body*. London: Routledge.

Simcock, G. and H. Hayne (2002). 'Breaking the barrier? Children fail to translate their preverbal memories into language'. *Psychological Science*. 13: 225–31.

Simon-Thomas, Emiliana R., Jakub Godzik, Elizabeth Castle, Olga Antonenko, Aurelie Ponz, Aleksander Kogan, and Dacher J. Keltner (2012). 'An fMRI study of caring vs self-focus during induced compassion and pride'. *Social Cognitive and Affective Neuroscience* 7(6):635-48. doi: 10.1093/scan/nsr045.

Skar, Patricia (2004). 'Chaos and self-organization: emergent patterns at critical life transitions'. *Journal of Analytical Psychology*. 49: 243–62.

Solomon, Hester McFarland (2004). 'Self creation and the limitless void of dissociation: the 'as if' personality'. *Journal of Analytical Psychology*. 49: 635–56.

Spence, Donald P. (1987). 'Turning happenings into meanings: the central role of the self'. In: *The book of the self* (P. Young-Eisendrath and J. Hall, editors) pp. 132–50. New York: New York University Press.

Sperry, R.W. (1968). 'Hemisphere deconnection and unity in conscious awareness'. *American Psychologist*. 23: 723–33.

Sporns, O., D.R. Chialvo, M. Kaiser and C.C. Hilgetag (2004). 'Organization, development and function of complex brain networks'. *Trends in Cognitive Sciences*. 8: 418–25. doi: 10.1016/j.tics.2004.07.008.

Sporns O. and J.D. Zwi (2004). 'The small world of the cerebral cortex'. *Neuroinformatics*. 2: 145–62. doi: 10.1385/NI:2:2:145.

Stam, C.J. (2004). 'Functional connectivity patterns of human magnetoencephalographic recordings: a 'small-world' network?' *Neuroscientific Letters*. 355: 25–28. doi: 10.1016/j.neulet.2003.10.063.

Stam, C.J. and J.C. Reijneveld (2007). 'Graph theoretical analysis of complex networks in the brain'. *Nonlinear Biomedical Physics*. 1:3. doi: 10.1186/1753-4631-1-3.

Stein, Murray (1998) *Jung's map of the soul: An introduction*. Chicago, IL: Open Court.

Steklis, H.D. and A. Kling (1985). 'Neurobiology of affiliative behavior in nonhuman primates'. In: *The psychobiology of attachment and separation* (M. Reite and T. Field, editors) pp. 93–134. Orlando, FL: Academic Press.

Stern, Daniel (1985). *The interpersonal world of the infant*. New York: Basic Books, Inc.

——(1989). 'The representation of relational pattern: Developmental considerations'. In: *Relational disturbances in early childhood* (A.J. Sameroff and R.N. Emde, editors) pp. 52–69. New York: Basic Books.

Stevens, Anthony (1982/2003). *Archetype revisited: An updated natural history of the self*. Toronto: Inner City Books.

Stevens, Anthony and John Price (1996). *Evolutionary psychiatry*. London and Philadelphia: Routledge.

Stewart, Louis H. (1987) 'A brief report: Affect and archetype'. *Journal of Analytical Psychology*. 32(1): 35–46.

Sugerman, A. and L.S. Jaffe (1990). 'Toward a developmental understanding of the self schema'. *Psychoanalysis and Contemporary Thought*. 13: 117–38.

Sullivan, R.M. and M. Leon (1986). 'One-trial olfactory learning enhances olfactory bulb responses in 7-day old rats'. *Developmental Brain Research*. 35: 307–11.

Suzuki, Daisetz Teitaro (1949). *The Zen doctrine of no-mind*. London: Rider and Company.

Thelen, Esther and Linda B. Smith (1995). *A dynamic systems approach to the development of cognition and action*. Cambridge MA and London: A Bradford Book, MIT Press.

Toib A., Lyakhov V. and Marom S. (1998). 'Interaction between duration of activity and time course of recovery from slow inactivation in mammalian brain Na2+ channels'. *Journal of Neuroscience*. 18: 1893–1903.

Tooby, John and Leda Cosmides (1992). 'The psychological foundations of culture: Evolutionary psychology and the generation of culture'. In: *The adapted mind: Evolutionary psychology and the generation of culture* (J. Barkow, L. Cosmides and J. Tooby, editors) pp. 19–136. New York: Oxford University Press.

Tomkins, Sylvan S. (1962). *Affect imagery consciousness: The positive affects* (vol. I). New York: Springer.

——(1963). *Affect imagery consciousness: The negative affects* (vol. II). New York: Springer.

——(1991). *Affect imagery consciousness: The negative affects anger and fear* (vol. III). New York: Springer.

Tresan, David I. (1996). 'Jungian metapsychology and neurobiological theory'. *Journal of Analytical Psychology*. 41(3): 399–436.

Turing, Alan M. (1950). 'Computing machinery and intelligence'. *Mind*. 59: 433–60.

Turk-Browne, Nicholas B., Justin A. Jungé and Brian J. Scholl (2005). 'The automaticity of visual statistical learning'. *Journal of Experimental Psychology: General*. 134: 552–64.

Turk-Browne, Nicholas B., Do-Joon Yi and Marvin M. Chun (2006). 'Linking implicit and explicit memory: Common encoding factors and shared representations'. *Neuron*. 46: 917–927.

van der Hart, O. and B. Friedman (1989). 'A reader's guide to Pierre Janet on dissociation: A neglected intellectual heritage'. *Dissociation: Progress in the Dissociative Disorders*. *2*(1): 3–16.

van der Kolk, B. A. and O. van der Hart (1979). 'Pierre Janet and the breakdown of adaptation in psychological trauma'. *American Journal of Psychiatry*. 146(12): 1530–40.

van Orden G.C., Holden J.G. and M.T. Turvey (2003). 'Self-organization of cognitive performance'. *Journal of Experimental Psychology: General*. 132(3): 331–50. doi: 10.1037/0096-3445.132.3.331.

van Pelt J., M.A. Corner, P.S. Wolters, W.L.C. Rutten and G.J.A. Ramakers (2004). 'Long-term stability and developmental changes in spontaneous network burst firing patterns in dissociated rat cerebral cortex cell cultures on microelectrode arrays'. *Neuroscience Letters*. 361: 86–9. doi: 10.1016/j.neulet.2003.12.062.

Varela F., J.-P. Lachaux, E. Rodriguez and J. Martinerie (2001). 'The brainweb: Phase synchronization and large-scale integration'. *National Review of Neuroscience*. 2: 229–39. doi: 10.1038/35067550.

Vezzoli Caterina, Cinzia Bressi, Giorgio Tricarico, Paolo Boato, Chiara Cattaneo, Umberto Visentin and Giordano Invernizzi (2007). 'Methodological evolution and clinical application of C.G. Jung's Word Association Experiment: a follow-up study'. *Journal of Analytical Psychology*. 52: 89–108.

von Franz, M.-L. (1982). *Marie-Louise von Franz. Bollingen. September 1982*. Casette recording. Stifung für Jung'sche Psychologie.

Wagenmakers E.-J., S. Farrell and R. Ratcliff (2005). 'Human cognition and a pile of sand: a discussion on serial correlations and self-organized criticality'. *Journal of Experimental Psychology: General*. 134(3): 108–16. doi: 10.1037/0096-3445.134.1.108.

Watson, John B. (1912). 'Instinctive activity in animals'. *Harper Magazine*. 124: 376-382.

——(1924). *Behaviorism*. New York: Norton and Co.

Watts D. and S. Strogatz (1998). 'Collective dynamics of "small-world" networks'. *Nature*. 393: 440–42. doi: 10.1038/30918.

Weaver, Ian C.G, Nadia Cervoni, Frances A Champagne, Ana C. D'Alessio, Shakti Sharma, Jonathan R. Seckl, Sergiy Dymov, Moshe Szyf and Michael J. Meany (2004). 'Epigenetic programming by maternal behavior'. *Nature Neuroscience*. 7(8): 847–54.

Werner, Gerhard (2010). 'Fractals in the nervous system: Conceptual implications for theoretical neuroscience'. *Frontiers in Physiology*. 1. PubMed Central ID: PMC3059969, doi: 10.3389/fphys.2010.00015.

Werner G. and V. B. Mountcastle (1963). 'The variability of central neural activity in a sensory system, and its implications for the central reflection of sensory events'. *Journal of Neurophysiology*. 26: 958–77.

——(1964). 'Neural activity in mechanoreceptive cutaneous afferents; stimulus-response relations, Weber functions, and information transmission'. *Journal of Neurophysiology*. 28: 359–94.

Williams, Mary (1963). 'The indivisibility of the personal and collective unconscious'. *Journal of Analytical Psychology*. 8(1): 45–50.

Wilkinson, Margaret (2004).'The mind-brain relationship: the emergent self'. *Journal of Analytical Psychology*. 49(1): 83–101.

——(2006). *Coming into mind: The mind-brain relationship: a Jungian clinical perspective*. London and New York: Routledge.

Wilson M.A. and B.L. McNaughton (1994). 'Reactivation of hippocampal ensemble memories during sleep'. *Science*. 265(5172): 676–9.

Woo, C.C. and M. Leon (1988). 'Sensitive period for neural and behavioral responses to learned odors'. *Developmental Brain Research*. 699: 192–200.

Woodman Marion (1980). *The owl was a baker's daughter: Obesity, anorexia nervosa and the repressed feminine*. Toronto: Inner City Books.

——(1985). *The pregnant virgin: A process of psychological transformation*. Toronto: Inner City Books.

Woodruff Smith, David and Amie L. Thomasson, editors (2005). *Phenomenology and philosophy of mind*. Oxford: Oxford University Press.

Yakovlev, P.I., and A.-R. LeCours (1967). 'The myelogenetic cycles of regional maturation of the brain'. In: *Regional development of the brain in early life (*A. Minkowski, editor) pp. 3–70. Oxford: Blackwell Scientific.

Yonelinas Andrew P., Leun J. Otten, Kendra N. Shaw and Michael D. Rugg (2005). 'Separating the Brain Regions Involved in Recollection and Familiarity in Recognition Memory'. *The Journal of Neuroscience*. 25(11): 3002–8.

Young, Jeffrey E., Janet S. Klosko and Marjorie E. Weishaar (2003). *Schema therapy: A practioner's guide*. New York, London: The Guilford Press.

Young-Eisendrath, Polly and James A. Hall (1987). *The book of the self: person, pretext, and process*. New York and London: New York University Press.

Zhou C., L. Zemanová, G. Zamora-López, C.C. Hilgetag and J. Kurths (2007). 'Structure-function relationship in complex brain networks expressed by hierarchical synchronization'. *New Journal of Physics*. 9: 178. doi: 10.1088/1367-2630/9/6/178.

Ziehen, Théodor (1898). *Psychophysiologische Erkenntnistheorie*. Stuttgart: G. Fischer.

Zietsch B. And G.N. Elston (2005). 'Fractal analysis of pyramidal cells in the visual cortex of the Galago (Otolemur Garnetti): regional variation in dendritic branching patterns between visual areas'. *Fractals*. 13(2): 83–90. doi: 10.1142/S0218348X05002829.

Zillmer, Eric A., Mary V. Spiers and William C. Culbertson (2008). *Principles of Neuropsychology: 2nd Edition*. Belmont, CA: Thompson Wadsworth.

Zinck, Alexandra (2008). 'Self-referential emotions'. *Consciousness and Cognition*. 17: 496–505.

Index